By God's Grace

I Will Get Up Again and Win

Autum Augusta

SEXUALLY ABUSED?

OR HAD TIM BEEN FRAMED?

THE STORY OF A TEACHER WHO TRIED TO HELP ONE OF HER STUDENTS.

Trafford rev. 11/06/2012

 www.trafford.com

North America & international
toll-free: 1 888 232 4444 (USA & Canada)
phone: 250 383 6864 ♦ fax: 812 355 4082

TABLE OF CONTENTS

CHAPTER I

TIM AND LORI JONES

The white electric alarm clock shook Lori from her terrifying dreams. It was 6:30, and time for another stressful day to begin. Lori pulled her sleepy body from the warm, king-sized bed. She walked into the kitchen and put a small amount of water on the new gas range, then hurried to the bathroom to put on her makeup and comb her red hair.

After putting on powder darker than her pale skin, Lori applied brown mascara to her white eye lashes and eye brows. "Dear Lord, please, let me have more natural color in my next life," she prayed.

Lori took a long look into the small, gold-framed mirror hanging above the white sink. Could that middle-aged, heavy-set woman looking back at her really be Lori Jones? Lori thought. She sighed and put on her dark-rimmed glasses. Lori hurried back to the bedroom where she quickly put on her school clothes. She paused a minute to look at her sleeping husband. "Maybe Tim can catch up on the sleep he lost last night while he was working in the field," Lori whispered to herself.

Lori walked back into the kitchen. She took the hot water off the stove and poured it over some instant coffee. It was only 7:15. "I guess I have time for some cereal before bus time," Lori told herself.

Lori enjoyed her simple breakfast as she thought about her present circumstances. She was thankful that her principal allowed her to ride the bus to work. Tim said it cost at least five dollars every time Lori had to drive the car to school and back. It was convenient when she lived only a few blocks from school and could even walk if she wanted to.

1

Now she lived fifteen miles from town, but she enjoyed the quietness of the farm. "I wish riding the school bus didn't make me so nervous," Lori thought.

It was soon time for the bus. Lori looked out the east living room window through the gold velvet curtains. She saw a small orange object, with clouds of dust rolling up behind it, coming west on the country road. It looked like a jet with a brown air stream.

As the bus came to a stop, Lori stepped back from the road to miss most of the dirt swirling around the vehicle. She stepped into the large bus and sit down in the front seat just behind the lady bus driver.

I wish farming conditions were better so I wouldn't have to go to work in this noisy bus, Lori thought again. She looked out the window at the sand blowing across the road.

Lori dusted some of the dirt from the window sill of the bus. "I don't guess I'll ever get used to this blowing dirt," she told the bus driver.

"Me either!" Doris replied. "It's really bad around our place this morning," she said.

Lori liked Doris. She had five children of her own and worked hard to make her own kids, as well as the other kids on the bus, behave. Sometimes, when she corrected the other kids, she had trouble from parents. Lori returned to her thoughts as she gazed out the window into the dust storm.

What a rough country to try to make a living in, Lori thought, but my dad made a good living on these dry plains. He left mother plenty in the bank and a nice home when he died. Lori remembered hearing her folks talking about hard times during the Dust Bowl and Depression era, and how hard they had to work just to survive. But her mother still looked young for her age.

Elizabeth, Lori's mother, had spent a lot of time at the cemetery the first few months after Lori's father died. Then she eventually married Authur who was a farmer and rancher. He lived fifty miles west, was a good church worker and well liked by Elizabeth's family, but Lori seldom saw her mother since she had moved out to the ranch.

The county had a lot of history for Lori. She and her two younger sisters had grown up on a farm ten miles west. Lori had lived all but two years of her life here. She had lived those two years in Texas while Hollis, her first husband, was in the army. The Korean War had ended the same week Hollis finished boot-training, so he didn't have to go overseas.

Lori and Hollis had dated during high school. Hollis graduated a year before Lori. He had attended a technical college that year. They were married the same weekend Lori graduated from high school. Everyone liked Hollis. Everyone thought that the couple would "live happily ever after".

A year and a half later, Lori's first baby had been due. Her twelve-year-old sister was staying with them in case Lori needed any help when the baby arrived. Lori had been thankful that Elaine was there because Hollis was at the army base when Lori went into delivery labor. Elaine had run for help. A local doctor drove her to the hospital on the army base. Lori could remember him yelling at her all the way there, "Slow down on your pains, miss. I don't want to deliver your baby in my new car."

Lori smiled as she remembered Hollis rushing into the hospital room that morning. "Just be brave, Lori, everything will be okay!" he shouted.

"It sure is. Your son is already an hour old," Lori replied, laughing.

After Hollis was discharged from the army, he and Lori had returned to the county. Almost every night after that, Hollis was gone until past midnight. Hollis told Lori it was none of her business where he spent his time. Lori tried to fill the lonely hours by getting involved in church work.

Hollis had been busy building a new business. His social life seemed to take the rest of his time. Lori tried to stay busy with her young son, her music, and teaching Sunday school and Bible School. Lori and Hollis drifted farther and farther apart.

Lori thought how different married life had been from her girlish dreams of married bliss. Instead of the bliss, she ended up night after night watching the clock and wondering where Hollis was, and what he was doing. It was a little more bearable if Hollis came in by midnight. If it was later than that, Lori couldn't sleep and watched the clock hour, after hour. She was tired and angry when Hollis finally came in. Lori tried to talk to Hollis, but he would never talk to her when he came in at night. She was always tired and cranky with Mike the next day.

Lori had not wanted any more children. She felt that it would be unfair to bring another child into such a miserable marriage. Hollis had wanted a girl, and when Mike was four and a half, Mitch was born. Although the baby was Hollis's idea, he didn't spent one evening at home during Lori's pregnancy, or until the baby was two-years-old. He told Lori how ugly she was and would not be seen with her while she was pregnant.

Lori was so discouraged that she promised herself that if Hollis was gone when she went into labor, that she would just have the baby by herself. Lori's water broke late one night. Hollis was not there, but her labor did not start until the next morning. Hollis drove Lori fifty miles to another town because the local doctor was in Denver at the Stock Show. Her only labor was hard labor and she would not have been able to drive herself.

When Mitch was born, Lori had to have a lot of surgery because he was a "breach" birth. Lori and Mitch would have died if she had tried to have the baby alone. The Lord had protected both Lori and her son from a tragic death.

The doctor told Lori that she could not go home until her fever had gone down. Lori had infection in her stitches and thought she could get rid of the infection if she was at home. She took the fever thermometer out of her mouth as soon as the nurse left the room and shook it down to normal. She put the thermometer back in her mouth when she heard the nurse coming back into the room. The doctor had let Lori go home that day.

At home, Lori soaked her stitches by sitting in a large pan of hot water and Epson Salt for an hour twice a day. Elizabeth stayed to help Lori the first few days.

"Lori, I think I'll go home now. I think Hollis will be more comfortable if I'm not here and stay home a little more," Elizabeth said.

After Elizabeth went home, Lori became constipated and tore some stitches. Hollis hadn't wanted Lori to nurse Mitch, so Lori had been given a shot at the hospital to keep her milk from "coming down". The shot didn't work and Lori's milk came anyway and caked in her breasts. They were as hard as rocks and hurt terribly. Lori's fever went up and she felt like she was going to die. She struggled to take care of Mitch and Mike.

Hollis came home after work and put on clean clothes. "I'm really angry. There is a poker party I wanted to go to, and my friend is having a party tonight, and I can't go to both places!" Hollis exclaimed.

"Why don't you stay home with me and the kids? We need you so badly," Lori had shouted.

"Because I don't want to! I just wish you would get out of here and never come back! I don't love you anymore, anyway!" Hollis shouted. He slammed the door as he left the house.

Lori fed Mitch his bottle and cooked Mike some supper. She gritted her teeth to stand the pain she felt in her womb, breasts, and heart. Mitch was asleep in his basket, so Lori put Mike to bed early, even though he wasn't sleepy. Then she went to bed and cried until Hollis came in at 2:30 a.m. Hollis didn't say anything. Lori tried to cover up the sounds of her sobbing. <u>Maybe when I loose some weight and look better, Hollis will love me again,</u> Lori was thinking.

Lori gradually regained her health, but it was two years before she had enough energy to enjoy her boys. Hollis continued to be gone most of the time.

Mitch had been four-years-old when Lori was visiting with a friend.

"I am going to start to college this fall with two friends," Rita said.

"Where can you go to college? There aren't any colleges around here?" Lori asked.

"We're going to Dannon Community College. It is only seventy miles from here. We have our classes arranged to where we can take a full load and only go to school three days a week," Rita explained. "Would you like to come with us and share in the driving?" Rita asked.

"Maybe I will," Lori replied. "If Hollis is going to be gone all the time, I should have time to go to school," she added.

That evening, Lori said, "I have decided to go to college."

Lori expected Hollis to be angry. Lori was surprised when Hollis asked, "What are you going to do with the boys while you're gone?"

"Mike is in school and Mitch likes to play at the neighbor's house. Maybe Mary can take care of him. I'll only be gone three days a week, anyway. If the good Lord wants me to go, He'll make a way," Lori said.

The Lord was willing and Lori started to college that fall, ten years after she had graduated from high school. She didn't realize how busy she would be by carrying a full load of classes. The days at home meant catching up on all her regular work, and many hours of studying. She was too busy to miss Hollis quite so much as she had before.

Lori and Rita had attended a university ninety miles away their last two years to obtain BA degrees in Elementary Education. The other ladies quit.

One time Lori had been discouraged when a friend told her, "Lori, don't quit, because you know what I heard the other day?"

"No what?" Lori asked.

"The guys at the cafe were teasing Hollis about his wife going to college. Hollis told them he thought he'd let you go until you flunked out, and got it out of you're system. Then you'd be glad to stay at home," the friend explained.

"Then I won't quit!" Lori said with determination. She graduated with a three-point-six average, and started teaching sixth grade that fall in the same school Mike and Mitch attended.

Lori was remembering a certain day in the past. It was May 18, the day after her and Hollis's twenty-third anniversary. Mitch had just finished his junior year of high school. It was the day Hollis moved out.

Although the marriage had not been a happy one, Lori was heartbroken. When Hollis moved out it was just like a death. Lori had to get rid of all the things he did not want. He was dead to her but alive to someone else.

Lori did not realize how much she loved Hollis until he was gone. She had even gone to Hollis's home and begged him to come back. "It doesn't matter if another woman is involved, I still want our family together again," Lori had pleaded.

"No, Lori, it's better for us to go our separate ways," Hollis said without any emotion.

Lori had been so hurt and devastated that she jerked off the wedding rings Hollis had given her for their twentieth wedding anniversary. She threw them at Hollis and shouted, "Then take these. I don't want them anymore!"

It had been another long night that Lori had cried herself to sleep. I wonder if I have averaged three hours of sleep a night for the last three years, Lori thought as she finally found relief in slumber.

Hollis ended up marrying his secretary that was eighteen years younger. This made Lori feel like she was a hundred years old. She was foolish enough to travel to California with a friend for a face lift. Lori had read a book about it and was excited. She walked into the doctor's office and was placed in a reclining chair. Both sides of Lori's head were opened up and the skin stretched, with nothing for pain. Lori's eyes were black and her head was swollen for two weeks.

Lori suddenly realized that she had been remembering the past again as she saw Hollis's wife driving to work in her new car. She sure is young and pretty, Lori thought with a terrible ache inside her. "I wonder why I still ache. Is it because of pride, or do I still have some love left for Hollis? Is it because I feel so old and broke? Is it because she can drive to work in a new car and I have to ride this old bus?" Lori asked herself.

Lori quickly stepped to the bus door, so she could be the first one out. Lori needed to be in her classroom a few minutes before her students came in. The whole day went smoother if Lori could have just five minutes to think through the day before her students came in.

The day was an average one with no exceptional events.

Shortly after 3:30, Lori boarded the bus while most of the other teachers went to the workroom for a cup of coffee and to relax and talk.

The dirt had blown all day and there was an inch of sand inside the bus. Lori dusted off a place and wearily sat down on the brown leather seat. It seemed almost impossible to rest or relax with all the screaming and teasing that took place on the bus. <u>I would never want to be a bus driver,</u> Lori was thinking. She was soon hidden again in her thoughts of the past as the bus headed south over the bumpy road.

Both of Lori's boys had done well in sports. Mike had a chance to play college football, but decided that he would rather work with cattle than go on to college. He had married his high school sweetheart who was then in nurses training. Lori's daughter-in-law, Stacy, was now a loved and respected nurse practitioner at the local hospital. Their son, Bryan, was one of Lori's greatest joys.

Mitch was still a bachelor. He had quit college and was now helping to build the gasohol plant in town. Both Mike and Mitch worked with Hollis in the cattle business.

Lori and Hollis's divorce had been difficult for the boys even though they were grown at the time. Mitch had been a senior in high school. Mike and Mitch had seemed to accept their new step-father, Tim, and their step-mother, Hollis's wife.

Lori felt of her face. It was grimy from the dirt that was blowing in through the bus window. She was remembering what it was like to be single. She was only seventeen when she and Hollis were married. Lori had never known any single life until after the divorce.

The year after the divorce, Mitch had been busy finishing school and working at the feedlot. He was gone most of the time.

Hollis had agreed to let Lori have the house through the divorce settlement. Lori was afraid she could not make the house payments and pay for all her other living expenses too. She was also thinking that if she could move out of the house, it would help her get away from hurtful memories, and forget Hollis. Lori sold the house and bought a new mobile home. The mobile home had two bedrooms and a bath on one end for Lori, and a large bedroom and bath on the other end for Mitch. The home was beautiful and even had a wood-burning fireplace.

Lori put all her energy into her teaching, cooking one meal a day for Mitch, and her church work. She loved teenagers and invited some young ministers to hold some weekend evangelistic meetings for the young people.

Many teenagers gave their hearts and lives to the Lord that week, and many of these same teenager had drug problems. Some of them began to spend a lot of time at Lori's house. They had many discussions and Bible studies in front of the fire place. Lori, and her friends, used scripture and prayer to help kids during withdrawal periods. Her house was often full of young people.

Lori remembered the trips she had taken that summer. First, she took kids to church camp and worked as a counselor. A few weeks later, Lori and a friend spent three weeks in Los Angeles. A week after Lori came home from California, she and her parents traveled to the state of Washington to visit two uncles.

The trips had been fun, but Lori knew she had been running from hurts of the past.

Lori was terribly lonely after Mitch left for college that fall, and her marriage to Hollis had left her feeling unloved. All this had made her a soft target when Tim came into her life.

Lori was thinking about the day she first met Tim. She had just finished washing all the windows and curtains in her mobile home and sit down to rest when the telephone rang.

"Hello, my name is Tim Jones," the voice said. "Are you Lori Brown?" Tim had asked.

Lori answered yes, and the caller continued.

"You probably know that I came home from work a few weeks ago and found that my family had left me," Tim explained.

"Yes, I heard that. Your twins were in my sixth grade. When they checked out of school that day, I thought that your whole family was moving. I heard later that you didn't go with them," Lori answered.

"Mrs. Brown, would you go out to dinner with me tonight?" Tim had asked.

"I don't date!" Lori exclaimed.

"We don't have to call it a date," Tim responded. "I hear that you went through a pretty rough divorce last year, and I need someone to talk to that knows what I'm going through right now," Tim said.

"You do sound terribly upset," Lori said. "Come by my house and I'll talk to you for awhile, but I won't go out with you," Lori explained.

"Thanks. See you at eight," Tim said and hung up.

Lori tried to remember if she had ever seen Tim Jones before. <u>I think I saw him a few years ago with his family. If he's the one I'm thinking of, he wears real thick glasses,</u> Lori thought.

Lori hung up the clean curtains. She soaked in the bath tub until she felt rested, then she put on a light-green, western-style, slack suit. After she put on her high platform shoes, she waited nervously for her visitor.

It was almost dark when a large, yellow sedan pulled up beside the mobile home. Lori walked to the door and saw Tim. He was the one she had remembered. Tim was blonde, short, and wore thick glasses. One eye looked off in a different direction from the other eye. Lori couldn't tell if the man was looking at her or not. He was dressed in a light-blue, western leisure suit.

"Come in," Lori said. "Stop barking, Silky, it's all right," she told her toy poodle.

Tim had introduced himself. Lori motioned for him to sit down. Tim sat in the large crushed velvet chair across from Lori. They sit looking at each other not knowing what to say.

"I guess I should offer to fix dinner for you, but I haven't cooked much since my youngest son went away to college. I don't know how to cook for just one," Lori said to break the silence.

Lori was thinking, <u>his man has driven the tractor all day and is probably hungry, and he has offered to take me to dinner. I guess it wouldn't hurt anything except for what people might say.</u>

"I guess it won't hurt to go out to dinner with you, but I don't want anyone to see us together. They might get the wrong idea, and this is a gossipy town," Lori said.

"You name the place," Tim replied.

They discussed three towns that were about fifty miles away and finally decided on one where they didn't think they would see anyone they knew.

Lori crawled into the yellow sedan and sit as far from Tim as possible. She had been a little nervous going somewhere with a man she did not really know.

"Mrs. Brown, why don't you date? I hear you have been divorced for over a year now. Can't you find anyone you'd like to go out with?" Tim asked.

"I had my heart broken over my first marriage. I think a lot of it was because Hollis and I didn't believe in the same things. I've made up my mind that I won't ever date unless the guy has the same beliefs I do, and is a Christian. You never end up marrying someone you don't date," Lori explained.

Tim slowed the car down to almost a stop. Lori thought he was looking for a side road to pull into. It was completely dark now. <u>What have I gotten myself into?</u> Lori thought.

<u>What have I gotten myself into?</u> Tim was thinking. <u>I hate religious people and they aren't any fun. I've ruined my Saturday night. I think I'll take her home. No, that wouldn't be right because I asked her out to dinner and I didn't ask her if she was a Christian or not. I guess I'll hurry up and feed her before I take her home, and hope I have enough time left to go to a dance somewhere.</u>

Lori was relieved when Tim started to drive faster. Now she wondered why he was driving so fast.

Tim started talking about his farming operation and Lori started to relax. She leaned over on her hand toward Tim so she could hear better above the noise of the bumpy road. Tim put his hand on Lori's hand. Lori quickly jerked her hand back. "Mr. Jones, I don't do things like that!" she exclaimed.

"Just as I thought," Tim told himself. He quickly drove the fifty miles and started looking for a nightclub that was still serving dinner. Every restaurant section was already closed for the evening. He finally found a Mexican fast foods place that was still open.

"You're much more attractive than I expected you to be," Tim said as he started to eat his first taco.

"Why? Is it because I'm a school teacher, or older, or red-headed?" Lori asked.

Tim didn't answer.

"Why did you call me? You don't even know me?" Lori asked.

"You wouldn't believe me if I told you," Tim answered.

"I'd like to hear your story, anyway," Lori replied.

"Okay. A few weeks ago I was farming about thirty miles from where I live. I came in late one night and the rest of the family had already eaten. The table was empty. My three boys had already gone to bed," Tim explained, starting his story.

"We always let people sit where they want to, but my wife told me where to sit. She picked up my glass that was already full of ice and started to pour me some tea.

I noticed that there was clear liquid in the bottom of the glass. I told her that the glass was dirty and I wanted another one.

She said it just had melted ice in it.

I was too tired to argue. I begin to eat my supper. Karen, my wife, said that the laundry equipment wasn't working. She said she was going to my mother's, eight miles away, to wash and dry some clothes.

I thought it was awfully late to wash clothes.

My daughter's boyfriend, Philip, was living with us. He said that he and Sally, my daughter, was going to go with Karen.

I said it was okay with me and poured myself a second glass of tea. I heard the car drive away from the house. I suddenly realized that I was eating slower and slower. My arms felt so heavy I could hardly get my fork to my mouth. The food had become tasteless. I was getting dizzy, so I started down the hall toward my bedroom.

The hall looked as if it was leaning over and I was trying to walk on the wall. I kept myself pushed against the wall as I worked to move my feet toward the bedroom door. Pulling myself through the door, I fell across the bed.

When I woke up, it was two-o-clock in the morning. I could hear loud noises coming from the kitchen. Dishes, pots, and pans were being moved around.

I never permitted any noise in my house when someone was trying to sleep. I tried to pull myself up out of bed, and see what was going on. I couldn't move. I tried to yell for the noise to stop, but I couldn't make any sound.

I thought that I must have the flue as I fell back into a deep sleep.

The next morning Karen called me to get up.

I tried to sit up, but I was too weak and uncoordinated.

The third time Karen called me, I managed to pull my heavy body out of bed. I stumbled down the hall and into the kitchen. I told Karen that I didn't want any breakfast because I wasn't feeling well. I told her to remember that she and Philip were to bring me my pickup when they brought be my lunch, so I would have a way to get home after work that night.

It took all my strength to pull myself up into my large four-wheel-drive tractor. I had hooked a large implement on behind it the night before. After I took a drink of cold water from the thermos jug that was in the tractor, I begin to gain some strength. By the time I reached the field, twenty miles away, I felt a lot better and started to cultivate a lot of ground.

I started to feel hungry and realized it was an hour past lunch time. There was no sign of Karen. I decided that she must be waiting for Philip to finish plowing the field he was working in.

By three o'clock, I had the feeling that Karen and Philip were not going to show up. I worked until almost dark. The tractor was getting low on fuel. I unhitched the implement and drove five miles to the nearest farm to find a telephone. I called my place. There was no answer. I called my mother to come after me.

Thirty minutes later, I crawled into my mother's car. She asked me where Karen was. I told her I didn't know. I did the driving and headed for my place as fast as I dared to travel over the unpaved, county road.

When we drove into my place, I noticed that the car and pickup were both gone. I parked the car beside the double-wide mobile home. The whole place was dark. I opened the back door and tried to turn on the light. The light didn't work. When I stepped into the kitchen my footsteps echoed through the whole house. Somehow, I knew the house was empty. I felt for a light and the light bulb wasn't there.

My mother handed me her flashlight and I looked through each room. Everything was gone except for a picture of my oldest son on one wall, two shirts, and two pair of pants in my closet. Even the curtains, light bulbs from all the lights, along with the rest of my clothes, razor, and other personal items were gone.

The house that had been bright and noisy with four kids, the night before, was now empty, dark, and as silent as death. 'My kids', I screamed in anger. I felt a knot in my stomach and I could hear my heart pounding in my ears. My hands were cold and clammy. My anger soon turned to a defeated, hopeless, sorrow.

My mother said that she wasn't surprised. "I guess Karen knew the only way she could hurt me was to take my kids," I told my mother.

I went home with my mother that night, but I couldn't sleep. The next day, instead of going back to the field, I was looking for an open bar. I drank until the bar closed. The pain was still there. I took some liquor home to get me through the night. My drinking caused me to lose the contract to farm the south farmland I had rented.

I had been drinking all afternoon and night, when I caught myself driving back to my mother's at a high speed. I told myself I was crazy to take such chances of having a car wreck, and killing myself. Then I realized that I didn't care if I lived or died.

The day after Karen left with my family, the sheriff brought me, what he called the biggest stack of papers he had ever served anyone. Among other things, there were papers to keep me from spending money or contacting my kids. I felt devastated.

My bar friends told me that what I needed was another woman to replace the one I had just lost. I told them that I wasn't interested. Many of my friends stuck telephone numbers of lonely women in my shirt pockets just in case I changed my mind.

I was fighting depression one night when I decided to look through the large number of names and telephone numbers my friends had given me. As I was dialing the first number, the name L. Brown came to my mind. There was no answer at the number I had just dialed. I dialed several more numbers, and each time the name L. Brown came to my mind. No one answered at any of the numbers I had called.

I wondered who is L. Brown. I checked the list of names that had been given to me and L. Brown was not on the list. I found a L.E. Brown in the telephone book, but I still didn't now if it was a man or woman.

I knew Ben and Linda Brown, so I called them and asked who was L. Brown. Linda told me you were her husband's aunt that had been divorced from his uncle for about a year. She told me to forget your number and not to call you because you didn't date.

"Is that when you called me?" asked Lori.

"Yes, I remembered all the gossip that was going around during your divorce. I felt like I needed to talk to you because you know what I'm going through right now."

"I'm afraid I do. I loved my husband, and after twenty-one years of staying home alone and waiting for him to come home, he left me for a beautiful woman who is young enough to be my daughter," Lori replied.

"Then you know what hurt pride is too," Tim said.

"Yes, it made me feel like I was ugly and old," Lori said. "You probably won't believe this now, but time does help to heal," Lori explained.

"Lori!" Tim said, jumping up from the table. "Do you realize it is past midnight and these guys are trying to close this place?" Tim asked. "I need to get you home!" he exclaimed.

"You're right," Lori said. She followed Tim to the car.

After they climbed into Tim's car, they continued their visiting. A police car pulled up beside them and a policeman got out. He had a "bully club" in his hand. Tapping on the window, he asked, "Lady is this man giving you any trouble?"

Lori tried to assure the cop that everything was okay.

When the cop was convinced, he said, "Would you please sit and talk somewhere else? The manager of this restaurant wants to close up and go home. He takes his money home with him. He is afraid that you are sitting out here waiting to rob him."

Tim and Lori both laughed and started home.

"Would you like to go to church with me this morning?" Lori asked.

Tim ignored the question.

A little further down the road, Lori asked again, "Tim, would you like to go to church with me this morning?" "I think it might help you get over your depression," she said.

"I guess it wouldn't hurt," Tim said gruffly, and continued to talk about his farming operations.

Tim was soon parking the car in front of Lori's mobile home. As Lori was crawling out of the car, she noticed a pack of cigarettes on the dash of the car. "Thank you for not smoking this evening," she said.

Lori walked around to Tim's side of the car. He had the window down. "I don't think you will go to church with me," Lori said.

"I haven't been inside a church for a long time. I didn't like it the last time I went, but if I said I'll go, I'll go!" Tim snapped.

Lori said goodnight and walked to her front door.

Tim waited until Lori had unlocked the door and was safely inside before he backed out of the driveway.

Tim went to church with Lori the next day and enjoyed it more than he intended to. They went on a picnic after church, and Lori had enjoyed Tim's company more than she had intended to.

Tim went to church with Lori again on Wednesday night. He accepted Jesus as his Savior after the service when Lori prayed with him. Although Tim had a rough reputation, Lori never saw him smoke, drink, or heard him swear.

Three weeks later, Tim received the baptism of the Holy Ghost and felt led to start a Full Gospel Church in his home. There were thirty-nine people, including two bankers and their families, at the first meeting. Lori could hardly believe it.

Lori remembered the day Tim had gone to court over his divorce. She prayed quietly for him as much as possible during school. Tim was waiting for her when she left the school building. "How did your day go?" she asked.

"I ended up agreeing to pay eight-five dollars a month on each of the boys. Karen tried to get me to pay that amount on Sally but the judge said no, since Sally and Philip are married now. They were married a week before they all left but I didn't know it. I felt like the kids needed their mother, so I only asked for, and was granted, visiting privileges. Jimmy, my oldest son, and Sally say they never want to see me again. I can't believe how much they have changed," Tim said.

"Guess what my twins, Timmy and Tommy, told the judge today?" Tim asked.

"I have no idea," Lori answered.

"It was concerning you," Tim said, looking in another direction.

"About me?" Lori asked.

"I hate to tell you this, but you'll hear about it anyway," Tim said. "They said that if they came to visit me, that you would . . . would sexually molest them."

Lori felt too shocked to say anything for a few minutes. She felt like she was just having a bad dream.

Tim continued, "The old judge said that he knew you and didn't believe it, but he had to consider everything when it came to what is best for the kids." "That's not the worst thing that was said," Tim added.

"You've got to be kidding!" Lori whispered.

"They tried to bring charges against me by accusing me of molesting Sally, my own daughter! Because the charges were reported so long after it was supposed to have happened, the judge just dropped it," Tim stuttered.

"The day they left, Karen convinced the sheriff's department that I was carrying a gun, and that I was dangerous. There were three lawmen at the double-wide that day with shotguns pointed in the direction I was farming. If I had come home that day, they probably would have shot me on sight," Tim explained. "Karen said she was sorry I didn't find a way to get home that day," he said.

"Man, she must really hate you!" Lori replied.

"Sally has been convinced that everything I've ever done for her was for the wrong reasons," Tim said with a sigh.

"As soon as the twins are out of school for the summer, they can come to visit me for two weeks," Tim said, smiling through tears.

Lori was very busy that winter. She sponsored the Jr. High and High School Pep Clubs, and tried to spend time with Tim. In early spring, she noticed that every time she rode the athletic bus, her arm hurt. With each trip, her arm grew worse. It was soon hurting all the time. The pain became so intense that it felt like her whole arm had been burned.

Dr. David sent Lori to the city where special x-rays were done. The first set of x-rays did not show any problem. The doctor checking the x-rays decided that an iodine x-ray would have to be given as a last resort.

Lori was wheeled into a large x-ray room where she waited for, what seemed, a long time. She had nothing on but a hospital gown and the hard x-ray table felt like ice. She had not felt this cold for a long time. Lori wished she had a blanket to put over her cold body. By the time two, young, male interns showed up in lab clothing, Lori was so cold, her whole body was shaking.

One of the young men gave Lori a shot in the vein of her left wrist. Then she was wheeled into another room and rolled over onto another cold, metal surface. This table was shaped like a cylinder, and it started to turn Lori into different positions. Lori felt herself getting terribly sick. When the machine positioned her with her head down and her feet up, she fainted.

Lori felt like she was swirling around and around in a small hole in the ground. Every muscle in her body felt tense. She could feel air blowing into her face and hair, because of the reeling motion. Then there was nothing.

"Please breathe, lady! Please breathe!" Lori heard the two young men yelling. They were shaking her as they shouted. Lori was sick to her stomach and had a terrible headache. When the two young men were sure she was going to be okay, she was put back into her hospital room and told not to turn over or try to get up for twenty-four hours.

It had been a terrible experience when Lori's heart had stopped. The x-rays showed two broken vertebras in Lori's neck. The vertebras were pinching some spinal nerves causing Lori's arm to hurt. Lori was scheduled for surgery.

"I feel so embarrassed about my physical condition," Lori told Tim. She pushed her back against the head of the hospital bed to relieve the pain.

"Why?" Tim asked.

"I've been healed of a crooked back, ulcers, and a lot of other things. I've prayed for other people's healing, but I can't pray about this. I feel too guilty for going with you before your divorce was final," Lori explained. "No matter what the judged said, or what you say, I'll still feel guilty," she explained.

Tim was silent for a few minutes. "Anyway Lori, everything will be okay, and I love you very much," Tim said.

Lori tried to prepare herself, mentally, for surgery.

The doctors operated on Lori's neck, and took a bone fragment from Lori's hip to fuse the broken vertebras. Lori believed for quick healing after surgery. She did not even need an aspirin for pain the days following her surgery. The surgery did cause Lori to loose her voice, and this caused Lori to miss three weeks of teaching school. It was during this time that Tim convinced Lori to get married so he could take care of her, and she would not be a burden to her family.

Although Lori's friends and family had been apprehensive about the marriage, she and Tim were married in a small church in another state.

Lori's folks, sister and niece, and Tim's mother were the only guests. Lori still had her neck in a brace, but she did remove it for a few minutes while her sister took some pictures.

Lori's father tied some tin cans on the back of Tim's car to cause attention as they drove through town. He also bought a nice steak dinner for everyone following the wedding. Lori felt loved and happy for the first time in a long time.

Timmy and Tommy came to visit in June. They had planned to run away the first night. The night was extra dark, and they decided they did not want to sneak out of the house. Lori and Tim felt sure that the twin's mother's relatives were waiting for them down the street.

The next morning when Lori cleaned up the bedroom where the twins had slept, she found bubble gum strung all over the bed and furniture. Lori believed that the twins had been told to do things like that, while they were there. Lori tried to clean up the mess. She never scolded the twins over it.

The twins tried to make Lori angry all that week. They even jumped up and down on the beds, which was juvenile for twelve-year-olds.

One after noon Lori had been busy in the kitchen cooking supper. "You're a big fat slob," Tommy said.

"I know. I need to lose some weight, don't I?" Lori responded.

Tommy looked surprised. "I don't know what I'm supposed to say next," he said.

Later, Timmy told Lori that their mother always punished him and Tommy if they ever said anything nice about their dad. "She cusses us every day," Tommy said.

"I don't want to hear anything about your mother," Lori ordered. "This week we are just going to forget the past and have a good time together," she explained.

During the second week, Lori, Tim, and the twins went to the field to work. Lori was driving one of the tractors. The twins were riding in the tractor with Tim when Tommy asked, "Dad, can I ride home with Lori in the little pickup tonight?"

"I think Lori would enjoy your company," Tim answered.

As Tommy had planned, Lori let him drive the small pickup until they reached the highway. Lori took over the driving from there.

"Lori, I can't believe the things that my relatives say about you, especially since I've watched you these last few days," said Tommy.

"What have you heard about me?" Lori asked.

"They say that you went to bed with one of your superintendents and that's why he got fired, and that's why your husband divorced you," Tommy answered.

"I have never gone to bed with any men, except two, and they happened to be the ones I was married to at the time," Lori said, trying to laugh.

"I thought so. I told my family that you didn't even get along with that superintendent because I saw you come out of his office once and you looked real mad," Tommy said.

"Thank you for your support," Lori replied. "Sometimes when people get divorced, they are hurt. When one of them remarries, they are hurt even more. They say things about the other person that they don't really mean," Lori tried to explain. "I did that once when my first husband divorced me for someone else," Lori added.

"You did?" Tommy asked.

"I sure did, and I've been sorry ever since," Lori answered.

The two weeks passed quickly. The night came when Lori and Tim had to take the twins back to their mother's relatives. Lori cried and Tommy had tears in his eyes when they said their good-byes.

A few weeks later, Timmy called. "I hate you, and I hate Lori, and I never want to see you again!" he screamed.

"What's the matter, son,?" Tim asked.

"Lori is going to school and telling her students that mom is sleeping with a different man every night! I hate her! I hate you! I never want to see you again as long as I live!" Timmy sobbed.

Before Tim could respond, he heard the telephone click. He tried calling Timmy back several times, but the boy was crying too hard to talk or even listen. Tim was never allowed to see the twins again.

In October, Tim and Lori gave a large, 65th wedding anniversary party for Tim's folks. Daddy Andy and mother Sarah enjoyed visiting with friends and family. Daddy Andy had a stroke in December that left him paralyzed on one side. Since he was six foot, three inches tall, and weighed 350 pounds, the family could not take care of him. Daddy Andy was in the hospital until his Medicare ran out. Tim had to put him in a Health Care Nursing Home center, and pay all the expenses in-between.

Tim and Lori moved to the farm and Lori's beautiful mobile home was moved close to the care center for mother Sarah. It was still costing Tim and Lori close to $2,000 a month to support Tim's parents.

It was a year later before Tim was able to get some government aid to help support Daddy Andy.

Tim was in Daddy Andy's room when Daddy Andy said, "Go get sheriff!"

"Why do you want the sheriff?" Tim asked.

"Shoot me!" Daddy Andy stuttered.

"Why?" Tim asked his eighty-four-year-old father.

"Me . . . Bank . . . Money," Daddy Andy tried to explain.

Tim checked at the bank and discovered that his folks owed the bank close to $100,000. He borrowed the money, with the farm as collateral, and paid the debt. He wanted Daddy Andy to be able to die in peace.

Lori had just come in from school when the telephone rang. Her mother was on the phone. "Lori, we have just put your father in the hospital. He has had another heart attack," Elizabeth sobbed.

Lori was thankful Tim was home. "I'll be right there, Mother," Lori said.

Lori's father, Gary, was close to death for a week. Then, his condition grew better. Daddy Gary was moved from an intensive care room into a regular room the same day that mother Sarah called. Sarah's only sibling, her sister Carey, Tim's only aunt on his mother's side, had just died. Tim and Lori left the hospital to pick up Sarah and take her to the funeral. They were gone for two days.

After the funeral Lori and the family went to Aunt Carey's home. There was a small table close to the front door. Lori noticed a Bible and a revolver on the table. Tim had told her that some young men had come to the house and demanded Aunt Carey's Avon collection. When they would not leave, Aunt Carey shot at them through the screen. They ran down the street and did not come back.

Another thing Lori noticed was splattered blood on some of the walls. Lori asked about the blood. "Aunt Carey drank herself to death," Tim's sister explained. "It was a terrible death," she added.

"Lori, would you mind reading Aunt Carey's will while we are all still together?" Tim's brother-in-law asked. "We just brought it back from the bank and we want you to read it," he explained.

Lori looked over the papers and started to read. Aunt Carey had left everything to Tim's sister. When she read that Aunt Carey's ring would also go to the sister, Sarah screamed, "That ring was supposed to be mine. It was given to Carey in 1930 and it was worth $25,000 at that time, and she said I could have it after she died!" Sarah was very angry.

Lori was visiting with Tim's nephew. "It seems so sad. We try to help old people by talking them into signing what they have over to us, which usually are not worth very much, and we give them a nice monthly income to live on," he said. "The sad thing is that right after we get them set up financially, they don't last much longer," he explained.

After Aunt Carey's funeral, Lori and Tim took Sarah home and returned to the hospital to see Daddy Gary. Lori's father had developed pneumonia and was in critical condition. Gary was in so much pain, that Lori, her family, and the nurses had to work continually to keep him on the bed.

Lori's folks always were holding hands, or Gary would have his arm around Elizabeth's neck. Lori had only heard her folks have one argument.

Gary was squeezing Elizabeth's hand one afternoon. He was in terrible pain as he looked at his wife of forty-eight years, and said, "Why does this have to happen?"

"I don't know?" Elizabeth sobbed. "We have been so happy together. I don't want to go on without you."

Lori was terribly tired when she returned home that evening. She made the mistake of telling Tim about a neighbor she had seen at the hospital. The neighbor and his wife had recently divorced.

"I don't want you to talk to single men like that," Tim shouted. Lori was in shock and before she could move, Tim struck her across the face. She fell into the wall and to the floor. Tim kicked her and grabbed her hair and dragged her down the hall.

Lori was still in shock as she tried to stand up. Tim looked at her with a strange look on his face. "I'm sorry Lori," he said and walked out of the house for awhile. Lori had a hard time believing what had just happened.

Gary was in such pain that the family decided to let him be sedated. He was unconscious most of the time after that. Lori had just checked on her father. It had been two days since the sedation was started. Gary was lying so still. Lori could not even tell if he was breathing or not. She watched the nurse at the foot of the bed. The nurse was watching the heart monitor. <u>He must be all right,</u> Lori thought.

Seconds after Lori left the room to check on her mother in the waiting room of the hospital, Gary raised up from his pillow. "I'm ready to go home," he said a fell back onto the pillow.

Lori heard the call "crash thirteen" come over the speaker. She heard a lot of commotion in the hall, but she did not know what it was. She had just sat down by Elizabeth when a nurse came in. "Your husband has passed away," the nurse told Elizabeth.

Lori was glad she was there with her mother. Her middle sister had made a hundred mile trip to take her baby sister to catch an air plane, so she could return home to her family and work. Lori was the only other family member there.

Arthur had just come to the hospital. Arthur and Gary had gone deer hunting together. Arthur asked if he could visit Gary. He wanted to ask Gary if he was ready to "meet the Lord", and pray with him if Gary wanted. He was told that Gary had just died. Arthur went to the hospital's mourning room to see if there was anything he could do to help the family.

It was a time of weeping. "Make sure that your mother drinks plenty of water. That is very important in a time of great sorrow," one of the nurses told Lori.

Lori tried to control her crying so she could be more help to her family. She and Tim had just come into town for the funeral when they saw the hearse coming down the street. Lori knew that it was carrying her father's body. She started to cry.

"You shouldn't be so sad. You got to now your father all these years. I've only had the privilege of knowing him for a short time. He was such a wonderful man that I feel that I have been cheated because I didn't have a chance to know him longer," Tim said.

Lori's sister wrote a poem about her father's large, loving hands. It was printed on the back of the funeral memoir. The song "Daddy's Hands" was sung during a nice memorial service.

As Lori watched her father's body being lowered into the brown earth, she thought she saw God's huge hands underneath the coffin, holding it in love. She was also reminded about the thief that was crucified beside Jesus, and accepted Christ's salvation at the end of his life. Jesus had said, "I tell you today, you shall be with Me in Paradise". Lori felt sure that her beloved father was now in Paradise.

Daddy Andy remained unable to talk or take care of himself. Tim and Lori traveled to the Nursing Home every Sunday to visit Daddy Andy, and to sing for the residents. Lori either played the guitar or piano. Mother Sarah helped them sing.

One Sunday Tim took Lori's guitar and pretended that he was playing it. He walked among the crowd of elderly people, singing, "We love you and God loves you." The residents thought he was the best guitar player they had ever heard.

Daddy Andy gradually shrunk from 350 pounds to 150 pounds, and was still losing weight.

Tim loved his kids and the loss of them was almost more than he could take. He was not permitted to see any of his children, yet he and Lori were making the $250 payment each month for their support.

The first Christmas Tim and Lori were married they managed to give each of their children, spouses, and the two grand children, fifty dollars each.

Tim heard that Sally and Philip were in the area visiting her mother's relatives. He went to find them so he could give each of them, and their baby son, a fifty dollar bill for Christmas.

Lori remembered that December day she came home from school and found Tim crying. "What's the matter?" she asked.

"I got to hold my grandson for ten minutes today. He's such a nice, quiet, little boy," Tim sobbed as he wiped the tears from his eyes. It turned out to be the only time he ever saw any of his grandchildren.

After Tim and Lori gave each person, in both their families, the fifty dollars the second year, Sarah learned that the twins thought that their extra money had come from their mother. By the third Christmas, farming conditions were so bad that Tim and Lori could no longer give Christmas money. No matter how bad finances were Lori and Tim still paid the $250 a month to help support Tim's three sons.

I just wish we could see his kids sometimes and I wish my own family would visit us once in awhile. It seems like it has been such a long, long time since I had any kids at home, Lori was thinking.

"Mrs. Jones, Mrs. Jones! Are you going to get off the bus today?" the friendly bus driver was asking. She laughed as Lori tried to shake her thinking to the present.

"I'm sorry. I guess I must have had my mind on something else," Lori said, apologizing. She quickly stepped off the bus and waved to her friend. She stepped back to avoid some dust, and watched the large, orange vehicle turn around and travel back down the dusty road.

Lori walked up the drive-way leading to the farm house. She unlocked the back door, opened it, and stepped back to avoid most of the dust that floated down from the top of the door. The dust always made her nostrils sting. She walked through the laundry room and into the kitchen. Lori started the coffee water again. She washed the grit from her face, put on her old clothes, and returned to the kitchen to relax with her evening coffee.

After resting for a few minutes, Lori filled a large bucket with water and started to the hen house. She loved to care for the forty, large, red laying hens and gather their eggs. She finished her outside chores and cleaned up the kitchen mess where Tim had fixed lunch. Lori straightened up the rest of the house and vacuumed up the dirt that had accumulated around the windows and doors.

Lori took time to play the piano before she started dinner. Music helped her to relax. She hurried to the large kitchen to start the evening meal. Tim always liked to eat as soon as he came in from the field.

Tim came in at 6:30. He kissed Lori hello on his way to the washroom. "What's for supper?" he asked.

"Steak and fried potatoes," Lori answered.

"Great!" Tim replied. "How was your day?" he asked.

"It went too fast to cover everything I wanted to cover in each class," Lori answered. "How was your day?" she asked.

"More breakdowns than farming," Tim said. "They don't build machines the way they used to. It wouldn't be so bad if I didn't have to drive so far for the parts," Tim explained. He held Lori's hand and asked the blessing over their food.

"Sometimes you're lucky if you can even find the parts," Lori said. She remembered the many hours she had spent going after parts when she was helping Tim in the field.

They ate in silence. Lori watched the unusual man she had married. His favorite things were simple: eating, loving her, riding a horse while working with cattle, and going to church. His only hobbies were cooking and belonging to the sheriff's posse. Through Tim's love, Lori had forgotten the day Tim beat her, the day before her father died.

Tim had made Lori feel loved for the first time in years. Hollis had hardly known she existed, and Tim didn't want to go anywhere without her. Lori's mother had said once, "Lori, you married one man that didn't seem to know you even existed, and then you married a man that doesn't even want to go to the bathroom without you. It looks like you could have married something in-between."

Lori had grown accustomed to Tim's eyes looking in opposite directions, and his thick glasses. Tim was just thankful he could see and never complained about his eyes except when the milo dust irritated them.

Many times when Tim was quiet, Lori knew he was missing his kids, but he seldom mentioned them anymore.

"What was in the mail, today?" Tim asked.

"Just a letter from the insurance company saying that they aren't going to pay us anything on the things we had stolen from your double-wide trailer after we moved out here," Lori answered.

"Why not?" Tim asked.

"They said it was because we didn't have receipts showing we had bought the things," Lori explained, handing Tim the letter. "Did the sheriff's department ever find anything?" she asked.

"Only that some of the finger-prints were small enough to be a child's," Tim answered, reading the insurance letter. "How can you show a receipt for a freezer full of meat since we fed the animal and had it butchered ourselves?" Tim asked, not expecting an answer.

"I don't know, but I know I messed up the finger-prints on the freezer. When I realized that our place had been broken into, my first reaction was to run over to the freezer and check it," Lori said. She remembered the Sunday night after church that they had stopped by the place Tim had lived before they were married.

"They did find more of your finger-prints than anyone else's," Tim said, teasingly.

"It makes you wonder who would have enough nerve to tear down the <u>front</u> door, next to the road, walk in, take everything, then sit down for a cigarette and a cup of coffee before they left," Lori replied.

"They sure weren't afraid of being caught," Tim agreed. "I thought that the sheriffs department would find some trace of the two new vacuum cleaners and my large air pump by now," Tim added.

"Tim," Lori said almost in a whisper.

"Yes, Lori, what do you want now?" Tim asked.

"Tim, Dr. David's daughter asked me, in class today, if I would like to have a white poodle puppy," Lori said. It was more of a question than a statement.

"Lori, I told you I didn't want you to get another poodle. You cried so hard when Silky died last summer, that I thought I was going to have to call the mortuary to have her put away," Tim said with a frown.

"I had Silky for fourteen years, so why wouldn't I cry?" Lori replied. "I need someone to talk to when you are busy working. Besides, you have your outside dog, Kato," Lori argued.

"Lori, as long as you are teaching and gone all day, I think it would be foolish to get another house pet. It would make messes in the house because you wouldn't be home to put it outside," Tim explained. He gave Lori a hug.

"I guess you're right," Lori agreed.

Lori started her outside chores the next evening after school. She decided to look for eggs in some of the old buildings away from the hen house. Lori gathered the eggs out of the hen house before she started looking in a large opened-ended storage building. The building was filled with what Lori called "junk" and Tim called "supplies".

There were four, clucking hens following Lori as she walked across the dusty cement floor of the large building. She suddenly was aware of a strange noise that was not coming from the hens.

"Maybe it is just a mouse," Lori said to herself. She listened and heard the noise again. "I don't think it sounds like a mouse, but what else could be in this old building?" Lori asked herself. She started looking through boxes and other junk.

Lori traced the sounds to a certain area. She got down on her hands and knees in order to look under an old refrigerator. She could see a tiny ball of gray fur behind the motor of the old refrigerator. It was too large to be a mouse, so Lori carefully put her hand under the refrigerator and around the ball of fur. She could feel the dust that covered the soft fur. Lori pulled out a tiny, gray and white tabby kitten.

The tiny kitten was so starved that every rib was poking out from its sides. The kitten was old enough that its eyes were starting to open, but it was too weak to stand up.

"You're from some of the wild cats that roam the fields, aren't you?" Lori asked. "Are you too starved to eat and live?" she asked the weak baby.

Lori forgot about the eggs. She took the tiny kitten in her arms and ran to the house to fix it some warm milk. The baby kitten surprised Lori by lapping up the milk. The baby was soon full and sleeping. Lori put some soft rags in an old box and tenderly placed the kitten in the rags. She washed her hands and prepared Tim's supper.

As soon as Tim climbed out of the pickup, Lori showed him the kitten. Tim held it up in his large hands. "He sure is marked pretty," he said.

Lori shook her head to agree.

"What are you going to call him?" asked Tim.

"I think it's a girl so I'll call her Tammi," Lori answered with a grin.

"I guess you finally got yourself the house pet you've been wanting. If you leave him, or her, outside, Kato will kill him, or her," Tim said. He petted the kitten and gave it back to Lori.

Lori fed Tim his supper and then she fed Tammi again, just before she and Tim went to bed. As Lori was crawling into bed beside Tim, she said, "It's really silly for us to make over Tammi so much, when there are so many kids in the world that need homes."

"I suppose you're right, but I don't know what we can do about it." Tim said, pulling Lori close to his own warm body.

CHAPTER II

THE GONZALESES

It was a beautiful, early spring morning in April. For once the wind wasn't blowing. The sun felt warm and friendly coming through the large kitchen window. Lori was ready for church, and cleaning up the breakfast dishes. Tim was in the bedroom putting on his Sunday clothes.

Tim came into the kitchen. "Are we ready to go yet?" he asked.

"You're earlier than usual getting ready," Lori said. "Let's go to church a different way since we have more time this morning," she suggested.

"Just as long as you do the driving. I'm so tired of driving by the end of the week after driving the tractor all week," Tim answered.

Instead of taking the main road to town, Lori drove east for two miles before she turned north. This road went past Rita's place. "Maybe we can see some of the authentic animals that Rita and her husband are raising," Lori said.

The wheat fields were bright green. The ditches along each side of the road were a different color of green where the weeds were just starting to break through the drifted sand.

"I see three white lamas in that pasture," Lori said, pointing behind the farmhouse on the property.

"There are five buffalo in the pasture north of the house," Tim replied.

31

"They are pretty, aren't they?" Lori said with a signed. "I wonder what this country looked like when there were thousands of them roaming over this land," she said. Lori turned the car north for a mile, then east again. They drove through an old run-down farm. There was a storage shed and barn on the north side of the road and an old house with four or five old buildings on the south side of the road. Three children were playing in the bare, sand-blown yard.

As Tim and Lori's car came closer, two more children came out of the old, weather-beaten front door. Tim and Lori waved at the kids, and the children waved back. They all had dark skin, eyes, and hair. They looked like they were of Spanish, or Indian, descent.

"I didn't know anyone was living on this old place," Tim said. "It's been years since anyone has lived here," he explained.

Lori drove another mile east and turned north again for the last seven miles of their journey. Suddenly, Lori almost stopped the car.

"What's the matter?" Tim asked.

"I didn't recognize those kids!" Lori exclaimed.

"What's so unusual about that?" Tim asked.

"Because I'm a teacher in this district. I know all the kids around here for miles, but I don't know those kids. That means those kids are not in school," Lori explained.

"I see what you mean, and why you are concerned," Tim replied.

The Jones enjoyed the church service and visited with friends after the meeting was over.

"Let's go through the old farm again on our way home," Lori suggested. "I would like to get a better look at those children," she explained.

This time, as Tim and Lori drove through the yard, there were two older boys with the others. "I know some of these kids should be in my classes," Lori said. She stopped the car.

Four of the children ran up to the rose-colored Cadillac. Tim and Lori said, "Hello" and the children responded with bashful "Hi s." The younger kids hid behind the older ones.

Lori introduced Tim and herself. "We're you're neighbors that live west of here," she said.

"How long have you guys lived here?" Tim asked.

"About four weeks," an older boy answered.

They don't even have a Spanish accent, Lori was thinking. "Where do you go to school?" she asked.

"We don't," the older boy said.

"I just wanted to know, because I'm a teacher," Lori explained.

"Oh, oh!" the older boy exclaimed.

Everyone was quiet. Lori and Tim knew the children were embarrassed. They said good-bye and drove out of the yard. They saw the children running back into the old house.

"They look awfully poor, don't they," Lori commented.

"Yes. I saw several windows missing from the house, and they had sheets across the windows, instead of curtains," Tim answered.

The next day Lori reported the new kids to the school migrant teacher. "They said that they moved into the community about four weeks ago," Lori explained.

"Thank you, Mrs. Jones. I'll check this out right after school this evening," Mrs. Medina said.

As soon as Lori got to school the next morning, Mrs. Medina told her, "I checked on the Gonzales family last night. They have at least five children that should be in school. There may be some older ones that I didn't learn about. Mr. Gonzales doesn't want to start the kids to school until next year since we only have five weeks of school left this year. I guess I won't bother them again until next fall."

"I can understand his reasoning," Lori replied.

The last five weeks passed quickly. As soon as school was out for the summer, Lori started to help Tim with his farming and ranching work.

When branding time came, Tim and Lori rounded up all the calves into the pens next to the house. A high school girl was hired to run the calves from the pens into the squeeze shoot where the animals could not move. Lori then gave each calf a shot to keep it from having certain diseases, and a shot of vitamins for health. After that, she doctored their ears with a powdery medicine. Last of all, Tim cut off their small horns.

While Lori was doing this, Tim was busy branding the calves. When a bull-calf came through, Tim waited for Lori to twist its tail up over its back. This made the animal stand in a peculiar position. Then Tim could castrate it by cutting the testicles open and pulling out the sacks that contained the substance that made it possible for the animal to get a cow pregnant. This made it impossible for the animal to develop into a bull. It would grow bigger instead, and have more meat and less fat on its body.

"Steers make the best meat," Tim had explained when Lori first became his "top cowhand".

Lori never forgot the first time she helped Tim castrate. The first calf they castrated made her feel like vomiting when she saw the blood spurting out. When they did the second one, Lori felt like she was going to faint. After they had finished their third castration, Lori dropped back on the bare sandy ground in the corral and cried. Tim had waited for Lori to regain her composure before taking the next calf.

After the first experience, Lori was a little tougher. She and Tim could take care of at least 150 calves in two days.

When equipment broke down, Lori hurried to town to buy new parts to replace the broken ones. She didn't have time to change from her field clothes to her good clothes. A friend told Lori one day, "I see you're coming to town looking like some of the rest of us."

That evening Lori told Tim what her friend had said. "I wonder what she meant?" asked Lori.

"Before I ever met you, I heard that you were one of the best dressed women in the country," Tim explained.

"I didn't know that. I guess I <u>did</u> always try to look my best when I went downtown," Lori said.

"I thought it was funny when I got to know you and found out that you bought a lot of your clothes at K-Mart," Tim said, laughing. "I guess what people don't know won't hurt them," he added.

"It doesn't make any difference where a person buys their clothes if they have a nice figure to put in them," Lori replied with a sigh. "I wish I could loose some of this weight so I could look nice in my clothes again," she said.

"Me, too," Tim said. "What's for supper?" he asked.

The cattle were soon put out on summer pasture. Tim and Lori were now busy driving tractors from early morning until late at night. The land had to be cultivated, and the crops planted. Tim and Lori never thought about the Gonzales family except when they waved at them on their way to church every Sunday.

In the fall, Mrs. Medina made sure that the children were enrolled in school. The Gonzales children were soon well-known by all the other students, all the staff, and all the administrators. The children were terribly behind the other students in their classes. Rosita was twelve and Ray was thirteen. They were both placed in the fifth grade with kids that were younger, and much more able to do their school work.

Ray was almost as tall as the teachers. He was handsome with thick curly hair. He was built like a heavyweight wrestler. The girls thought he was good looking until he insulted them with his dirty, four-lettered words. Ray loved pushing and hitting the other students. The other students were soon afraid of him.

Mr. Wilson, the elementary principal, spanked Ray several times. He took long bladed knives away from him almost every day. Punishment did not work with Ray. Mr. Wilson resorted to making Ray stay close to him during classes, between classes, at recess, in the lunch room, and even in going to the rest room.

Ray was the most disruptive student Lori had ever had. He tried to leave the room, or talk loudly, any time he wanted. The teachers wondered how they could discipline a child that didn't seem to be afraid of the devil, himself.

Rosita was tall and slender. She had long, black hair that looked unhealthy. It laid in tangles all over her head. Rosita wore long-sleeved, high-necked, ankle-length dresses, even in PE class. She wore high-healed shoes with dark-colored, holy socks, and she always carried a purse. Rosita wore PE shorts under her dresses. She looked a little more modest when she wrestled with the other students and her dress went up over her head.

Rosita was easy to spot on the playground among the other girls in their blue jeans. She was stronger than she looked and did well in the fights with other students. Rosita fought with all students no matter how young they were.

Teachers tried to correct Rosita. She usually sassed them and said, "You can't tell me what to do, and besides, the kids were picking on my little brother and little sister!"

Although Rosita, and Ray, were "street smart", they had severe problems in their academic work. Ray struggled reading on a second grade level, and Rosita had trouble with third grade reading material. It was hard to make Ray be quiet in class and Rosita would never answer any questions or respond to a teacher except in a negative manner.

Lori had to take a rubber band away from Ray on the playground one day. He had been shooting other students with it. A short time later, Lori caught Ray with another rubber band. She confiscated the second rubber band and made Ray turn his pockets inside out to prove he didn't have any more rubber bands.

A few minutes later, Ray was flipping kids with another rubber band. Several students came to Lori to show the welts on their arms where Ray had flipped them.

Lori took the third rubber band away from Ray, and made Ray show the inside of his pockets again. As Lori walked to another part of the playground, she watched Ray. Lori saw Rosita hand Ray another rubber band from her purse.

Lori walked over to Ray and took the rubber band before he could hurt another student. "Rosita, let me see if you have any more rubber bands in your purse," Lori demanded. She grabbed the purse, but Rosita would not let go. She screamed, cried, and was ready to fight. Lori gave up because she had so many other children to watch. "Don't go close to Ray, or I will send you to the principal," Lori yelled.

"I won't," Rosita whimpered.

The Principal checked Rosita's purse a few days later. He was shocked to find switchblade knives in the purse along with her large supply of rubber bands.

Ray and Rosita were in trouble so often that Lori dreamed about them at night. In her dreams, Ray was in a prison. She saw Rosita holding a sick, crying baby with no husband to take care of her.

Lori was so worried about Ray one night that she asked Tim, "What would you think about having a young boy in our home for a few weeks?"

Tim was reading the newspaper, but this quickly got his attention. "What are you talking about?" he asked.

"This boy, Ray . . . at school . . . I'm afraid that he is going to grow up to be a criminal . . . . You know the family that live on the old farm? . . . . Maybe, if we could keep him awhile and you could take him with you to feed cattle and things . . . . and we could buy him some nice clothes . . . and I could help him learn to read . . . . I think it might make a difference in his attitude and behavior," Lori tried to explain.

Tim did not answer right away. He was thinking about how his own kids had hurt him. Finally, he answered slowly, "We have all we can handle right now with the farming, the cattle, and your teaching, and I don't think we have time to try to change a problem kid!"

"You're right," Lori agreed. She never mentioned it again. Lori checked with Mrs. Medina. The school had obtained part of the Gonzales children's school records. The family had moved so often that the kids had missed a lot of school. "No wonder they can't read," Lori said.

"It seems that the older children have dropped out of school when they reached Ray and Rosita's age. Mrs. Gonzales can neither read nor write," Mrs. Median explained.

"Probably when the kids can read on a second grade level, the family considers them educated," Lori remarked.

Mrs. Medina nodded her head to agree. "They can't function on their grade level so all they know how to do is to use their energy to cause trouble," she said.

Every week Ray and Rosita told their teachers, and the other students, that they were moving. It was obvious that moving had become an escape for them when school got too tough, or when they had made too many enemies.

Ray was interrupting the class by talking loudly one morning. Lori looked straight into his brown eyes and said, "Young man, if you were the only student in this classroom, I wouldn't mind taking the time to hear what you have to say, but I have nineteen other students to think about. If you, in any way, try to stop me from teaching my lesson, I'll stop you in any way I can!" "Do you understand?" she asked.

Ray did not answer, but he sat quietly in his seat for the rest of the class period. He showed, by his body language, that he was not going to look at his book or listen to the lecture about the country they were studying.

Lori let Ray pout for a few minutes. "You can waste your time if you want to, Ray, but the rest of us are going to learn something this morning," she said quietly.

The lunch bell rang. Lori dismissed all of the students but Ray. "Ray, you stay where you are," she ordered. Lori waited until the other students had left the room. She sat down in the empty desk in front of Ray. Lori turned around so she could face the boy.

Ray had his fists clenched, waiting for another lecture.

"I hear that you guys are getting ready to move again," Lori said.

"Yeah," Ray answered. "Whatcha want to know for?" he asked.

Lori looked at her rebellious student. He was still a boy, but he would soon be a man. With tears in her eyes, she started to talk softly. "Ray, you're headed the wrong way. Do you realize where you'll end up if you keep going the way you are going now? I'm willing to do anything I can to help you change; even taking you home to live with me and my husband if your folks would let me. Maybe we could help you learn your school work, and help you start feeling different about yourself, and about others."

Ray had been looking down at his desk. He slowly looked up and Lori saw tears in the big bully's eyes. "Why wouldja want to do that for?" Ray asked.

"Because, you silly kid, I like you and I care about what happens to you," Lori said with a smile. "Now go on out and eat your lunch," she ordered.

Ray tried to be good in class, but his classes were too difficult for him. He always ended up getting restless and causing trouble.

Rosita settled down enough to answer a question now and then. The Gonzales family did not move.

One evening, Lori had just come into the house from doing her chores. She heard Kato barking. Lori looked through the kitchen widow just in time to see a red and white pickup pull into the driveway. It was Mr. and Mrs. Gonzales, and six of the kids. Lori walked out to the Ford pickup and greeted her neighbors.

Carlos introduced himself, his wife Juanita, and his two small granddaughters that were in the front seat. "We are raising these little girls for my son," Carlos explained. Ray, Rosita, Becky, and Leos were quietly sitting in the back of the pickup.

Juanita was pretty, but much over-weight. She looked more Indian than Spanish with a large black braid hanging almost to her waist. This is where Ray gets his good looks, Lori was thinking.

Carlos was dark, slender, and tall. He looked more Spanish with a large mustache and lots of black, curly hair. Rosita favors her father as much as Ray favors Juanita, Lori was thinking. "Would you like to come in?" Lori asked her guests.

"We're too dirty to get out," Carlos apologized with a Spanish accent. "We have been working in the garden. Ray and Rosita have been pestering me all week to bring you, their teacher, a watermelon and some cantaloupes," Mr. Gonzales explained. He grinned, proudly at his kids in the back.

Lori looked over at Ray and Rosita. She smiled and said, "Thank you". The kids looked down at their feet, bashfully. I've never seen them

<u>so quiet,</u> Lori was thinking. She took the heavy box of fruit that Carlos handed her and placed it on the sidewalk.

Carlos talked about the weather, cattle and the coming winter. Juanita agreed with everything he said by shaking her head. Lori wondered if Juanita could talk English.

Carlos noticed that Lori was watching the two, cute little girls. "We had to cut their hair off like a boy's so Juanita could take care of it. Juanita isn't well," he explained. Carlos lovingly patted each girl on the head.

Lori guessed the girls to be about one and three years old.

Carlos saw that the little girls were getting restless. "We must go now and get the kids home for supper," he said. "You can come over any time," Carlos said through a big smile.

"Thank you for the invitation. I just might stop by some day," Lori replied. She waved as the pickup backed away from the yard and started east on the country road.

Everyone waved back as the vehicle traveled out of sight in a cloud of dust.

CHAPTER III

THE ACCIDENT

It was December the fourth. The weather had been more like a warm summer day rather than a cold winter day. It was Saturday, and all the Gonzales children were home. Carlos had been around the house since he had fed the cattle early that morning. Juanita was busy cleaning house, washing clothes, and fixing tortillas. Carlos helped by taking care of the younger children and making the older children help their mother.

"While I finish the cleaning, Carlos, would you like to go to town and buy a few groceries?" Juanita asked.

"Sure, Mama. Tell me what you need so I can write it down," Carlos answered.

Juanita named several items. "Come right back, Carlos. I am very tired," Juanita said in her native Spanish.

"Okay mama," Carlos replied. "Does anyone want to go to town with me?" Carlos shouted happily in English.

Six-year-old Becky, and five-year-old Leos yelled, "We do. We do!"

"Well, don't just stand there. Get into the truck. We have to hurry," Carlos ordered, laughing.

The two kids crawled into the pickup. Carlos carefully shut and locked the doors. As he crawled into the driver's seat, Becky and Leos waved to Rosita and the little girls standing with Rosita at the kitchen door.

Carlos started the pickup. He was crossing the yard when he saw Juanita carrying the trash to the trash barrel on the other side of the yard. "Shall we see if we can run over mama?" he said, teasing Becky and Leos.

"No!" the kids both squealed with laughter.

The kids were giggling as Carlos pulled toward Juanita. Juanita shook her head "no" at her funny husband and pointed a finger toward town.

Carlos saluted his wife and started backing up the pickup in order to circle around the house. At the same time, two-year-old Sita called, "Me too!" The little girl ran from the house and behind the pickup. She ran so fast that Rosita could not catch her.

Carlos backed the pickup on back. He felt a terrible bump that he could not understand. He could not remember seeing anything in the yard that he could have backed over. It felt like a post or something. He looked toward the house where Rosita was screaming. She was jumping up and down. He looked toward the trash barrel and saw Juanita waving her arms and running toward him. She was screaming, "My baby! My baby!"

Carlos jumped out of the vehicle. He saw little Sita lying on the ground. She was covered with dirt and there were tire marks across her small body. She was lying very still and whimpering.

Juanita gently lifted Sita up into her arms as she motioned for all the other kids to get into the family car. She was screaming orders in Spanish. "To the doctor!" Juanita screamed at Carlos.

Carlos felt numb. "This can't happen," he whispered. He let out one sickening sound and touched Sita's tiny hand. By the time Carlos had walked around the car and crawled under the steering wheel, Juanita was in the front seat with Sita, and the other kids were in the back seat. Ray was the last to crawl into the car. He checked both back doors after he had locked them.

The new, blue Chivvy was the most expensive thing Carlos owned. He spun the car around and was soon on the main road traveling eighty miles an hour.

Sita was still whimpering. Juanita tried to make her more comfortable, but nothing seemed to help. The other children were giggling in the back seat to cover up their fear.

Carlos drove the thirty-five miles in thirty minutes, but it seemed more like two hours. Before the car had completely stopped, Juanita was running into the hospital with her small grandchild folded in her arms.

Juanita ran into the emergency room and laid Sita on the examining table. The nurse couldn't understand what Juanita was saying in Spanish, and through her sobs, but she could tell what had happened when she was the marks on the baby's body. She called the doctor, and he was there in ten minutes.

The doctor carefully examined the baby and said, "She has internal injuries. We must operate right away because she is bleeding on the inside." He shouted for the nurses to call everyone that was needed for the surgery while he went to wash his hand, and put on his surgical clothes. "Time is important!" he shouted.

"Go find your brother and his wife so that Sita's mama and papa will be here for the surgery!" Carlos shouted to Rosita. "Ray, you watch the little ones?" he ordered.

Rosita ran swiftly across the small town to her brother's house. No one was there. After catching her breath, she ran toward the local bowling alley in another part of town. She only stopped twice to catch her breath again before she reached the metal, blue and white building that was the main source of recreation for many miles.

"Thank you God!" Rosita said when she saw her brother's car parked in the parking lot. She ran into the building and quickly spotted her sister-in-law, Molly. Molly was a full-blooded Indian. She was dark, tall, and very skinny, with long, straight, black hair. "Molly, Molly, Sita has been hurt bad!" Rosita shouted.

"Now don't get so excited," the teenage mother said. She took another drink of her coke. "It can't be that bad," Molly sighed.

"But it is! It is! Papa ran over her!" Rosita shouted through sobs.

"Well, get in my car and we will find out how bad it is," Molly ordered.

"Where's Joey?" Rosita asked.

"He's working ten miles out east of town," Molly said.

"We have to get him, too. Sita is in the hospital. They are getting her ready for surgery. Papa said for me to bring <u>both</u> of you back to the hospital!" Rosita shouted.

"Well, if that's what he said, that's what you better do," Molly said and turned the car around and drove toward the place where Joey was working.

When Rosita finally returned to the hospital with Molly and Joey, Sita had been in surgery for two hours. They walked into the waiting room and quietly sit down beside Juanita and Carlos.

Rosita quietly took Sita's sister, Bitina, from Juanita's lap and cuddled her in her own arms. She tried to comfort the restless child while they waited.

Thirty minutes later, the doctor came out of the operating room. He walked slowly toward the family. His face was pale and sweaty. He smelled like medicine.

Carlos stood up and met the doctor at the door of the room. The doctor slowly explained, "We have completed surgery, and we have stopped the bleeding . . . We have done all we can do."

Before the doctor finished talking, two nurses came out of the operating room pushing a hospital bed. Tiny Sita was just a small lump under the white sheets. An I.V. bottle was attached to the head of the bed. The nurses were halfway to the recovery room when one of them called, "Doctor, come quick!"

The Gonzales family watched as the doctor and nurses wheeled Sita back into the operating room and worked over her. Ten minutes passed. The doctor came out of the operating room and walked toward the family for the second time. He looked even more tired and pale.

"She was terribly crushed . . . We did all we could do . . . She had lost a lot of blood . . . I'm sorry we couldn't save her . . . If there is anything

I can do to help . . ." His voice trailed off as he sadly walked back to the operating room and closed the door.

Carlos fell back into a chair. "I killed her! I killed her!" he screamed.

Juanita kept screaming, "My baby. My baby!"

Rosita shouted, "No! It's my fault, papa. I should have made her stay in the house until you were gone out of the yard. It's my fault!"

"No! It's my fault, Rosita!" Carlos screamed.

"No! It's my fault!" Rosita screamed back. With a cry of anguish, Rosita ran from the hospital. She ran down the front sidewalk. She was soon across the street, and running wildly down a dark alley before Joey caught her.

Rosita felt someone grab her arm and fought like a wildcat.

Joey tried to hold Rosita. "Rosita Sita was my daughter and it wasn't anybody's fault, understand?" Joey said, shaking his sister.

Rosita screamed again, "It's my fault!" Her face started to sting as she realized that Joey was slapping her. Rosita jerked back and looked at Joey. She felt dizzy.

"Let's go back to the hospital and see her before the mortuary comes to pick her up," Joey said gently. "We have a lot of work to do to make her the prettiest little girl anyone ever saw for the funeral," he said. Joey gently pulled Rosita back to the hospital and into the room where Sita's body lay.

Rosita did not want to see Sita, but she was in the room with the rest of the family. Baby Sita looked like she was asleep. Rosita had never seen her so still. She had always been moving, even when she was asleep.

Juanita was screaming and crying. The rest of the family were trying to help Juanita. Rosita walked across the room and patted the still warm hand. "Why God?" she asked.

The small community heard about the accident and many people gave money to help with the expenses. The family picked out a pretty, tiny casket, a blue organdy dress with lots of lace, and new shiny white shoes. Juanita wasn't well enough to help the rest of the family with the funeral preparations.

The next evening Carlos came home with the clothes Sita had been wearing at the time of the accident. Juanita started to cry uncontrollably.

"You must do away with these clothes," Carlos told Rosita.

Rosita picked up the box of clothes, but before she could put them away, Carlos grabbed the box and hid it somewhere in his and Juanita's bedroom.

Carlos had just sit down to rest when he heard a noise. He jumped to his feet. The noise came from the back porch and Carlos knew what it was. Juanita was having another epileptic seizure. Carlos ran to the porch. Rosita was already there trying to help her mother.

Juanita was standing like a stiff board in the corner of the two-foot ledge above the basement stairs. Carlos could hear his heart pounding.

Rosita was pulling with all her strength to keep Juanita from tumbling head first over the fatal drop-off. Juanita was frozen with her eyes rolled back into her head.

Carlos edged his way to Rosita, grabbed Juanita, and yelled, "Get the high-chair from the kitchen, Rosita!"

Rosita moved swiftly around Carlos and Juanita. She jumped to the first step, ran across the porch, grabbed the baby's high-chair, and was back in seconds. Rosita handed the chair to Carlos.

"Hold her again," Carlos shouted.

Rosita gritted her teeth as she pulled as hard as she could toward the opposite direction of the stairs. She could taste the salt from the sweat running down her face, <u>or was it tears?</u> Rosita wondered.

Carlos ran down the stairs. He pushed the high-chair against Juanita's stiff body. Inch by inch, they slid Juanita sideways from the terrible ledge, and laid Juanita's clammy body on the porch floor.

Carlos tried shaking Juanita, but she wouldn't respond. "We have to get her to the car, Rosita, so we can take her to the doctor," he shouted. "I can't get her to move at all!" Carlos shouted.

Rosita looked around to see if the three younger ones were all right. She saw Ray, Becky, and Leos peeking out from behind the kitchen door. Becky was holding Bitina.

Rosita called them to her. She put her arms around them like a mother hen protecting her chickens. "Everything is going to be all right," Rosita said.

It was difficult to put a large woman, whose muscles were frozen, into the car. With Ray's help, they slid Juanita into the back seat. The kids were giggling again because they were afraid, and they seldom had a chance to ride in the front seat.

The doctor said that Juanita had to stay in the hospital. It was up to Rosita to dress the little ones, get the meals, and see that everyone looked their best for the funeral. It seemed to Rosita that everyone always showed up at meal time. Besides the family, including some older brothers and sisters, many friends showed up at the farm the morning of the funeral.

Rosita was sure everyone was out of the house and in their cars ready to drive to the funeral. "I have to run back into the house because I forgot something," Rosita said. With her usual speed, she ran into the old house and to her father's bedroom. She knew that Carlos had forgotten about Sita's clothes.

Rosita quickly reached under the bed and pulled out the small box. She took out one of Sita's small shoes and put it in her purse. "No one can ever take this part of you away from me, Sita," Rosita whispered. "Maybe papa will think it got lost when he burns up these things before mama gets to come home," she told herself. Rosita was back in the car so fast that Carlos didn't think much about it.

Rosita was proud that the funeral was so pretty. Sita looked like a big Christmas doll in the new blue dress and white shoes. Juanita's preacher did a fine job of reading the scriptures. Rosita was thinking, <u>Mama is a very religious person but none of our family goes to church with her much . . . . Rosita, you will always try not to hurt mama and papa the way the other kids have . . . You will always be a good girl and protect</u>

the others . . . and help in any way that you can . . . . Mama and papa have been hurt enough!

The service was a short one. The preacher gave a short message about Sita being in Heaven and that everyone needed to accept Jesus as their Savior and live for Him so they could see Sita again, someday. Rosita didn't think that some of the others were listening to what the preacher was saying, but mama would be happy to know what had been said.

After the preacher finished his talk, a lady from the church sang, "Flowers for the Master's Bouquet". The preacher prayed and everyone marched past the tiny casket. "Good-bye Sita," Rosita said as she looked at the small body for the last time. "I will miss you," she whispered.

The group drove slowly to the cemetery. There were trees and grass there, which made it one of the prettiest places in the area. There would be many flowers in the spring and summer. Rosita was glad the cemetery was a pretty place even on this dreary winter day.

After another prayer, the people watched the small casket as it was lowered into the brown earth. It was already getting colder, the wind was staring to blow, and there were a few flakes of snow in the wind.

The family sadly walked away. Joey walked beside Carlos. "Don't blame yourself no more, papa," Joey said. "You did the best you could. Maybe Molly and me shoulda tried to raise her, but Molly is so young, and you know mama wanted to raise the girls . . . Just don't blame yourself no more," Joey repeated.

Carlos shrugged his tired shoulders and nodded in agreement. He felt so helpless and defeated.

The family was silent as they drove back to the old farm. Each one was lost in their memories of little Sita. Rosita had the tiny shoe her coat pocket so she could squeeze it without anyone knowing what she was doing.

CHAPTER IV

CHANGE OF LOCATION

Carlos didn't know what to do. Juanita was still in the hospital, and the doctor said she would have to stay there for quite awhile. She may never be strong enough to come back to the farm and see the place where Baby Sita was run over, Carlos was thinking.

Each time Carlos had gone to see Juanita, she started crying and screaming, "My baby! My baby!"

"I must be with her as much as I can, anyway," Carlos said to himself. The kids needed him at home and he had his farm job to think about. The boss had moved in more cattle for him to take care of. If he didn't do a good job, he would not have a job and a place to live, or money or food.

I'm glad that Joey and Molly have decided to take care of Baby Betina until Juanita is strong enough to come home, Carlos was thinking. "How can I do everything and send Bobby to high school, and the others to grade school?" Carlos asked himself aloud. "My Rosita, she is working too hard to help me," he said with a sigh.

Carlos was thinking about some neighbors that were fine Christian folks. They had told him, even before the accident, that if they could help in any way, to let them know.

"That's it. I'll ask them to keep my kids for a few days until things get better. Juanita won't mind because they are Christians," Carlos said.

Carlos stopped by the neighbor's farm on his way to the hospital that evening. As he drove into the McCormick driveway, he looked at their new, beautiful, two-story home. If the inside was as pretty as the outside, his kids would think they were living in a palace.

Three large, but friendly, dogs greeted Carlos as he walked up to the front door. About the time Carlos knocked, Lee opened the door. Carlos saw Judy and their three girls standing behind Lee.

"Hello Carlos. Come right in," Lee said with a smile. "How's Juanita?" he asked.

"She's still in the hospital, and I need your help," Carlos answered humbly.

"We'll help in any way we can," Lee replied.

"I need someone to keep the kids in school for me until Juanita comes home. The hospital is in one direction, and school is in the other direction. It is very hard for me go to each place. Rosita works hard to take care of the others, but she is too young for so much responsibility," Carlos explained. "Maybe it wouldn't be for very long," he added.

"Do you think we can find room for five extra kids for awhile?" Lee asked Judy.

"Sure, but I'd like for you to bring them over this evening so I can be sure they are ready for school in the morning," Judy replied.

"Thank you," Carlos said. He hurried to the car to make the trip back to his house. "I'll have them back here in an hour," he called over his shoulder.

"I can take care of everyone, papa!" Rosita shouted.

"You're a good girl. I'm glad for your help, but it will be better for all of you to stay with Lee and Judy for awhile," Carlos said sternly.

"Yes, papa," Rosita replied, bitterly. She tossed wrinkled clothes into two boxes and stuffed more clothes into brown paper sacks. Rosita put several pairs of old shoes into more paper bags.

Ray and Bobby packed their own clothes.

Carlos left the kids and their belongings. "Thanks again for your help. I must hurry if I get to the hospital before visiting hours are over," Carlos said and waved good-bye.

"We understand. Don't worry," Judy said.

Everyone waved as the blue Chivvy turned around and headed toward the main road.

The Gonzales children were looking at the McCormick family.

Lee was a tall, slender, light-skinned man with a black mustache. His hair was black and thinning on top.

Judy was a tall, pretty, brown-eyed blonde, with a nice tan complexion.

Kathy, the oldest daughter, was Rosita's age, but she was two grades ahead of Rosita in school. She was tall and blonde. Kathy was even more slender than Rosita. She was quiet and reserved, and she was a straight A student in school.

Jill was only four-years-old. She had black hair and light skin, and favored Lee. Jane was three. She was another brown-eyed blonde, and she favored Judy.

"Rosita, would you like to share my bedroom with me while you're here?" Kathy asked.

Rosita had fought all her life just to survive. She didn't know how to get along with a girl her own age. "I suppose I'll have to," Rosita said hatefully. She took her paper sacks and slowly followed Kathy upstairs.

"I hate you!" Rosita said as soon as the girls were in the bedroom.

"Why?" Kathy asked in surprise.

"You're rich, living in a place like this. My mother deserves a place like this, not your mother. You get everything you want from nice clothes to pretty horses, and that's why I hate you!" Rosita answered with a sneer.

"We're not rich, and I'm sorry you feel the way you do," Kathy replied.

Judy assigned places for each of the guests to sleep. She supervised each child's bath. Judy made sure everyone's skin and hair were clean before the kids crawled into clean beds.

The kids were finally all in bed. Lee helped Judy wash, iron, and hang up the Gonzales's clothes. It was past midnight when they wearily climbed into bed.

Kathy had never had to share her bedroom, and parents, before. She tried to get along with Rosita, but the girls fought continually. The second day Judy worked hard to get the six kids on the bus did not go any smoother than the first day.

After breakfast, Kathy went to her bedroom to finish getting ready for school. "Rosita! That's my best pair of panty hose. I only wear them to church. Please don't wear them to school. You'll get a hole in them," Kathy yelled.

"That's okay. Your mother is rich and she can buy you another pair," Rosita said.

"Mom, make her stay out of my things," Kathy yelled down the stairs.

The next morning Kathy thought she saw Rosita with one of her rings. "Rosita, what do you have in your hand?" Kathy asked. Rosita's slender hands and fingers were moving so fast that Kathy wasn't sure she had really seen anything. Rosita wouldn't steal my jewelry, Kathy tried to convince herself.

Rosita replied, "I don't have to tell you everything I do, nosy!"

Kathy went downstairs to talk to her mother.

Judy listened above the noise of the other kids playing. "Kathy, I know you're upset, but Rosita hasn't had nice things. If she has your ring, I'll find out," Judy said. "Every time I try to scold Rosita, she takes something out of her purse and goes into the bedroom and cries. Just be patient a few more days, dear, and they will all be going home. Things will soon be back to normal again," Judy said.

Kathy had started back up the stairs when Judy called after her. "Kathy, by the way, I've decided to put Rosita and Becky in the same bed and let you sleep with your little sisters," "God will be pleased with you for helping this family in their time of need," she added.

"Thanks mom. That will help," Kathy replied.

That night everyone was in bed, and the house was quiet. "Becky, hold out you hand. I have something for you," Rosita whispered.

"What is it?" Becky asked. She held out her hand as Rosita put an object into it. "It's a ring," Becky squealed.

"See if it fits one of your fingers," Rosita whispered.

"It does. I want to see what it looks like, and it's too dark in here," Becky said.

"If you can't wait until morning, then pretend that you're going to the bathroom and look at it in there with the door shut," Rosita instructed.

Becky crawled out from under the covers and tip-toed into the bathroom. She soon returned and crawled back under the covers.

"Do you like it?" Rosita asked.

"Unhuh," Becky said with a giggle.

"Don't let anyone see you wear it except at school, or when we move back home, understand?" Rosita whispered under the covers.

"Unhuh," Becky answered. She snuggled up to Rosita's warm body and was soon asleep.

Kathy slept a lot better with her sisters. That evening after school, she found several pieces of her jewelry missing. Kathy asked Rosita bout it.

Rosita started to cry. "You probably just lost it. You accuse me of taking it just because I'm a different color than you," she said with a sob.

Kathy had put up with Rosita long enough. She stomped down the stairs and into the kitchen. Judy was busy fixing dinner for her large family. "Mom, I need to talk to you," Kathy said.

Judy sat down to listen.

"Mom, Rosita has taken some more of my things, and now she says she didn't!" Kathy exclaimed.

"Maybe someone else did take them, dear," Judy said.

Kathy was a gentle, intelligent girl, but she felt that she could not take any more of Rosita. "I know she took them. If Rosita is here after school tomorrow, I will not come home after volleyball practice, nor will

I <u>ever</u> come home until she is gone!" Kathy said. "You can just raise her and I will let grandpa and grandma raise me!" she shouted.

Kathy ran to her room before Judy could answer. She didn't come downstairs for supper that night, or for breakfast the next morning. Kathy came down from her room just in time to get on the bus the next morning.

Judy had not slept well. Kathy had never been any trouble. She really wasn't selfish. <u>Maybe Lee and I are selfish to expect Kathy to give up everything so we can do our Christian duty and help Carlos and his family,</u> Judy thought. She knew she had to do something. Judy finished the dishes and made the beds, before she went to town. She knocked on Lori's classroom door.

Lori was glad to see her neighbor and friend.

"I need to talk to you, Lori," Judy said.

"Sure," Lori replied. She stepped back into the classroom and gave an assignment to her class. "I have a visitor outside. I need for you to read the next two pages in your textbook and we will discuss them when I come back in. Please be quiet," Lori instructed. She stepped back into the hall.

Lori and Judy had taught school together. Now they only lived two miles apart. Judy had stopped teaching for a few years to stay home with her two little girls. Right now, Judy looked unhappy.

"Lori, I know you've heard about Mr. Gonzales accidentally running over his little granddaughter?" Judy said, slowly.

Lori shook her head yes. "I feel so sorry for the poor man. I know he really loved the little girl," Lori replied.

Judy continued, "Sita's death has put Mrs. Gonzales in the hospital with epilepsy seizures."

"How sad," Lori whispered.

"Mr. Gonzales didn't feel that he could do his farm work, visit Juanita in the hospital thirty five miles away, and take care of all the kids, and keep them in school," Judy explained. "I can take care of all the kids, except for Rosita," Judy said in desperation. "She has caused so many problems that Kathy says she is going to stay with her grandparents until Rosita is gone," Judy explained.

"Judy, I can't imagine Kathy talking to you like that. I taught her for two years, and I haven't ever heard her say a cross word to anyone," Lori replied.

"I know, but this situation seems to be more than she can handle," Judy replied.

"I know Rosita can be a problem at times," Lori agreed.

"Lori, if you and Tim could just take Rosita, I can take care of the others. I hate to ask you to do this, but I don't know what else to do. You don't have any kids at home for her to fight with," Judy said.

"Sure, we'll keep Rosita," Lori said. "Tim and I are the ones that should be taking care of those kids. We have a large house with three extra bedrooms. You have your girls to think about!" Lori exclaimed. "I'm sorry we haven't been any help until now," Lori added.

Judy started to leave when Lori said, "You can bring Rosita's clothes over to my house and leave them by the back door before we get home." "Our biggest problem will be separating her from the other kids. She feels like she has to take care of them," Lori explained.

"You do know her pretty well, don't you?" Judy said. "What do you think Tim will say?" she asked.

"There's not much he can say in circumstances like these, and I'm pretty sure he won't mind anyway," Lori answered.

That evening when Lori stepped into the bus, Rosita was pounding the back of a seat with her fists. She was angry because Judy had picked up all the kids but her.

Lori waited until the bus was a few miles out of town before she said, "Rosita, you're going home with me tonight."

Rosita pointed a long finger at Lori and shouted, "Oh no, I'm not!"

Lori had to talk above the noise of the bus. "Judy and I had a talk today and she asked me if you could stay with us for a few days," Lori explained.

"She hates me!" Rosita screamed.

"No she doesn't, but she does have her own girls to think about. Besides, I need a girl at my house. Judy has three girls and I don't have any," Lori yelled above bus noise.

"We'll see!" Rosita screamed. She crossed her arms to pout.

The bus stopped at Lori's house. Rosita refused to get out. Doris knew what was going on, and she refused to drive on with Rosita still on the bus.

The other kids started yelling at Rosita to get off the bus so they could get home.

Rosita realized that she was out numbered. She reluctantly got off the bus with Lori.

"Rosita, you might as well try to make the best of our situation. It will make it easier for you. We'll do everything we can to make you happy while you are here," Lori said as she unlocked the back door. Lori picked up Rosita's clothes that Judy had placed beside the door.

Rosita didn't offer to help carry the clothes. "You can't make me happy. I guess I'll stay here just so I won't worry mama," Rosita said. "What am I supposed to call you around here, anyway?" Rosita asked hatefully.

"You can call me Lori, if you still call me Mrs. Jones at school," Lori answered. "I taught my youngest son and he had to call me Mrs. at school, too," Lori said.

Rosita didn't smile. She found a large chair to fall into and pout.

"Rosita, would you like to go with me to feed the chickens and gather eggs?" Lori asked.

"No! I'm not going outside and be your slave!" Rosita screamed.

"I'll be back in a little while," Lori replied, ignoring Rosita's nasty attitude.

Rosita turned her face toward the wall. She had her upper lip sticking out, still pouting.

As soon as Lori was out of the house, Rosita jumped up to explore the house she was going to stay in for a few days. She quickly went from room to room, remembering where everything was located.

Rosita had already seen the laundry room where the washer, dryer, and freezer were located. She opened the freezer and was pleased to find some ice-cream bars. At least I won't starve, Rosita was thinking.

Next to the laundry room was a large eating area that was part of the large kitchen. The area had two cabinets, a table, and four chairs on rollers, and an old chest with a TV on top. An eating bar was between the dinette and kitchen.

The kitchen had dark cabinets with bright copper handles. On the top of one cabinet was something that looked like an outside barbecue grill. The carpet was brown, orange, and yellow. It had names of food written on it. Rosita stepped on the words and read, "beans, flour, and corn." There were some other words she could not read.

The next room was the dining room. It had a thick, white carpet, and large, pretty, dark wood furniture. A buffet, china cabinet, table and chairs all matched. Rosita noticed some important looking papers in the china closet.

The next room was Rosita's favorite. It was the library. Rosita was not interested in the walls of books, but the room contained a piano, organ, guitar, and accordion. Rosita ran her long, slender fingers over the white, smooth, ivory keys of the piano and organ.

Knowing that Lori would soon be back, Rosita quickly continued her exploration.

The living room was large. It had two couches, three large chairs, a TV, fireplace, three coffee tables, and two end tables. The windows were covered with gold-colored, velvet drapes, with white satin ties.

"This must be Mrs. Jones's bedroom," Rosita said. The room had a large bed, other bedroom furniture, a small red couch, a red bean-bag chair, and a large white rocking chair. The bed and windows were covered with red-colored velvet.

"There is the third telephone," Rosita said. She remembered one in the kitchen, and one in the music room. "At least I can make calls when I want to," she said.

Rosita returned to the music room and opened a door. It opened up to a small bedroom that had old, but shiny furniture. She returned to the large bedroom and went through the door on the opposite side. Here she found a small hall. At the end of the hall was a two-part bathroom with blue fixtures and red carpet.

On the other side of the hall was another door. This was a middle-sized bedroom with white walls and wooden floors.

"This must be all of it," Rosita said. Then she saw another door. Here she found a fourth bedroom. The furniture in it looked like it had been made from wagon wheels.

Rosita saw another door. She opened it and found herself back in the kitchen eating space.

Rosita heard footsteps outside. She knew Lori was returning. Rosita ran back to the chair she had been sitting in when Lori left and acted like she had been there all the time.

Lori came in and hung up her coat in the laundry room. "It sure is cold outside," she said, rubbing her hands together.

"I'm going outside to walk around!" Rosita screamed.

"Be sure to put on your coat and don't go too far away from the house," Lori ordered.

Rosita put on her heavy, old fashioned coat. She put her nose up in the air as a sign of defiance, and marched out the back door.

The row of trees surrounding the house had been covered with green leaves when her family stopped by last fall. Now the trees were bare. They looked like long, brown, skinny figures, swaying in the strong winter wind.

The outside buildings were white with brown roofs. They had lost most of their paint. The bare lilac bush swayed outside the large living room window. The yard had no grass, just bare ground. The double, dirt driveway was outside the row of trees west of the house. At the end of the driveway was a large garage with no doors.

Rosita walked to the garage and peeked in. It had a dirt floor. She walked around the empty garage and noticed a door on the back side. The door was propped open by a pile of sand. "Someone must have lived in here a long time ago," Rosita said. "Now it's filled with old furniture, and a lot of sand, boxes, and junk," she added.

Rosita walked to the east side of the house. Through the blowing dirt, and snow, that was beginning to fall, she saw a building beyond a large butane tank. Rosita pulled her coat tightly around her slender body and pushed her cold hands into the coat's fuzzy pockets. The hard snow and sand stung her face as it was tossed by the howling wind.

The old building had two rooms. One had an old stove, some cabinets, and an old table. There were some broken chairs in the room. An old refrigerator was full of important looking papers. The other room had an old bed, dresser, and closet.

As Rosita left the bunkhouse, she noticed an interesting object a few yards to the south of her. There was barely enough daylight to make it shine. Rosita was shaking from the cold, but she was determined to see what the object was.

Rosita walked toward the object. It was much larger than it had appeared from the bunkhouse. Rosita realized that it was a camper trailer. Her fingers hurt from the cold when she pressed in on the frozen door handle. The door opened after the third jerk. It was caught by the wind and slammed against the side of the camper.

"How pretty!" Rosita exclaimed as she squinted her eyes to see better through the dim light of dusk.

The camper had a bathroom trimmed in gold, a tiny kitchen, and lots of seats, and a table, covered in a bright material of pink flowers. I can come here to hide and be by myself, Rosita was thinking.

Rosita rubbed her hands after she closed the camper door. She could barely see a hen house, a small building, a large building, and some cattle pens to the north.

"I'll explore the rest later when it isn't so cold and dark," Rosita said to herself. "If I don't go in before it gets completely dark, old lady Jones will be out here looking for me," she told herself.

Rosita entered the house through the back door. She threw her coat over the washer. Rosita walked into the kitchen where the smell of onions and potatoes filled the air. She did not see Mrs. Jones anywhere. Rosita heard footsteps outside and ran to her chair and turned her face toward the wall.

Lori came in and hung up her, and Rosita's, coat on the coat rod next to the washer.

"Where have you been?" Rosita screamed.

"Following you so you wouldn't get lost in a strange place," Lori answered.

"It's not nice to spy on people!" Rosita shouted.

"It's not safe to be outside in the dark when it is staring to snow," Lori said without looking at Rosita.

"What's your husband's name and whatcha fixen for supper?" Rosita asked.

"Tim, and steak and potatoes," Lori answered.

"I don't like it fixed like that! I only like tortillas and I only like my mama's!" Rosita shouted.

"You might get rather hungry around here because I don't know much about fixing Mexican food," Lori replied.

"What makes you think I'm a Mexican?" Rosita yelled.

"I didn't say that you were, but you should be proud of what you are," Lori replied.

"I am!" Rosita shouted.

Tim drove in from feeding cattle. He entered the house and threw his heavy work coat on the washer. "What's for supper?" he asked on his way to the bathroom to wash his hands. "What do we have here?" he asked with a smile when he saw Rosita.

Rosita smiled and hid behind Lori.

"This pretty young lady is going to be our guest for a few days. Her name is Rosita," Lori answered.

"Welcome to our house and make yourself at home," Tim said, and continued to the bathroom.

Rosita refused to eat any supper. While Lori was cleaning up the kitchen, Rosita found some hard candy in the living room and ate part of it.

Lori finished the dishes and sat down in the living room where Rosita and Tim were sitting and looking at each other. "Rosita, your hair looks dry and matted. I'm going to wash it and condition it for you," Tim said.

Lori was surprised when Rosita walked to the kitchen with Tim and let him wash her hair in the kitchen sink. She found her best hair conditioner, and she and Tim gave Rosita's hair a health treatment.

"What's your cat's name?" Rosita asked.

"Tammi," Lori answered.

Rosita petted Tammi, and then she took a long bath using some of Lori's bubble bath. Rosita put her dirty clothes back on and came into the kitchen to watch TV with Tim and Lori.

"Rosita, as long as you're here living with us, you will put on clean clothes after you take a bath," Lori said.

"I don't have to, and I won't be here long, anyway!" Rosita shouted.

They watched TV for two hours. Tim turned off the TV after the ten o'clock news.

Lori walked Rosita to her bedroom which was the bedroom across the hall from her and Tim's. "Now I want you to take off those dirty clothes and put on you pajamas or nightgown," Lori ordered.

"I sleep with my clothes on and you can't make me take them off!" Rosita screamed.

Lori sat on top of Rosita and pulled off the girl's dirty, holly socks. "If you insist on wearing socks to bed, here are some of my clean, white ones," Lori said.

Rosita was crying so hard by this time that the bed was bouncing when Lori returned with some pajamas. "I guess just clean socks will do for tonight," Lori sighed.

"I hate you. I want to go to Judy's house, right now, where Becky is!" Rosita demanded between sobs.

Lori sat down beside Rosita and patted her. She pulled the covers off her face so she could talk to the crying girl. "Rosita, we can't take you to Judy's. You'll have to stay with us until your mother is well, like you said earlier this evening," Lori said.

Rosita pulled the covers tightly over her head again and cried harder. Lori gently pulled the covers off Rosita's head again and reached for Rosita's hands. "Rosita, what do you have in your hand?" Lori asked.

"None of your business!" Rosita shouted.

"Its a little girl's shoe," Lori said in surprise. "Rosita, is this Sita's shoe?" she asked.

"Yes," Rosita answered. She hugged the shoe and sobbed. "It's the one she was wearing when she was run over," Rosita explained.

"It's nice that you have a part of her to always take with you," Lori said, softly.

"When papa found out I had it, he tried to take it away from me. I promised him I'd never let mama see it, because it will make her cry," Rosita explained.

"My grandmother died when I was about your age," Lori said, remembering the past. "Grandma always made jelly roll cakes for us on our birthdays. She had made me a jelly roll cake for my birthday just a few days before she died. A few days after the funeral, I decided it would be nice to eat grandma's last cake. I took it out of the freezer and put it on the table. My mother saw it and was reminded that it was the last cake her mother would ever make. She started to cry. My daddy scolded me and told me to throw the cake away," Lori said.

"People act funny sometimes when they are awfully sad," Lori continued. "Would you like for me to pray with you before I go to bed?" she asked.

"Yes, but _you_ do it," Rosita answered.

Lori prayed that the Gonzales family would soon be over their sadness and soon be back together again. She prayed that Rosita would sleep well. Lori kissed Rosita on the forehead, left the room, and closed the door. She heard Rosita crying again.

Lori walked back to Rosita's bed. "Rosita, why did you cry when I closed the door?" she asked.

"Because I can't sleep by myself," Rosita sobbed.

"You have a nice bedroom and a nice comfortable bed. Isn't this enough?" Lori said, patting Rosita's arm.

"No! I've never slept by myself. I've always slept with Becky, Bitina, and Sita," Rosita said. She was crying again. "When I close my eyes, I see the accident all over again," Rosita whispered between sobs.

"I'm sorry Rosita, but I don't know what to do about it. I have to get some sleep so I can teach school tomorrow. Now go to sleep," Lori said, sternly. "Rosita, would you like for me to leave the door open?" Lori asked.

"Yes," Rosita whispered.

Lori was almost asleep when she had the feeling that someone was looking at her. She opened her tired eyes. With the help of the outside yard light, Lori saw Rosita on her hands and knees just inches from her face.

"Please let me sleep with you," Rosita pleaded.

Lori pulled her tired body up into a sitting position. "I guess it won't hurt this time. It looks like this is the only way we're going to get any sleep around here," she said.

Lori thought Tim was asleep when Rosita crawled into bed beside her, until he said, "Just a minute, if she's going to sleep with us, I'm going to put my clothes back on."

Lori put her arms around the crying, shaking girl, and held her tight.

"Do you know what happened to me once?" Lori asked, not expecting an answer.

"No what?" Rosita asked, ready for another story.

"I was almost eighteen when my grandpa came to visit us one morning. He liked to tease me and when he found out I was still in bed asleep, he came into my room and dropped a wet wash cloth on my face," Lori said. "I put on my housecoat and visited with him for awhile. When he started to drive back to town, where he lived, I told my mother that I wanted to order special flowers for him and grandma to wear at my wedding. My wedding was only two weeks away.

At about that time, my mother and I heard daddy calling us. We ran to the road in front of our farm. We could see grandpa's car partly in the ditch. When we got to the car, grandpa was already dead. His face and old bald head were purple. His old heart had finally stopped.

I was so upset that I slept with my folks for the rest of the week, and that was just two weeks before I was married," Lori said, finishing her story.

"That's kind of funny," Rosita said. Lori felt Rosita relax a little.

Lori was wide awake by this time. She could hear Tim lightly snoring on one side of her and Rosita breathing heavily on the other side. A few times Tim rolled over and put his arm around Lori. Lori made sure his hand never touched Rosita. Lori was glad that Tim and Rosita could sleep, anyway.

CHAPTER V

ADJUSTMENTS

A week went by before Rosita could go to sleep in her own bed. Tim and Lori gave her so much attention that she started to enjoy living with them, although she would never say so.

When Rosita thought about the other kids, she pouted and threatened to run away. She spent all her play time at school playing with Leos and Becky. Rosita never cared to play with students her own age, anyway.

It was on a Saturday morning that Lori knew Rosita was thinking about running away. She knew Rosita could travel the two miles to Judy's house in no time. Rosita was probably thinking the same thing.

"I'll take you to Judy's house if you promise me you'll leave without a fuss when it's time to come back home," Lori said.

"I promise," Rosita said, pleadingly.

Lori finished what she was doing. She and Rosita crawled into the car and drove the two miles south. When they crawled out of the car, they could smell baking cinnamon and sugar.

Judy and Lee had taken all of the kids to a wooded area to get a Christmas tree. The younger kids were helping Judy make Christmas cookies to hang on the tree. Lee, Bobby, and Ray were putting up the ten-foot tree in the two-story part of the living room.

Becky and Leos let out happy squeals when they saw Rosita. They hugged each other, and went off into another room to play.

Judy sat down to rest and visit with Lori.

Lori let Rosita play for over an hour, before she called, "It's time to go home now, Rosita."

"That's not my home and I'm not leaving unless Becky can come with me!" Rosita screamed.

"You promised not to argue when it was time to go home," Lori said.

"I don't care! I'm not going without Becky!" Rosita shouted.

Becky started to cry.

Judy was looking down at her lap. "I wish I could take care of all of them," she said.

"I feel just awful," Lori said. "We walked into a peaceful house just a short while ago. Now everyone is upset. I wish we hadn't come!" Lori exclaimed. She did the only thing she knew to do. Lori picked up the screaming, fighting girl, and started toward the front door.

Rosita was almost as tall as Lori. Lori could feel a pain in her lower back as she carried the girl across the floor.

Lee crawled down from the tree top to help. He took Rosita. Lori held the front door open. She opened the door of her car and Lee pushed Rosita into the front seat.

Lori was under the steering wheel by this time. She locked Rosita's door while the girl was still screaming and kicking.

"I'm sorry we upset everything," Lori yelled out of the window. She spun the car around and started home.

Rosita didn't try to force the door open once Lori was driving faster.

Lori pulled the car into her own yard and started honking the horn.

Tim came running out of the house. He calmly asked Rosita to get out of the car. Rosita refused. Tim asked her three times, and then he opened the door and pulled Rosita out of the car and carried her into the house. Rosita was hitting Tim on the head and shoulders all the way into the house.

Rosita was still fully dressed and had her shoes on when she sobbed herself to sleep that night. She was lying on top of the bed covers so Lori put a blanket over the sleeping girl.

The next morning, Rosita was the first one up and ready for church. She was hoping that Carlos would be there. Carlos had been in church the previous Sunday, and some of the church people gave him money to help with his expenses.

Rosita plopped down on the church bench next to the entrance door. She would not move. Lori and Tim did not want to cause a scene, so they sit next to her instead of where they usually sat.

Carlos didn't come.

Rosita pouted all the way home and refused to eat dinner.

Lori finished the dishes. She heard Rosita trying to play the piano. Lori sat down on the piano bench beside Rosita. "Would you like to learn how to play the piano?" she asked.

"Unhuh," Rosita whispered.

"Okay," Lori said. She pressed Rosita's fingers down on certain keys and had the girl to listen to the sound. It took Lori about thirty minutes to show Rosita how to play the C, G, and F chords. Rosita practiced the chords over and over. With her sharp mind and nimble fingers, Rosita was learning easily.

"Do you like to sing?" Lori asked the next evening.

"Yes," Rosita answered.

"Tim, come in here and let's teach Rosita some Christian songs," Lori called.

Tim had been reading in the living room. He came in with a smile on his face. "What ones do you want to teach her?" he asked.

"What would you like to learn?" Lori asked Rosita.

"Mama likes the song, This Is the Day That the Lord Has Made," Rosita said.

Lori, Tim, and Rosita sang the song, and then Rosita sung the song in Spanish. For the first time, they were having fun together.

"That was beautiful. Maybe we can go to the hospital soon, and you can sing for your mother, Rosita," Lori said.

"I can't do that," Rosita said bashfully, looking down at her lap.

"Sure you can," Lori replied. "I can take the guitar and help you sing the English part, and then you can sing the Spanish part," Lori explained.

"Okay," Rosita said with a giggle.

"Rosita, your hair is beginning to look shiny. Would you like for me to brush it for you?" Tim asked.

Lori could hardly believe it, when Rosita ran into the bedroom and found a hair brush. Tim brushed the girl's hair while Lori looked through her closets. She wanted to find some more stylish clothes for Rosita to wear.

Lori had Rosita try on some clothes she had worn when she was slender before she married Tim. The clothes were a little large, but they looked cute on Rosita. Lori even let Rosita wear her new denim platform sandals. Rosita felt proud when she went to school the next day in her stylish clothes. She even got into fewer fights than the day before.

Lori was getting ready for school the next morning. Rosita knocked on the bathroom door. "May I come in?" she asked.

"I guess its okay. I'm just putting on my makeup," Lori replied. She opened the door. "I'm not used to anyone watching me do this," Lori said, feeling embarrassed.

"Why do you put that stuff all over your face?" Rosita asked.

"So I won't look pale and sick," Lori answered.

"I don't ever look pale and sick," Rosita said proudly. "What's that green stuff you're putting above your eyes?" she asked. "It looks awful," Rosita added.

"It's called eye shadow," Lori answered. "I smooth it out like this," she said, trying not to get angry. "This is called rouge to make my cheeks pink. This is called mascara to make my ugly white eyelashes dark," Lori explained.

"My mother doesn't put on stuff like that," Rosita said. She went back into her bedroom to finish dressing for school.

"She doesn't hat to, she's pretty enough," Lori called after Rosita.

As soon as Lori left the bathroom, Rosita rushed in and closed the door. She unzipped the small blue bag and put on some eye shadow and rouge.

Lori was thinking that Rosita looked like she had circles under her eyes on the bus that morning. "She seems to be feeling all right, though," Lori told herself.

Rosita helped Lori with the chores after school. She cleaned her room and came into the laundry room to help Lori fold clothes.

Tim came home from town with some candy, a new blouse, and a pretty coat for Rosita. "The candy and blouse is from me, but the owner of the store in town gave me the coat for you," Tim said, smiling. He handed Rosita the things.

After payday, Lori went to the store and bought some white, silk-looking socks to replace Rosita's dark, holy ones.

The evenings were spent with Tim brushing Rosita's hair, and Rosita learning new church songs. Tim, Lori, and Rosita sung the special song at church the next Sunday.

Tim bought Rosita something every time he went to town. Every time they went somewhere in the car or pickup, Rosita always ran ahead of Lori so she could sit in the middle of the front seat next to Tim. She always ran out to meet Tim when he came home from work.

Rosita laughed at Lori the first time she watched her put rollers in her hair. "My mama doesn't make her hair do that," Rosita said.

"She doesn't have to. Her hair is long enough to braid, and it looks pretty that way," Lori replied.

"She never cuts her hair and I want long hair like hers," Rosita said.

After Rosita washed her hair Saturday morning, Lori talked Rosita into letting her curl it with the curling iron. The girl looked pretty with soft, shiny curls around her face.

Lori decided that if Rosita was going to wear makeup, she might as well learn how to put it on correctly. She let Rosita wear just enough to give a pink glow to her dark skin. The boys begin paying as much attention to Rosita as if she was a new student.

Rosita was now bathing and putting on clean clothes from the skin out. She still slept in her clothes, and never wore the nightgown Tim bought her.

One evening as they were sitting in the music room singing and laughing, Tim said, "I wish you could be our little girl forever. I wish we could adopt you."

Rosita stopped singing. "I only belong to my mama and papa, and don't you forget it!" she shouted.

"I'm sorry. I just forgot," Tim said, apologizing.

Rosita was soon singing with Tim and Lori at the Nursing Home. The old folks loved her. Daddy Andy always laughed and tried to talk when he saw Rosita. His condition was so bad, that he didn't even know all of his family when they came to visit.

The only way Tim and Lori knew how to communicate with Daddy Andy was through music. He usually laughed, and shouted, "Praise the Lord!" when they sung to him.

"And to think he was eight-three years old before he became a Christian," Tim said. He was remembering the times Daddy Andy had chased people off his place when they came to invite him to church.

Rosita was fitting into Tim and Lori's lives more than they could have ever imagined. The girl always wanted to be close to Tim until the night of the Christmas party at the Nursing Home.

CHAPTER VI

ROSITA'S MYSTERIOUS CHANGE

It was the night of the Christ party at the Nursing Home. Tim picked up Lori and Rosita right after school. Rosita ran ahead of Lori so she could sit next to Tim. They visited happily the hour it took to reach their destination.

Tim stopped by a fast-food place where Lori bought a bucket of fried chicken and some potato salad.

Sarah was waiting for them at the door of the large Tumble Weed recreation room where the Joneses sung for the people on Sundays. Inside the room were four long tables covered with dishes of food. Lori and Rosita put their food on one of the tables and joined Sarah and Tim. They were standing beside Daddy Andy in his wheel chair.

The room was so crowded that it was hard for people to get from one place to another. Each family was trying to find a place where the whole family could sit together. Some people, like the Joneses, needed to find places large enough to accommodate wheel-chairs too.

Tim was pushing Daddy Andy's wheel-chair when he heard someone say, "You people can sit here, Mr. Jones". Tim looked up and saw one of the workers pointing to a place near the end of a table.

Tim pushed Daddy Andy's chair up to the table near the corner. The rest of them sit down around Daddy Andy. Paper cups containing a pink-colored drink had already been placed on the table. It was hot in the room and they drank some of the liquid before it was their turn to fill their plates.

The Joneses were waiting their turn when a man rushed up to them and shouted, "You are sitting in our places and drinking our drinks!"

"We're sorry. We'll move. We didn't know this place was taken," Tim replied.

"You might as well stay there now! We wouldn't want to drink after you! Some people are too rude to care about anyone else! You!@#$%^$$#%," the man shouted as he stomped away into the crowd.

Tim clenched his fists and started to follow him. "He has no right to talk to us that way!" he said.

Lori pulled Tim back into his chair.

Rosita was sitting between Tim and Sarah. She stopped laughing and looked at Tim in anger. "Are you going to let that man get away with talking to us like that?" she asked. "Why don't you fight him?" she yelled.

"Because I don't want him to," Lori answered.

Tim asked Lori to go back to the food tables and refill his plate about thirty minutes later. Lori was reaching for a piece of fried chicken when she felt a large hand grab her arm. She turned around and looked into the eyes of the angry man.

"Our family is just as good as yours!" the man shouted. "Because you took our place, we can't sit by my dad and he might not be alive next Christmas!" he yelled. "Someone needs to put people like you in your place!" the man said with a snarl. He squeezed Lori's arm harder and begin to shake her viciously.

"I'm sorry we took your place, but we wanted to sit by our dad too, and he might not be alive next Christmas, either!" Lori shouted back. "You're hurting my arm!" she yelled.

The man loosened his grip for a second and Lori jerked her arm loose. She hurried back over to her own table. Lori told Tim what had happened because she was afraid the man might try to cause more trouble. "Let's just forget it if we can," she said.

They saw the man eating at another table. "I thought I recognized him," Tim said. "He was in a car accident a few years ago, and he hasn't acted quite right since then. I would hate to fight a man in that condition," he explained.

"You mean you're going to let him get away with hurting Lori?" Rosita asked.

"He didn't hurt me, and I don't want Tim to do anything about it," Lori repeated.

"I don't understand," Rosita said. She looked disappointed.

Everyone was soon eating and having a good time again.

Tim was feeling extra happy when he forgot and said, "I wish we could adopt this little gal so we could all be a real family."

"I think that would be nice," Sarah said. She smiled and gave Rosita a big hug.

Again, Rosita pretended to be mad at Tim for wanting to adopt her. She soon forgot about it and was sitting close to him again.

After the meal, Rosita helped some of the old people open their Christmas gifts. They enjoyed her special attention. She helped one little, old lady open her gifts. Rosita was taking off the tape and paper of one present when she asked, "Have you been a good girl this year?"

"Oh dear, I'm afraid I haven't been as good as I should have been," the lady answered. "Hey, girl, can you help me with this ribbon?" the little lady asked. "It's tied too tight for me," she said in desperation.

Rosita carefully took the package and pulled the ribbon and paper off. "Looky!" she exclaimed, and lifted up a new watch from the box.

The old lady squealed happily. Then she looked serious. She put her wrinkled hand over her mouth and shook her white head. "I know I haven't been <u>this</u> good. I don't know why I'm getting so many nice things." she said.

<u>She has really started believing in Santa Clause again,</u> Lori was thinking. <u>I'm glad she doesn't know the gifts have been sent by her family that live near by, and didn't take time to attend her party,</u> Lori thought.

Lori was lost in her thoughts for a few minutes. <u>It's not easy to come here. The smell of urine almost makes a person sick when they first come through the door. It isn't easy to see your relatives fed and diapered like</u>

<u>babies, but the old folks are so lonesome when people don't visit them. Maybe that is why some of them quit eating and die. I guess the families ease their consciences by sending gifts. the people are enjoying their gifts, anyway,</u> Lori was thinking.

"Time for beddy by," one worker said. She pushed the little old lady's wheel-chair into the hall leading to the individual rooms.

Lori and Rosita waved to her. "She was so cute," Rosita said with a giggle.

Tim, Lori, and Rosita helped clean up the Tumble Weed room. Then they stopped by Daddy Andy's room to pray with him and kiss him goodnight.

Lori waited for Rosita to run past her and jump into the car beside Tim.

Rosita stood behind Lori and exclaimed, "You get in first! I don't want to <u>ever</u> sit beside him again!"

Lori shrugged her shoulders in bewilderment, and crawled in beside Tim. Rosita slid in close to her.

They followed Sarah to the mobile home, kissed her goodnight from the car, and started their long journey home.

"Did I make you mad when I said I wanted to adopt you?" Tim asked.

"Kinda," Rosita answered.

"Did I make you mad when I wouldn't fight that man?" Tim asked.

"Kinda," Rosita answered, again, and snuggled up against Lori.

"Why don't you want to ride beside me?" Tim asked.

"I don't know," Rosita said. She was soon asleep.

Tim said something to Rosita the next morning before she left for school. "Don't talk to me, Bug Eyes!" Rosita snapped.

Tim looked puzzled. He didn't say anything else to the girl before the bus arrived. <u>She must be awfully tired from last night,</u> he thought.

Before the night of the Christmas party, Rosita would bathe, then wait in her room for Tim and Lori to come in, talk about the day's events, pray, and kiss Rosita goodnight. Even the night before the party,

Rosita had called Tim into her bedroom and told him about a fight she had at school. Tim had told her how important it was not to fight at school.

The night after the party, Tim started to walk into Rosita's bedroom with Lori. Rosita screamed, "Get out of my room, Fatso!"

Tim was hurt, but he walked back out of the room. Lori went ahead and prayed with Rosita and kissed her goodnight.

Rosita never rode next to Tim again.

Lori asked Rosita, a few weeks later, "What happened at the Christmas party to cause you to hate Tim?"

Rosita started to say her usual, "I don't know." She looked at Lori with a puzzled look on her face, and said, "I forgot."

CHAPTER VII

CHRISTMAS

Lori and Rosita walked into Juanita's hospital room. Lori was carrying her guitar. Juanita hugged Rosita and said, "My baby. My baby."

Rosita hugged her mother and the two of them sit on the edge of the bed, sobbing in each others arms. Lori felt like an intruder, watching this precious reunion of mother and daughter.

Rosita and Lori sung for Juanita. Carlos and some of the older brothers and sisters came in, and Lori and Rosita sung more songs for them. Carlos had a proud smile on his face as he listened to his daughter sing. Lori thought she could see a lot of new wrinkles on Carlos's dark face.

"It's time to go home now, Rosita," Lori said, with apprehension.

To Lori's surprise, Rosita kissed her mother good-bye, hugged Carlos around the neck, said good-bye to the rest of her family, took Lori's arm, and walked out of the room. She didn't even whine, and she was smiling.

"Praise the Lord," Lori whispered. She was remembering the terrible scene at Judy's house.

It was almost Christmas. Lori took another chance and let Rosita invite Becky to spend the Saturday with them. Lori found an old Christmas tree, and some decorations in the attic of the old farmhouse. She dug out her own decorations that she had moved from her mobile home. The two girls decorated the tree and much of the house.

"I didn't put up a Christmas tree last year," Lori said.

"Why not?" Rosita asked.

"Because I didn't have any kids around to help me or to enjoy it," Lori explained.

Rosita and Becky finished their decorating by putting tinsel and candy canes on all the light fixtures in the house.

Becky was more upset than Rosita when Judy came to take Becky back to her house.

"If your mother is still in the hospital on Christmas Day, would you like to go home for a few days?" Lori asked later that evening. "I worry about your papa spending too much time alone, and thinking about Sita," Lori explained.

"Yes! Yes!" Rosita exclaimed, hugging Lori.

Rosita was in bed. Tim and Lori were talking about their financial problems. "Lori, it's been three years since I've made as much money from my crops as it has cost to raise and harvest them," Tim said.

"My salary is swallowed up in farming expenses and child support," Lori responded. "I wish we could do something that would <u>make</u> money rather than <u>take money</u>, she said.

"Lori, I know we're almost broke, but I have to hire some help," Tim explained.

"I can help you in another week, when I get out for Christmas vacation," Lori said.

"This week's work is too crucial for me to wait for your help," Tim replied.

Tim went to town the next day, and hired a black man from Dallas.

Terry Lee did not know anything about farming, but he promised he would "work reeeal hard, man," He was over six-and-a half feet tall, and built like a football player.

<u>I sure can use the help of all that muscle at the farm</u>, Tim was thinking when he hired Terry Lee. "Bring your family out to my farm this afternoon and I'll let you live in our twenty-three foot camper trailer," Tim said.

"I can't do that, man," Terry Lee replied.

"Why not?" Don't you want the job?" Tim asked.

"Cause I ain't got no wheels man. The only way I can get my family out to your place is for you to take us out there, man," Terry Lee explained.

"That's okay. Get your family ready. I'll be by to pick you up before I leave town. I have to do some shopping for my wife," Tim said.

Tim did some shopping for Lori, and bought some things for Rosita. He stopped by Terry Lee's relatives to pick up Terry Lee, his wife Lois, his four-year-old son, Danus, and a few belongings.

Lori heard Tim drive in. She was stunned when she looked through the living room window and watched Tim unload the black family from the purple and white Dodge pickup.

"Lori, can you find enough groceries for this family until I pay Terry Lee?" Tim asked as he came in the back door.

Lori took some canned goods and potatoes from the large pantry. Tim went to the freezer to get some meat. "Won't they be crowded living in the camper?" Lori asked.

They act glad to have it," Tim said with a smile. "They have been staying with relatives, and not getting along too well with them since Terry Lee has been out of a job," Tim explained.

"Tim, I never know what you're going to do next," Lori said with a tired sigh.

"Now I'll have someone to play with," Rosita squealed, jumping up and down. "I'll love taking care of the little black boy," she said.

"Don't call him black boy. His name is Danus," Tim said.

Lori gave Lois time to put their things away before she went over and introduced herself. While Tim showed Terry Lee around the farm, Lori took some food and got acquainted with her new neighbor.

Lois was pretty, young, and in her last stages of pregnancy. Danus loved Rosita right away. They were soon outside running around the farm yard.

The next evening, and every evening after that, Danus asked, "Can I's goes over to my daddy's boss man's wife's house and see her and her girl?" He was knocking on the back door almost as soon as Lori and Rosita came in from school.

Lori always fixed something special for the kids to eat and drink. If Rosita had more refreshment than Danus, Danus would measure the treats. Then he would stick out his thick lower lip, put his fuzzy head down, roll his large brown eyes up at Lori, and say, "Bigger dan me."

Lori soon fell in love with this child that followed her around the house, calling her "ma". Lori was rocking the little boy one day when she noticed that his hair was so thick, it was impossible to find his scalp.

"Why do you braid all you guys' hair the last of every week?" Lori asked Lois.

"If we don't braid it, it will get too fuzzy to comb," Lois explained. "Braids embarrass Terry Lee, so that's why he wears his sock cap," Lois said with a giggle.

Lori was resting in one of the rocking chairs in the living room one evening after school. Danus crawled into her lap. Lori continued to rock, and Danus put his head on Lori's shoulder and was soon asleep.

Lori never forgot the sweet strawberry smell coming from the sweaty, curly head lying on her neck. It was some kind of hair product the black people used to help control their hair. Lori never forgot looking at her own white hands that were holding the small black feet with light colored bottoms. She knew the baby in her arms was as precious as any other child in the world.

The black family ate with Tim, Lori, and Rosita almost every evening. Lois was a hard worker. She did a lot of deep house cleaning for Lori. She also helped with the dishes and did a lot of cooking. Lois was so much help that Lori offered to do their laundry. Lori thoroughly enjoyed the friendship of the black lady.

Things weren't going so well outside. Tim took Terry Lee to the different pastures where the cattle had to be fed and ice broken in the stocks tanks. "This has to be done every morning, and every evening," Tim explained.

Terry Lee did not even want to get out of the pickup. "It's too cold, man," he complained.

<u>I don't think he likes to get his hands dirty, either</u> Tim was thinking. Tim let Terry Lee use the little Luv pickup to do his work. He was angry the day Terry Lee took the pickup to town without permission. Terry Lee had driven the thirty miles to town and back just to buy a pack of cigarettes. "Don't you ever take the pickup to town again without my permission!" Tim yelled.

Lori's folks had given the black family some money for Christmas. Lois told Lori that Terry Lee had spent part of the money on liquor when he bought the cigarettes.

Tim checked the stock tanks one morning and discovered that Terry Lee had not broken the ice when he fed the cattle. The cattle had gone several hours without water. Tim bawled out Terry Lee and Terry Lee promised that he would do better.

The weather was warmer. Tim decided to put Terry Lee on a tractor while he took care of the cattle. This didn't work well, either. Terry Lee came to the house several times a day for Tim to fix simple problems on his tractor or implement.

Every time Tim became angry, Terry Lee would say, "Hey, man, I'll do it right tomorrow. Give me another chance."

Lori was in the kitchen when she asked Rosita, "Where is that pan I use when I make meat loaf?"

Rosita laughed and said, "A big niggerman came and got it."

"You mean to tell me that Terry Lee came in here and took my meat loaf pan from my kitchen?" Lori asked.

Rosita turned red. She looked at Lois. They were all embarrassed. "I'm sure you'll never use that phrase again," Lori said.

"Terry Lee, you need to put another spare tire in your pickup before you go out to the field today. The one in the back of the pickup looks pretty worn," Tim said. "You can find a better one in that building over there," Tim explained, pointing toward the north side of the garage.

"I'm tired of that Dude telling me what to do," Terry Lee whispered to himself. He did not get another tire before he left for the field. That evening when he started home, he ran over a nail. Terry Lee had to put on the spare tire. It went flat when he put the weight of the pickup on it. "Man, what do I do now?" Terry Lee asked himself, aloud.

Terry Lee saw a farm on a hill some distance away. He quickly started walking toward the small dot on the horizon.

When Terry Lee left the pickup, the weather was just a little cold. Before he reached the old farm, a storm was blowing in from the northwest. The wind was blowing harder and harder. It was beginning to snow.

"I'm tired of this cold wind. I' think I'll go back to Dallas," Terry Lee said. He pushed his large hands into the small pockets of his light denim jacket.

Terry Lee was almost running when he entered the sand-blown yard and knocked on the door of the Gonzales home. He did not know where he was. After knocking several times, Terry Lee realized that no one was home. He tried opening the back door. Terry Lee was surprised to find that the door was not locked. "I'll take my chances and go on in," he told himself. "They won't mind if I stay in here long enough to call Tim to come after me, and warm up a little, while I'm here." Terry Lee said aloud.

Terry Lee stood close to the small butane heater a few minutes. The warm heat penetrated his cold legs and thighs. He turned around to warm the back of his legs and body. He looked around the room he was facing. Then he looked more closely in the dim light.

"I don't see no phone, man!" Terry Lee exclaimed. He searched the whole house in panic. "If I stay here, the people might not be home for hours. If they do come home, they might shoot me for tresspassin. I guess I'll have to take my chances and try to walk home before the storm gets any worse," Terry Lee said. His voice was shaking from the cold and maybe from fear of survival as he walked.

The snow blew hard against Terry Lee's face. At first his face and hands hurt from the cold. Then he started to lose the feeling out of his hands and feet. Terry Lee ran every few yards to try and raise his body temperature.

"I don't want to die in this God forsaken place, and I'm too young to die anyway!" Terry Lee shouted into the howling wind. He begin to stumble and fall, but each time he found the strength to pickup himself back up and press on into the raging northwest wind.

It was time for Terry Lee to be back. Tim checked to see if the young man had taken an extra tire. He shook his head in disbelief when he found all the other tires still there. Tim started toward Terry Lee's field in the large 4-wheel drive pickup. The snow was already piling up into drifts around the trees and house.

"I just can't make it through this drift," Terry Lee moaned. He fell face down in the white, frozen enemy, but it didn't feel cold anymore. Terry Lee thought he was trying to swim in a warm lake in Texas. He was struggling to get up out of the "warm water" when Tim saw him.

"Hey, man, what took you so long. I've never been so cold in my whole life!" Terry Lee exclaimed, shaking his head to come back to reality. Tim pulled the large man to his feet and pushed him into the large pickup. Terry Lee started rubbing his aching legs.

"Why didn't you take a spare tire?" Tim asked.

Terry Lee didn't answer. His hands were too cold and stiff to help Tim put a tire on the Luv pickup. He had to force himself to drive the pickup back to the farm. Terry Lee was too cold to talk the rest of the evening.

The sun was shining the next morning and Tim sent Terry Lee back to the field. After Tim finished taking care of the cattle, he stopped by the field to check on his hired hand.

"There's something wrong with this, Dude, it ain't running right, Terry Lee said, complaining.

Tim listened to the engine. "I think I know what's wrong," he said. "Just keep the tractor moving while I go to town and get the part I think it needs," Tim instructed.

"Why don't you run this baby, man, while I go to town and get the part?" Terry Lee said, hatefully. "Just because I'm black doesn't make me a slave to you white folk!" he snarled.

"You run the tractor. That's what you're getting paid for. I'm not paying you for running to town!" Tim shouted.

Tim told Lori what had happened and what Terry Lee had said when she came home from school that evening. "I can't believe he would talk to you like that," Lori said, angrily.

Latter that evening, Terry Lee came in to pick up their clean laundry. Lori said, "I wash your dirty, stinking laundry. Does that make me a slave to you black folk?"

Terry Lee looked embarrassed. He picked up the laundry basket full of clean clothes, and walked out without a reply.

Many people in the community brought Christmas gifts to Judy and Lori's for the Gonzales family. Rosita had already received two watches.

The evening before the school Christmas parties, Lori gave Rosita some money to buy gifts for her teachers and closest friends. Rosita made wise choices in spending her money. She chose every gift carefully, and made sure the wrapping and name card were perfect.

The next day, Lori and Rosita went to pick Lori's three-year-old grandson, Bryan. Bryan was excited about going to the party. Rosita is always happier with a small child on her lap, Lori was thinking as she drove back to the school building.

The sixth-grade students took turns pushing Bryan around the basketball gym on a sled with rollers. Rosita watched closely to see that Bryan was not hurt in case the students got too rowdy. One sixth-grade boy was running around the gym with his shoe laces untied. "Hey, boy, tie your shoes!" Bryan shouted every time he saw the boy.

The parties were soon over and the students were on their way home for Christmas vacation. "It's time to take down the Christmas decorations and put them away for another year," Lori said. She went to the storage room and brought back some boxes. "The chairs have to be stacked and the whole room made ready for vacation cleaning," Lori explained.

"Bryan and me want to help, too," Rosita said. She took Bryan by the hand, and walked over to where Lori was working.

Bryan noticed one of the smaller desks. "Look, a table just my size," he said.

Rosita laughed. "Let's take this old silver tree apart for your grandma, Bryan," Rosita said.

"One of my students gave me this old tree about ten years ago. He was an only child and he thought he was getting too old for it. It's probably about twenty years old by now," Lori explained. "But, it still looks pretty," she added.

Bryan was pulling branches out of the wooden trunk of the tree. "Here's one for mommy, one for daddy, one for grandma, and one for Uncle Fudd, and one for . . ." Bryan was saying.

"I don't think anyone would want a branch off of an old Christmas tree, Bryan, so let's put them in this box so we can use them next Christmas," Rosita said. She was laughing at every thing Bryan was saying, and doing.

Lori had never seen Rosita so happy. <u>She doesn't look, or act, anything like the girl I took home with me just a few shorts weeks ago</u>, Lori was thinking.

The room was soon finished. Lori took Bryan home smelling like peppermint candy.

Carlos came after Rosita early that evening. Lori helped them load the pickup with the presents from the community, and two boxes of meat she took from the freezer. "Merry Christmas," Lori said as she shook Carlos's hand and hugged Rosita good-bye.

"Thanks for everything," Carlos said with tears rolling down his thin face.

Lori waved good-bye, but Rosita was turned around talking excitedly to Carlos. <u>How lucky he is to have her</u>, Lori thought. She had such a large lump in her throat that it hurt to swallow. She coughed several times.

Lori looked at the western sky stretching across the flat dry plains. She could barely see the dark gray clouds rolling in with the strong wind, because of the tears that were in her eyes. Lori was thinking of the precious little girl that had followed her every where and tried to do what she saw her do. "I hope I haven't been a bad influence on her," Lori said with a sigh.

Lori heard a noise beside her. She looked down and saw Danus with tears rolling down his face. Lori picked Danus up, and carried him into the house. She sat down on one of the chairs at the kitchen table. Danus sit still in Lori's lap. He had his lower lip stuck out. His eyes rolled up at Lori. "I want dat girl. I want dat girl," he sobbed.

Lori had Tim's supper ready when the men came in from the field. It was after dark before she saw the lights turn into the driveway.

"Sure is quiet," Tim said when he went to wash his hands. "The house sure seems big tonight," he said when he sit down to eat. Tim was missing Rosita and was overeating. "How could we have gotten so attached to her in such a short time?" he whispered.

"I don't see how you can think so much of her when she talked to you the way she did," Lori said.

"I guess I always dreamed that she would change and want to stay with us and treat me right," Tim replied.

"I guess I did too, but I won't miss hearing her sass you," Lori said. "Did Terry Lee work better today?" Lori asked, trying to change the subject.

"A little, I guess," Tim answered.

"Why do you put up with his attitude?" Lori asked.

"I guess because I need any little help I can get right now, but I think the main reason I put up with him is because I feel sorry for Lois and Danus," Tim answered.

Tim ate another plateful of food. "Lori, Terry Lee and Lois are going to be away from their families Christmas since Lois's folks have moved back to Texas," Tim said. "Let's scrape enough money together to surprise them with Christmas gifts. They'll be here Christmas Eve, and we don't have anything else planned since your family is going to be out of town," Tim suggested.

"Tim, we don't even have enough money to buy each other presents," Lori protested.

"Lori, we have so much, and they don't have anything," Tim argued. "I found out that Terry Lee has a rabbit-fur coat on layaway in town and he still lacks fifty dollars of paying it off and," Tim said.

"You thought you'd see to it that Lois gets that coat for Christmas," Lori finished.

Tim shook his head yes.

Lori smiled. She rolled her chair around the table and snuggled up in Tim's large arms.

The next day Tim went to town and paid off the coat with grocery money Lori had saved. He had it gift wrapped. Tim bought Terry Lee a nice shirt and a pair of dress pants. "We have enough food stored in the pantry and freezer to get by for now," Tim told Lori.

One of the teachers told Lori about a poor family in town. The father wasn't working and the children would not be getting any Christmas presents. Lori had ordered two stuffed toys to give to Rosita and Becky. The Gonzales family had received so many presents that Lori decided to give the stuffed toys to children that weren't going to get much for Christmas. She and Tim were too broke to buy much else anyway.

Tim and Lori traveled to the city to do some last minute shopping Christmas Eve. On their way they stopped by the poor family's house. Tim waited in the car for Lori to deliver the two Christmas presents to the children.

Lori ran up to the door with the gifts. She knocked. Someone yelled, "Come in." The house was clean, but sparsely furnished. Lori was invited into the living room by a pregnant mother. She saw a small boy and girl standing in a shadowed corner of the room. They looked thin and pale.

The healthy-looking, handsome father was sitting in a chair. He said hello and gave Lori a welcome smile, but he did not get up to greet her. Lori could not see any Christmas packages anywhere. She finally managed to say, "I don't want to embarrass you, but I heard that your children wouldn't be receiving any presents for Christmas this year. The community had brought in many gifts for the Gonzales family, because of the accident, that I decided to bring these two to your children."

The mother smiled and said, "We really appreciate this. If none of our relatives bring gifts tomorrow, our children won't have a Christmas this year."

"These gifts are from the community," Lori reminded. She handed the gifts to the children and turned to leave.

"Pleas stay to watch the children open what you have brought them," the mother said.

Lori watched the children walk across the room and sit on a worn out couch. She noticed that the little girl was crippled.

The children squealed with joy when they un-wrapped the stuffed toys. One toy was a mother panda bear holding her baby, and the other toy was a mother kangaroo with her baby in her pouch. Lori saw the happy expressions of the children as they hugged their new toys.

"Thank you very much," the father said.

"Please come back and visit us," said the mother.

Lori hugged the children and said, "I'll try, but now I have to hurry. Tim and I haven't done our last minute shopping yet." She slipped out the door and ran through the cold wind back to the car.

Lori was quiet the first several miles. "Tim, I just can't understand what I saw in that home. The father went to school with Mike. He came from a fine, hard working family. He was good in band, football, and wrestling. He was an A student, graduated as Salutatorian, and was offered several college scholarships. He has a college degree now, but he can't keep a job or support his family. Many people around here have tried to help him by giving him work, but he always gets fired or quits. His family suffers. His wife is expecting their third child," Lori said. "It's just hard to understand how someone with so much ability could turn out be such a failure," she added.

"I guess that proves that college doesn't have all the answers," Tim said, remembering that about all he had was a grade school education. He pulled Lori close to him as he drove toward the city.

Tim and Lori took the last of their money to buy two gifts for Lori's family gift exchange, and presents for Bryan and Danus. Lori remembered how much Danus enjoyed playing with her electric guitar, so she bought him a little, plastic one with real strings.

It was after dark when Tim and Lori returned to the farm. Tim helped Lori unload the car and put the presents under the Christmas tree. While Lori was fixing supper, Tim went over to invite the black family to spend the evening with them.

Lois hurried over to help Lori in the kitchen. Danus was right behind her. He was soon running from one end of the large house to the other.

"I know it must be hard for Danus to be confined in that tiny camper all day," Lori said.

They had a large supper. Lori and Lois took the dishes from the dining room to the kitchen. The men went to the living room to visit. Lois worked so quickly that she and Lori soon had the dishes in the dish washer and the kitchen clean. They joined the men folks in the living room. Lori sat down in one of the large chairs and nodded to Tim.

Tim walked over to the Christmas tree. He picked up three packages and said, "Hummm, these seem to have your names on them."

Lois and Terry Lee were surprised. Danus grabbed his package. He tore off the wrapping and screamed, "It's a geetar, just like my daddy's boss's man's wife's one!" Danus put the strap over his fuzzy head and entertained them with his music for the rest of the evening.

Terry Lee was as surprised as Lois over the fur coat. The coat did not go around Lois's pregnant tummy, but she was proud of it anyway.

Terry Lee told Tim, "I thanks ya for the pants, but I feel nakud in button shirts, so I won't be a wearin it."

Carlos always made his home large enough for more people. He brought home a young alien couple and their baby daughter. They had come in from Mexico and they had no place to live.

There were plenty of groceries in the Gonzales house. The Mexican woman was too timid to help Rosita in the kitchen. Rosita did all the cooking for four adults and several kids. It seemed like her older brothers and sisters only came by at meal time.

On Christmas Day, Rosita fixed dinner and did the dishes before the whole family went to the hospital to see Juanita. The doctor told Carlos "I don't think I can take a chance and let Juanita out of the hospital to go home to the scene of the accident. I think it will upset her and she will be right back in here."

The day after Christmas, Carlos's boss accused him of stealing gasoline from the farm gas tanks. "I didn't steal no gas, and you didn't pay me my wages last month," Carlos told his boss.

"I think it's time for you to move on, Carlos," the boss said. "I want you all off my farm and property by next week!" the boss ordered, shaking his finger at Carlos as he drove off in his new car.

Carlos had no where to move and lot of people were depending on him. Now he didn't even have a job. During the next few days, Carlos took extra good care of the cattle. He was hoping the boss would change his mind. The hospital bills were stacking up, and Carlos did not know where to put Juanita.

Things looked hopeless late one night. Carlos was trying to figure out what to do. He thought about a friend he had in town. Able was a tall, pale-faced man. He was about twenty-five years old. He didn't think as good as most people. Abel's folks had died and left him several houses. Able lived in one house and rented the other houses. He had told Carlos that one of his houses was empty.

"Maybe Able could eat his meals with us in exchange for rent money," Carlos told himself. "I'll ask him tomorrow when I stop by to visit Juanita," Carlos said. He was soon asleep, knowing that his problems could be worked out.

The two men agreed the next morning. Juanita moved into the house that afternoon.

Able was happy to have someone to cook his meals. <u>It's just like having my own family</u> Able thought. Able also thought he had the right to walk into, and through, the Gonzales house anytime he wanted: day or night.

Carlos and Rosita were eating supper with Juanita and Able before they returned to the farm. "Carlos, do you know what the people are saying?" Juanita asked in her broken English.

"What do you mean, mama?" Carlos asked.

"I know Molly was very young when Sita and Bitina were born, and that's why I wanted them," Juanita said.

"Yes, mama, go on," Carlos demanded.

"Molly, she is still very young. It's a good thing that she takes care of Bitina, now, I guess." Juanita said.

"Mama, tell me what the people say!" Carlos said.

"They say that Molly went to a lot of people's houses after Sita was . . . They say that Molly ask for money for hospital and funeral bills. Now the people want to know if the hospital and mortuary has been paid," Juanita explained.

Rosita's eyes were wide open in surprise. She watched Carlos sadly sake his head.

"All those expenses have been billed to me. Not a cent has been paid and Molly hasn't given me no money. I don't know if she did it or not, mama," Carlos answered.

"I think you need to talk to her," Juanita said.

"They are dirty liars!" Molly screamed. "Do you believe everything you hear, Carlos!" she asked, loudly.

"I don't know what to believe, or how I'm going to pay the bills," Carlos said. He got up to leave his son's house.

"I ain't blamed you for Sita's death, Don't blame me for nothin, either. If you hadn't run over her, there wouldn't be any bills!" Molly shouted through the screen door.

The next morning Carlos was called to the county jail. He followed the sheriff down the hall between the cells. He saw his oldest son standing in one of the cells. "What now?" Carlos asked.

Carlos looked and sounded so weary that the angry law officer had a feeling of pity for him. He answered Carlos in a gentle manner. "Jimmy was arrested while robbing one of the grocery stories here last night," the sheriff explained. "He and two buddies tore up the back door to get in," he added.

"Why, Jimmy?" Carlos asked.

"For food, papa," Jimmy answered.

"I hope so, son," Carlos replied. "Why didn't you tell me you needed food, son?" he asked. "I thought that you were getting along pretty well since you went to work," Carlos said.

"I had too many back bills to pay to keep my house and car, papa. We have been too much trouble to you already. You have so many others to take care of that I . . ," Jimmy tried to explain.

"You are my son, and I'll always try to help," Carlos said. He turned toward the sheriff and asked, "What will it take to get him out here, Sheriff Barns?"

"Did I hear you say that Jimmy has a job now?" the sheriff asked.

"Yes Sir and he has his wife and child to take care of," Carlos answered quickly.

"Since all the things they stole are back in the store, if you'll sign a note to pay for damaged door, I'll let him out on probation under your care, Carlos," Sheriff Barns said.

"Thank you. We'll pay for the door as soon as we can, and I'll watch him real good, Sheriff Barns," Carlos answered in a shaking voice.

The sheriff unlocked Jimmy's cell. "Look here, young man, if you pull anything else like this, your pa will be in bad trouble, and I'll throw the book at you. Understand?" Sheriff Barns shouted.

Jimmy nodded his head yes and followed Carlos to the car. He was soon back at work.

Carlos went over to Juanita's. Another son was there. "Mark, I'm glad that you are a good boy and cause me no trouble. When you gonna get married to that preacher's daughter?" Carlos said laughing. He patted Mark on the back.

"Just as soon as we save enough money for the weddin, papa," Mark answered.

"That won't take too long with both of you a working," Carlos said.

Mark stopped laughing. "Mama, you better tell papa what you just told me," he ordered.

"Papa, I hate to put more worries on you, but you know Betty, Rosita's best friend. She has lived with her pa since her folks divorced," Juanita started.

"Betty's pa saw me in the grocery store today and told me that my sixteen-year-old son, Dano, got his fourteen-year-old daughter pregnant. He thinks that if Dano doesn't marry her, that he should at least help with the expenses," Juanita explained.

"Oh that Dano. He's too young for tricks like that!" Carlos shouted.

"That's not all, papa," Juanita said.

"What else can happen?" Carlos said, throwing up his hands.

"My friend that goes to my church said that Dano is wanted for doin bad checks in Texas City," Juanita said. "My Dano is one I can't understand. He writes and sings songs to be about Jesus and then goes out and does these things. I just don't understand my Dano," Juanita said.

Juanita finished the dishes and sit down. "Leslie and Antonio are coming here to live with me," Juanita said. Leslie had a good job, and then Antonio came to live with her. He has a family in Mexico, so they can't get married. Now she has quit her job and they are coming here. Antonio, he eats so much," Juanita said. "But, don't worry none, Carlos. God will take care of us, somehow," she added.

"Maybe if I stay on the farm, I can get my job back," Carlos said, thinking aloud. "Maybe I should look to find a better job. Maybe we should go to south Texas and let the whole family work in the fields," Carlos mumbled.

"Don't take the kids out of school to work in the fields if there is any other way, Carlos," Juanita begged. "I don't want them to grow up dumb like me," she said.

CHAPTER VIII

ROSITA'S RETURN

Lee was driving by the Joneses one afternoon. He saw Tim in the yard and stopped to visit. "The Gonzaleses are moving to Palinsville," he said. "Carlos has lost his job and Juanita can't go back to the farm where the accident happened," Lee explained.

'Thank you for keeping us informed," Tim said.

As soon as Lee left to go home, Tim went to the old farm. "Please, Carlos, let us take Rosita and keep her in school until school is out this spring," Tim begged.

"I don't want her to go," Carlos answered. "She is my youngest one. She is my good one, but I know she would be better off with you and Lori," Carlos said. "Let met talk to mama some day when she is feeling good. I'll let you know," Carlos promised.

"She was starting to do much better in school since Lori has been helping her, Carlos," Tim said. "If she could just stay in the same school for a whole year, it would really help her," he added.

Carlos nodded in agreement, and repeated, "I'll let you know."

Carlos took his part of the family to Plainsville to eat supper with Juanita and her part of the family. He told Juanita that Tim and Lori wanted to keep Rosita for the rest of the school year.

"That would be good for Rosita," Juanita said, hurting inside. "They are good to her and there's so much trouble around here right now. I worry about her doing wrong things when she is with older ones," Juanita said, almost to herself.

Rosita came in from playing with Becky and Leos. Juanita sat down next to Rosita on the old worn out couch. She took Rosita's hand and squeezed it. "Rosita, you must go back to live with Lori and Tim for awhile," Juanita said.

Rosita was thinking <u>I like living with Lori. I like to look nice and be popular. I like having my own room and nice clothes, but I love my mama and my papa, and they need me.</u>

"I want to stay with you and help you mama," Rosita said, squeezing her mother's hands.

"I'll be okay, and Becky is old enough to help me now. Besides, Mrs. Jones can help you with your school work and your music," Juanita said.

"But mama, you can't even read or write and you need me to do this for you. You have so many to cook for and take care of, I need to be here to help you," Rosita said.

"This is why you must go and live with Tim and Lori. I want you to be educated. I don't want you to be like me," Juanita said. "I want you to learn many things. That is why you must stay with them for now," she ordered.

"But, mama, I want to be like you. I want to stay and help you," Rosita argued again.

"Becky and papa can help me. You must go to them. You must enjoy living like a little girl again, and stop living like an old woman who takes care of everybody!" Juanita exclaimed.

"Yes, mama, but I will miss you," Rosita said. She started filling paper sacks with her clothes again.

Carlos took Rosita and her sacks to Tim and Lori's. Tim was angry, and Lori cried when they discovered that Rosita no longer had any of the cute clothes Lori had given her. Rosita had let her older sisters and sister-in-laws take all of them.

"I thought that you gave me the clothes," Rosita said.

"We did," Tim and Lori both said.

"Then, they were mine to do with what I wanted, and I wanted to give them away," Rosita said, casually.

Rosita had nothing to wear to school except her old lady dresses, and dark, holy socks. She knew that Lori and Tim would find a way to dress her in nice clothes again.

Rosita pouted the first few days she was back. She didn't do well in school. Rosita gradually thought that her family was doing all right. She started to enjoy living like Lori's little girl again. Rosita cleaned her room each day. She helped Lori with a lot of her work, although Lori never asked her to. Lori knew Rosita had worked hard at home. She didn't want her to work too hard now when it wasn't necessary.

Rosita's attitude toward Tim had not changed. She often said, "Lori, I want to be you little girl. If you'll leave Tim, I'll be your little girl forever." Rosita's personality completely changed the minute Tim came home.

Tim always said pleasant things to Rosita, and did things for her. Rosita always sassed him and called him, "Fatso, Ugly, Dummy, or Bug Eyes" in return.

"You'll be happy living with us some day," Tim said over and over.

"I'm happy living with Lori, but not you!" Rosita screamed at Tim, over and over.

"Rosita, if you love me, you'll be nice to Tim," Lori repeated for the hundredth time.

It was Saturday. Lori had just finished putting away the breakfast dishes. She had time to do some mending before starting lunch. Lori picked up a pair of Tim's old work jeans, a needle and some thread, and sit down on the black leather love seat in the music room.

Rosita was practicing at the piano.

Lori mended one torn place on Tim's pants while she listened to Rosita's music. "Come over her and sit by me, Babe. I need to talk to you," Lori said.

Rosita sprung up from the piano bench and bounced over to the couch. She plopped on the love seat like she was diving backward into a pool of water. Rosita snuggled close to Lori's side, and said, "Oaky. Doaky."

"Rosita, why do you hate Tim?" Lori asked.

95

"I don't know," Rosita answered in the way she always did when she didn't want to talk about something.

"Rosita, why do you sass Tim every time he says something nice to you?" Lori asked, looking straight into the girl's dark brown eyes.

Rosita dropped her head and looked down at her lap. She started playing with her fingers.

"He's very good to you. I can't understand why you act so terrible when he's around. I'd shake you good if you talked to me like that", Lori said. "You know why you do it, and I demand that you tell me why," Lori said quietly, but sternly.

Rosita was quietly for awhile. Lori sat waiting for an answer. "It's because . . . because, I'm afraid of him!" the girls whispered, still looking down at her feet.

Lori was shocked. "Has he ever hurt you, or touched you in the wrong places," she asked.

"No! He'd never do anything like that" Rosita shouted.

"Has he ever said anything to embarrass you?" Lori asked.

"No! He wouldn't do that either!" Rosita yelled.

"Then, why on earth, are you afraid of him?" Lori asked.

"Because of his eyes," Rosita answered, feeling relieved that the truth was finally known. "They look so big and they look in different directions, and I can't tell when he is looking at me," she explained.

Lori felt Rosita's slender body shivering beside her. "That's not his fault. When he was young, he almost went blind. The doctors removed the lenses from his eyes and replaced them with his thick glasses," Lori tried to explain. "That's better than being blind, don't you think?" she asked.

When Lori realized that she had Rosita's undivided attention, she continued. "The doctors had to cut his eyeballs in half to take out the back lenses. That's why his eyes aren't round like other peoples. Back in those days, it was a new kind of surgery. The first operation went okay. Before his second operation, his doctor was killed in a plane crash. The doctor that took over the second surgery broke his leg in a skiing accident. He went ahead with the surgery, anyway. He slipped on his crutches during the second surgery, and cut the muscle in Tim's eyes. That's why it turns out in the opposite direction from the other eye," Lori explained. "You'll never hear him complain, though. He just thankful that he can see," Lori said.

"There's another reason I'm afraid of him," Rosita whispered.

"What's that?" Lori asked.

"It's because of what I've heard about him," Rosita said.

"Did it have anything to do with his daughter?" Lori asked.

"Unhuh," Rosita answered.

"Tim was only seventeen, and his first wife was only fifteen, whey they were married. They were too young to really know what they were doing. Tim didn't want his daughter to make the same mistake. He wanted her to finish high school before she got married. He wouldn't let her date much. He tried to get his daughter to break up with her only boyfriend," Lori said.

"Tim's ex-wife wanted her daughter to get married. The situation turned into a family fight. Tim and his wife ended up getting a divorce. Tim's daughter ended up getting married. She ended up hating her father," Lori tried to explain.

Lori continued her story, "Tim has now lost all contact with his children. Since that time there have been some horrible stories going around about Tim trying to hurt his daughter sexually. The stories didn't even make enough sense for the county judge to believe them when they tried to take Tim to court." "I don't believe the stories because I know Tim. I can't imagine him ever doing anything like that," Lori said. "I think Tim's family is just trying to ruin his reputation, and make people not trust him," she added.

"There have been some terrible stories made up about me, and I know that they aren't true," Lori said. "Now, what are you going to believe; what you hear, or what you have seen since you came to live with us? Do you think Tim could have done the terrible things that they say he did?" Lori asked.

"I don't think so, but Betty, my friend wouldn't lie to me," Rosita replied.

"Probably not, but after all, she is just repeating what she has heard and not what she <u>really knows</u>, right?" Lori said.

"I guess so, but why would people say those things if they aint true?" Rosita asked.

"Rosita, do you believe that I would do the kinds of things that you have heard that Tim has done?" asked Lori.

"No! Never!" Rosita screamed. "Nobody ever better say anything like that about you or I'll give them this!" Rosita shouted, doubling up her fist and shaking it in the air.

"His ex-family has told people that I did. I can't figure out why, in the world, they would say things like that about me," Lori said.

"They'd better quit saying things about you!" Rosita shouted again.

"Rosita," Lori said. She lifted the girl's head up so she could look into her brown eyes. "Rosita, just to make you more comfortable while you're living here, will you promise me that if Tim ever does anything, or even says anything he shouldn't, that you will come and tell me immediately?" Lori asked.

"Yes! I'll be glad to get even with him for calling me <u>his</u> little girl," Rosita said. She fell into Lori arms and gave her a big hug.

Rosita's long, soft hair brushed across Lori's chin. It smelled nice, and Lori could smell perfume on the girl's neck. <u>How different she smells now,</u> Lori was thinking.

When Rosita first came to live with Tim and Lori, she had a very peculiar odor. It was a sharp, almost sickening smell. The odor did not seem to wash off with daily baths. Lori was afraid that Rosita had some type of infection. She took her to the clinic in town. Stacy had given Rosita a complete physical.

"Rosita is healthy, untouched, and the only thing I can find wrong with her is that she is a little dehydrated," Stacy reported. "She needs to drink more water," she said.

"What is causing the odor?" Lori had asked.

"It could be caused from the high-spiced foods that she is used to eating," Stacy said.

"I really like her," Rosita had told Lori on the way home that evening. "She was so nice that I wasn't afraid at all, and I tried to tell her the truth on every question that she asked me," Rosita had said, proudly.

The odor had gradually gone away.

Lori held the dark, slender girl in her arms. <u>Sometimes she acts like a little girl, and sometimes she acts like a mature woman. What hurts is that she is such a part of me, and yet, she will never really be a part of me,</u> Lori was thinking.

Without any warning, Rosita jumped back and smiled at Lori. "Lori, do you know what?" she asked, excitedly. "Me and Betty are almost related!" Rosita exclaimed, bouncing up and down on the love-seat.

"How are you almost related?" Lori asked.

"She is going to have my brother's baby!" exclaimed Rosita.

"How old is Betty, and how old is your brother?" Lori asked.

Betty is fourteen, and Dano is sixteen," Rosita said. "I can hardly wait for the baby to be born. I'm anxious to see if it's a boy or a girl, and who it looks like! I just love babies!" the girl squealed.

"Rosita, your friend should still be a little girl without any worries, and doing fun things that girls do. Now she has given up the only childhood she will ever have just to please a boy that doesn't even love her, or feels any responsibility to her or to the baby. She will suffer to have the baby. She will suffer to raise it. It hasn't cost your brother anything!" Lori shouted.

"Dano is anxious to see the baby," Rosita said.

"Is he anxious to marry Betty, and give the baby a last name? Is he anxious to support both of them and give them a home? Is he anxious to accept the responsibilities of his actions?" Lori asked.

"Of course not! He has another girl friend now," Rosita said. She did not understand why Lori was angry about Betty's pregnancy.

"Is he even planning to help support the baby in any way?" asked Lori.

"Of course not. He can't do that because he doesn't have a job and our family doesn't have much money," Rosita said. "I'll help Betty take care of the baby as much as I can," she added.

"Rosita quit trying to take your brothers', and sisters' responsibilities. Make them take care of their own messes that they get themselves into," Lori ordered.

"I <u>want</u> to help!" Rosita said. She was still happily bouncing on the love-seat.

"Rosita, it isn't good for your brothers and sisters not to take care of their own lives. Betty's situation <u>is not anything for you to be happy about!</u>" Lori shouted.

"Why not?" Rosita asked.

"The thing that you might understand is, this," Lori began slowly. "Dano and Betty have hurt your mother as well as mixing up their own lives, and they have broken God's law," Lori tried to explain.

"But, babies are so cute," Rosita argued.

"I wish you weren't so crazy over babies!" Lori exclaimed.

"That's what my mama told me," Rosita said. "She said she loved babies and had thirteen of them in fourteen years, and she doesn't want me to do that. She said that loving babies could get me into trouble, but I love them anyway, and I want a lot of them," Rosita explained.

"Can't you just enjoy your nieces and nephews until you get a little older?" Lori asked.

"I do enjoy my oldest sister's babies almost every day," Rosita replied.

"Where does your sister live?" Lori asked.

"In south Texas," Rosita answered, laughing.

"Then how can you enjoy her children every day?" Lori asked.

"I'm not supposed to tell anyone, but you know my little brother, Leos, and my little sister, Becky?" asked Rosita.

"You know I do, but what do they have to do with it?" Lori asked.

Rosita continued. She sounded like she was, at last, giving up a dark, family secret. "Leos and Becky aren't really my brother and sister. I'm the youngest of our family. Becky and Leos are really my sister's kids," Rosita explained.

"My sister was young and she was having a difficult time taking care of herself, Becky, and Leos. She decided to let Becky and Leos be adopted. Papa found out. He went to mama, and cried and cried. He said the babies needed someone to love them, and he asked mama if they could raise them.

We get a small check from the government every month to help take care of them. I decided that I'll help take care of them too," Rosita said, finishing her story.

"Betty can be getting herself into the same kind of situation that your sister was in, Rosita, can't you understand that?" Lori said. "Is that why you get into so many fights trying to protect Becky and Leos at school?" asked Lori.

"Unhuh. Some of my sisters aint supposed to have babies, though," Rosita said, wanting to share another family secret.

"Why not, Babe?" Lori asked, as she continued to patch Tim's work pants.

"They have epilepsy," Rosita explained. She looked down at her feet again. Rosita started talking almost like she was talking to herself as much as wanting to tell Lori something. "Lori?" Rosita whispered.

"What now, Babe?" Lori asked.

"The reason I don't like for you and Tim to talk about me like I'm your little girl is, because a long time ago, my papa used to drink a lot," Rosita started her next story.

"He doesn't now, does he?" Lori asked.

"No, he quit. He used to come home drunk. He would hit my mama and he would beat on my bothers and sisters. He never hit me. He would sometimes get a gun and shoot at us. Sometimes he would bring young, pretty women home with him and mama would get up and fix them something to eat, like her special tortillas, before they went to bed."

"Your mother deserves a reward for that. I don't know of any other woman on earth that would do that for her husband. I sure couldn't" Lori said.

Rosita shook her head "yes". "One night papa came home real drunk. He hurt mama, and he beat on the other kids until they ran out of the house. Papa went to his truck and got his gun. He started shooting at us.

Some neighbors called the pigs, I mean cops. They came and took papa to jail. The next day some people came and told mama that she couldn't keep us kids no more until papa stopped drinkin. The people put each of us in a different home until papa got better.

I was real little, but I can remember. I was afraid of the people that took me even though they were nice. My brother, Dano, was about seven-years-old then. He would run off from his foster home and walk clear across town to come and see me.

Dano wasn't supposed to be where I was, so I hid in the weeds all the time he was there, so no one could see us. When he was there, I wasn't scared no more, and I knew we would all be together again, sometime," Lori said.

"I can see why you think so much of Dano. He seems to be your favorite," Lori replied.

"Yes, he has always kept me from being afraid," Rosita said.

"I don't care how much you love Dano, don't let him teach you that the wrong things he does is right," Lori ordered.

"Dano is really a good person, Lori," Rosita argued.

"He and Betty have broken God's law," Lori reminded.

Rosita was still sitting next to Lori. She was looking at her feet, and rocking back and forth. Lori could not tell if the girl was agreeing with her or not.

CHAPTER IX

DISCIPLINE

Three weeks after Christmas, Terry Lee and Tim had another argument.

"This farm work is too hard, man. It's too cold breakin up the ice and feeden the cattle. I ain't never bee so cold in all my life. I guess I jest can't get used to a little guy, like you, a given me orders, man. Itsa maken me feel like I's a slave, man, like my great grandpappy was," Terry Lee said.

Tim put his hands into his pockets, and clenched his fists. He walked back to his pickup. "If I can just put up with him for at least three more months, the weather should be getting a little warmer, and it won't be so rough on Danus, and Lois, and the baby when I fire him and they will have to move. The baby should be born by then," Tim said to himself. Tim did not know that Terry Lee was fighting with Lois at home, too.

The next morning Tim was filling the large gas tank on the back of the 4-wheel-drive pickup.

Terry Lee walked up beside him. "I can't go to work today, man," he said. Terry Lee sounded more concerned than argumentative.

"Why not?" Tim asked.

"If I leave for work, my wife will leave me while I'm gone, man," Terry Lee answered.

Tim knew that Terry Lee was not going to change his mind. He went to the house and asked Lori to go over and talk to Lois before she left for school. She knocked on the camper door.

"Come in! The door is not locked!" Lois shouted. When Lois saw Lori, she looked surprised, and said, "I thought you were Terry Lee. I'm sorry I shouted at you."

"Terry Lee is refusing to go to work this morning because he says you'll leave him while he's gone," Lori said.

"That was <u>yesterday</u> that I told him I was going to leave him. That wasn't <u>today</u>," Lois said. "I don't know what he's so worried about <u>today</u>," Lois remarked.

Lori would have laughed at the situation if it had not been so serious. "Please go tell Terry Lee that you'll be here when he comes home tonight, so we can all get to work," Lori said, with a smile.

"Okay," Lois said and followed Lori outside to where the two men were standing.

A few evening later, Tim, Lori and Rosita came home from town. The black family, along with a few other things, was gone.

"One of Terry Lee's friends must have given them a ride," Tim said. "I sure hope Lois and Danus are all right," he added.

"I heard at school today that Terry Lee left Lois and Danus stranded in Texas somewhere," Lori told Tim two weeks later.

"If I knew where they were, I'd invite them to come back and live in the camper. Lois could help you so they'd have a little income," Tim said.

"You're always worried about people, Tim. If they don't have everything they need. You always want to take care of them, even when we're having a difficult time making ends meet, ourselves. You always want to stretch out what we have to help others," Lori replied.

"I really miss Danus, and his black face, and his fuzzy hair," Rosita said one evening while she and Lori were gathering the eggs.

"Me, too," Lori said with a sigh. "I guess there's no such thing as a prejudice feeling on <u>this</u> place," she said.

The next morning, Tim left, right after breakfast, to load two, two-year-old steers. He was going to take them to the local packing house. One animal's meat was enough to meet his family's needs. He planned to give the other animal's meat to Carlos for is family.

Tim ran the large animals into the pen leading to the shoot where animals were forced into a truck or trailer. He was trying to make them run into the narrow space leading into the horse trailer. One of the steers turned and ran through the old wooden fence. Two boards snapped as the steer escaped.

Tim knew if he did not get help fast, the steer would be a mile away within minutes. If he left the hole in the fence, while he went after help, the other steer would probably get through the broken fence and start running in the opposite direction. He did not have time to wire the hole shut.

Tim pushed the steer into the furthermost corner from the damaged fence, and ran a fast dash to the house.

Rosita was in the kitchen watching Saturday cartoons.

"Quick, Rosita, run out to the holding pen and stop that steer from getting through the hole. Lori and I will try to catch the one that got away?" Tim yelled. He ran through the house calling for Lori.

"I'm not going to go out there and get dirty. You do it yourself, Bug Eyes!" Rosita screamed.

For the first time, Tim lost his temper. Without thinking, he ran back across the kitchen, and slapped Rosita across the face, and shoved her toward the door.

"I'll get even with you for that!" Rosita screamed and ran from the house.

Tim was running from one room to another calling for Lori.

Rosita ran across the yard when she saw Lori coming out of one of the old buildings. Lori had the egg bucket on her arm. Rosita ran into Lori's arms, crying, "He slapped me! He slapped me!"

"What on earth did he do that for?" Lori asked.

"I don't know. I was just sitting there watching TV, when he came in and slapped me really hard!" Rosita cried, rubbing her face.

"That's difficult to believe," Lori said. "Are you sure that's all that happened? Are you sure you didn't do or say something that upset him?" Lori asked.

"I'm sure," Rosita said between sobs.

"No matter what you did, he had no right to slap you. That's what bottoms are made for," Lori said. She patted Rosita, trying to console her.

Tim could not find Lori in the house. He ran back outside. "Quick, Lori, the steer broke through the fence and has run behind the old shop building, and he's headed for the road?" Tim shouted. Tim ran back to the loading shoot.

"What steer?" Lori yelled.

"The one I was taking to be butchered. Make Rosita watch the one that is still in the pen, so he won't get out. You help me corner the one that is out. Run around on the other side of the shop and keep him from going out to the road!" Tim shouted.

"Run and do what he says, Rosita," Lori ordered. She ran to help Tim.

Rosista walked back to the house, instead of doing what she was told to do.

It took Tim and Lori thirty minutes to get the steer back inside the gate. The other steer was still inside the fence. They loaded both steers, and returned to the house.

Rosita was watching TV again. She heard Tim and Lori come in and started rubbing her cheek and crying. "You slapped me," she screamed at Tim.

"You wouldn't get up and help me when I asked you to," Tim said. "One of the steers I'm taking to be butchered is for your family. I won't charge them anything for it, either," Tim explained.

"You owe it to them for letting me stay here!" Rosita shouted.

"I'm sorry, but you sassed me, and I was in a terrible hurry," Tim tried to explain.

"I don't doubt that, but you shouldn't have slapped her," Lori said.

Rosita smiled as Tim and Lori argued. <u>Maybe they will separate</u>, Rosita was thinking. "I'm going to make them fight ever chance I can," Rosita said to herself.

After the steer incident, Rosita ran to Lori and tattled over every little thing she saw Tim do, and every little thing she heard him say.

Tim continued to buy things for Rosita. This always made Lori angry. "We can't afford to buy Rosita all these things," Lori said many times. Lori and Tim had arguments every time Tim went to town, and every time he returned. Rosita always stood next to Lori and shouted at Tim during these arguments.

Carlos and Dano came over one evening. Rosita saw the red and white pickup drive up to the house. She ran out of the house to meet them. She was rubbing her face and crying, "He slapped me! He slapped me!"

"If he slapped you, girl, you deserved it," said Carlos. "What did you do?" he asked.

"Nothin, papa," Rosita answered, sobbing.

"I know better than that, girl. You probably sassed him or something. I know these folks are good to you. See how spoiled you are?" Carlos said.

Tim and Lori came out of the house to greet Carlos and Dano. Carlos looked at Tim. "Make her mind, Tim," he ordered.

Tim felt embarrassed. He smiled and said, "Yes, she did sass me. I did slap her, but everything is okay now."

Carlos and Dano walked into the kitchen and sit down in chairs at the table. While they were all visiting, Rosita secretly motioned for Dano to follow her outside. They left the house unnoticed. Rosita led Dano through the dark to the old bunkhouse.

"Rosita, I miss you. I'll be glad when our crazy old man comes to his senses and lets you come home again," Dano said. He took Rosita in his arms and held her tightly. "Did he really hurt you?" Dano asked.

"Yes," Rosita answered. Her thin body shivered.

"If I had a gun, I'd kill him," Dano said.

"I think I can get you one," Rosita whispered.

"Great! Go get it right now, and I will kill him," Dano replied.

"I'll have to get it later," Rosita explained.

"That's okay, Rosita, because right now, I think I'll go in there and beat him up for you, That is what papa should do and he won't," Dano said. "I'll kill him later," he added.

"Hold me tight, Dano, the way you always do when I'm scared," Rosita whispered.

Lori saw the kids coming back into the house. She didn't like the expression on their faces. I should have watched Rosita closer, she was thinking.

Dano stomped into the kitchen and grabbed Tim's arm. He tried to hit Tim in the face. Rosita was jumping up and down in excitement, shouting, Hit him hard, Dano!"

"Behave yourself, Dano!" Carlos yelled.

Tim blocked Dano's blow with his large arm. He looked down at Dano, who was half his size, and said, "Don't make me hurt you, kid, because I don't want to."

Dano threw another blow, and Tim stopped it with his other arm.

"Go to the truck, boy!" Carlos yelled.

"He hit my sister, and you're not man enough to fight for your own daughter. We don't need the junk he gives us that much!" Dano shouted.

With a tone of authority, Carlos said, "Dano, these are good people. They wouldn't hurt your sister. If I thought they would ever do anything but good to her, I'd fight, and I'd take Rosita home. But, they love her and they don't get after her as much as they should. See how spoiled she is? Now get into the truck before the fight has to be between me and you, and I'll have to hurt you."

Dano was curing. Reluctantly, he went outside and crawled into the pickup, and slammed the door. Rosita was disappointed that the fight was over.

Tim and Lori followed Carlos to the pickup. "Tim, I need a cook stove for my Juanita to cook tortillas on," Carlos said. "Do you happen to have one that you're not using?" he asked.

I wonder if Carlos has been over here sometime when we were gone and saw the old range we have stored in that old building? Lori was thinking.

"Yes, we do. But, we would like to have it back if you ever move out of this area," Tim answered.

"Thanks, Tim. It's getting late now. I'll come back over tomorrow and you can help me load it then," Carlos said.

It was very dark, except for the yard light. "I think that's the third time I've seen Rosita hand Dano a brown paper bag, but maybe I'm just imagining things," Lori said to herself. "What would Rosita be sending home with Dano, anyway," she wondered

Lori and Tim waved good-bye as their guests drove out of the yard.

"Rosita, what were in those sacks you handed to Dano a few minutes ago?" Lori asked.

"I didn't hand Dano no sacks!" Rosita snapped.

"I know you did, young lady, and I want to know what was in them," Lori replied.

"I don't know," Rosita said, whining.

"If you don't tell me, I'll have Tim talk to your father about them tomorrow," Lori said.

Rosita pouted a few minutes before she said, "It was some school-work papers that I wanted mama to see."

"Why didn't I see the papers?" Lori asked.

"I don't know," Rosita replied softly. She snuggled up against Lori as they walked into the house.

Lori did not know if Rosita was telling the truth or not. She soon forgot about the incident.

With her hair clean and shiny, cute clothes, and no fights, Rosita was soon popular at school. She was well liked by the boys as well as the girls.

Each of the other teachers told Lori, "For the first time, Rosita is trying to pass her class. I'm impressed with her change of attitude."

Lori gradually begin to notice that Rosita had two distinct personalities. One Rosita was sweet and religious like her mother. When Rosita was in this personality, she criticized everyone for everything from wearing makeup and slacks, to just inferring something that wasn't true.

The other "Rosita" was devilish and mean. When Rosita was in her second personality, Lori caught her stealing, telling lies, and causing all kinds of trouble.

About the time Lori thought that Rosita had really changed, Rosita would take on her second personality. Lori never knew what the girl would do next while she was in this personality.

The principal, Mr. Wilson, called all the fifth grade girls into an empty classroom. "Girls, someone in this room is stealing makeup and money from your lockers. You do not need to bring makeup or money to school, but whoever it is that is taking these things, that don't belong to them, should confess and give them back," Mr. Wilson said.

"Today, during the noon recess, someone took lipstick and eye shadow, and did some extensive art work on the girl's rest-room walls," Mr. Wilson explained.

"I'm going to keep all you here in this room until someone can give me some kind of information on this crime. You are missing classes, and you will have makeup home-work to do as long as we have to stay in this room," Mr. Wilson said. He sat down on the teacher's chair at the front of the room, crossed his legs, and folded his arms. Mr. Wilson slowly looked at one girl, then another.

One of the girls spoke up and said what the other girls were thinking. "Rosita has been wearing makeup lately. She has made fun of us for wearing it," she said.

Before Mr. Wilson could reply, Rosita shouted, "I got my makeup from Mrs. Jones's house, so there!"

Mr. Wilson left the room to talk to Lori. Lori verified Rosita's story. Mr. Wilson returned to the room. He explained to the girls what Mrs. Jones had said. He resumed his position at the front of the room, like he had all day to wait.

"Rosita always has her purse with her. She goes into the school building several times each day during noon recess," another girl said.

"I don't have anything in my purse, but my billfold, some pictures, letters from my family, and one little shoe," Rosita said. She opened her purse and dumped the contents out on her desk for everyone to see.

"What about going into the school building during noon recess?" Mr. Wilson asked, sternly.

"I can't help it if I need to go to the rest-room then," Rosita said with a giggle.

The other girls snickered.

"You're just accusing me because I'm poor and I'm a Mexican," Rosita said timidly.

Mr. Wilson realized that his carefully laid plans were not working. He dismissed the girls to go back to their classes. Mr. Wilson talked to Lori again.

"Mrs. Jones, this is a serious problem and I feel that Rosita could be guilty. I want you to watch her closely at home. If any articles, or money, show up at your house that you don't recognize, please let me know," Mr. Wilson said.

"I think everyone is judging Rosita by the way she used to be, and not the person she is now," Lori said. "She has changed a lot, but I will watch her. I don't expect to find anything, however," she replied.

Lori had driven the car to work that morning so she could buy some groceries after school. She stopped by the grocery store on her way home. Lori picked up a few items and put them into the grocery cart. She pushed the cart up to the cashier. While the cashier was quickly totaling her purchase, Lori opened her wallet to pay for the food in cash. She counted her money twice, and was sure she had a ten dollar bill missing.

Lori didn't say anything, but quickly wrote a check for the purchase. She tried to hide her concern over the missing money. Lori walked down the street to find Rosita. Rosita was in front of the drug store. She had just bought some ice cream cones for herself and two of her friends. Lori did not want to embarrass Rosita in front of her friends, so she only said, "Rosita, get into the car, Babe. It's time for us to go home, now."

Rosita bounced into the car. "Can we take Leslie and Bonny to their houses before we go home?" she asked.

"I guess, since they don't live very far away," Lori answered. She held the back car door open for her two students.

The girls were soon safely delivered. Lori and Rosita traveled toward home over the bumpy, dusty road. Rosita was chattering happily over the events of the day.

"Rosita, did you take a ten dollar bill out of my purse?" Lori asked. "I know you were in my purse when you were looking for two dollars to order that book you wanted," she said.

"No Mam. I wouldn't take any of your money without asking first," Rosita answered with complete confidence.

"Where did you get the money to buy refreshments for your friends?" Lori asked.

"Papa gave me some money that last time he was over to visit," Rosita said. She snuggled up to Lori's side.

<u>She can't sound so innocent if she is guilty,</u> Lori was thinking. "Why didn't I know anything about the money before now?" she asked.

"I didn't know I was supposed to tell you about it, Lori," Rosita said. "I'm sorry I didn't tell you if I am supposed to," she said. "I will tell you next time," Rosita added with a smile.

"Well, if you didn't take the money, then someone else took a ten dollar bill from my purse, sometime today," Lori explained.

"If I knew who did that to you, I would give them this," Rosita said, shaking her fist in the air.

Lori carefully thought through the day. <u>Rosita was the only one that had a chance to take the money. Her purse had been in her sight all day except when Rosita got the two dollars out to order her book,</u> Lori was thinking.

"She just couldn't have done it," Lori kept telling herself.

CHAPTER X

Carlos was still on the farm, hoping to get his job back. Juanita was living in town with Leos, Becky, and some of the older kids. Ray and Bobby had not changed schools yet. They were still living with Carlos on the old farm.

Tim had just finished his supper. "I'm going over to talk to Carlos," he told Lori as soon as Rosita was out of hearing distance.

Carlos was always glad to see Tim. He invited him into the old house. Tim sat down in an old, hazel-colored chair that had a large rip in the back. Carlos brought an old kitchen chair from another room and sit down across from Tim. "How are you and Mrs. Jones, and how is my little girl?" Carlos asked.

"Great! Carlos, I want to talk serious with you," Tim answered. He looked at the slender, dark, man with black hair, except for the white patches around his face.

"Has Rosita been bad again?" Carlos asked.

"No. This is more serious than that. Carlos, I want to adopt your Rosita," Tim replied.

Carlos leaned back in his chair. Tim saw sadness and heartache on the man's face. Carlos was unable to speak.

"Carlos, I want to show you something to help you make up your mind," Tim said. He stood up and motioned for Carlos to follow him.

113

Both men were silent while they drove over to Tim's farm. Together, they walked into the large farm house.

As soon as Carlos entered the house, Rosita squealed and ran from the music room. She threw her long, slender arms around him, and gave him a big hug.

Carlos squeezed his youngest daughter. <u>She looks so beautiful, clean, and shiny, and happy,</u> Carlos was thinking.

Carlos felt numb except for the pain he felt deep in his chest. <u>There was something special about this girl, his youngest of so many,</u> Carlos thought.

"Would you like to see the rest of the house?" Tim asked. "I don't think you have ever been past the kitchen, before," he added.

By the time Carlos saw the red bedroom, and the music room, he had tears in his eyes. <u>It looks like my Rosita is living in a palace,</u> Carlos thought.

Lori had refinished an old bedroom set of furniture, and put new bronze handles on the dresser and night stand drawers. She had made blue, crushed velvet drapes to match the bedspread. Rosita's room was as pretty as the rest of the house.

Carlos stood looking into the room. He was deep in thought. He had visions of his beautiful daughter living like "upper folks" with everything she would ever need. Carlos followed Tim back into the music room. Rosita played the piano while Lori played the guitar. Lori, Tim, and Rosita sung several songs for Carlos.

"I have to get back home and check on Ray and Bobby," Carlos said, jumping out of his chair.

Tim drove the pickup back to the main road. "What did you see tonight, Carlos?" Tim asked.

"I saw a beautiful house. I've seen nice houses before, maybe even nicer than yours, but I was never permitted to sit down in one before.

I saw a family, Lori and you, and my Rosita. I see your wife teaching Rosita beautiful music. I see you taking care of my little girl and taking her to church, and teaching her the right way to live. I see my Rosita growing up different from my other children, living right, in nice clothes, respected and loved. I see her growing up in a good crowd of people, and maybe even going to college. I see my baby daughter marring someone that will be nice to her, and will buy her nice things," Carlos answered. He was talking to himself as well as Tim.

Carlos continued, "My house is full of many children, more than I can take care of. Us Mexicans, we don't ever have much, a house full of kids, and maybe a nice car. We move many times. Sometimes the houses we live in don't even have all the windows. I can see my baby not living in places like that."

There were several minutes of silence. Tim left Carlos deep in his thoughts.

"You own land, Tim. When farming gets better, maybe you can remember old Carlos with maybe a quarter of land to grow old on, someday," Carlos said.

Tim knew everything that Carlos was going to say, except about the land. "If farming gets better, I might be able to help you get a quarter of land of your own," Tim replied. "That will probably have to be a long time from now," he said.

Carlos nodded his head sadly, and replied, "I understand. Let me find Juanita on a day that she is feeling better, and I'll tell her about what you have said. My Juanita, she knows that the older ones are causing our Rosita to do things we don't want her to do. Juanita wants what is good for Rosita."

Tim pulled the pickup up into the old farm-yard so Carlos could get out. The two friends talked for a long time about farming and family problems.

"Tim, you might wonder what kind of guy I am to let you take my daughter for a price, but I know it is best for her. I have a lot of others to try to take care of," Carlos said.

"I understand, and I realize the position I've put you in," Tim replied.

Tim and Carlos shook hands. Carlos walked into the old house for a short night's rest.

"Where, on earth, have you been?" Lori asked. "You've never been out this late before," she said.

"Carlos and I have just been talking," Tim answered.

"About what?" Lori asked. She raised her head and propped it up on her elbow on the pillow.

"Adopting Rosita," Tim answered.

"After the way she talks to you?" Lori asked.

"She will get over that," Tim said. He undressed and crawled into bed beside his warm wife.

"I sure hope so," Lori replied. She stretched out on her stomach next to Tim, and pulled the covers up over her shoulders. "What did he say?" Lori asked.

"He said just what I thought he'd say, after he saw how nice things are for her over here," Tim answered. "He said he'd talk it over with Juanita when she gets to feeling better. Carlos said he'd try to convince Juanita that Rosita is better off with us," Tim explained.

"I also reminded him that his last two daughters ran away when they were about Rosita's age," Tim said.

"Don't you think that was unfair?" Lori asked.

"Yes, but he was thinking the same thing," Tim answered. "Do you know what else he said?" Tim asked.

"I have no idea," Lori answered. She was wide awake now.

"He said that if we take Rosita permanently, one of these days, when farming gets better, and we start to make money, that we can remember him with a quarter of land," Tim replied.

"I guess that serves you right, considering the heart breaking position you had him in," Lori said. "I suppose you said <u>someday</u>, Lori commented as she tried to go back to sleep.

CHAPTER XI

CHECK OUT TIME

What a cold day to have playground duty. This wind is blowing right through my heavy coat, Lori was thinking, as she watched her eighty students playing in their designated area.

"Mrs. Jones! Mrs. Jones!" someone yelled.

Lori turned toward the school building. One of her students, Al, was running toward her. "What's the matter?" Lori asked.

"Mrs. Jones, Rosita's brother's wife is her to get her. She is getting all her things out of her locker. They are getting ready to leave right now!" Al shouted, trying to catch his breath.

"Thank you for letting me know," Lori said. She could not leave the area unless one of the other teachers took over for her. Lori looked around the playground, and the area around the lunch room building. She didn't see any other teachers except the other teacher on duty across the playground.

By the time Lori came in from duty, Rosita, Bobby, Ray, and Molly were going out the front door of the school building.

Lori called to Rosita, but the girl didn't even turn around. Lori ran down the sidewalk after them. "You can't take Rosita! I won't let her go with anyone but Carlos or Juanita," Lori yelled.

Molly turned around to face Lori. She seemed to have all the authority she needed. "They sent me after her!" the skinny, Indian woman shouted. "They want all the kids home tomorrow. They are even making the older ones come home," Molly said.

"Why? Is Juanita sick again?" asked Lori.

The young woman shrugged her shoulders and started walking toward the car again. Lori ran after Rosita. Rosita ignored her like she was a complete stranger.

Lori knew she could not stop them, and that she was causing a scene. Students and teachers were looking out of the classroom windows. "Bye Rosita," Lori said, trying not to cry. She hurried to her classroom to start her afternoon Reading class.

"Where is Rosita going?" the students asked when Lori entered the room.

"Home," Lori managed to say.

"Boy, she sure is lucky to get out of school this afternoon," one student said with envy. Some of the other students nodded agreement.

Lori ignored the comments. "Turn to page 159 in your Readers, she ordered.

Tim had gone to a cattle sale. He sold his truck-load of calves and picked up the money for them at the Sale Barn office. On his way out of town, he saw a large "SALE" sign in the window of a small dress shop and parked in front of the store.

Tim bought two pair of dress slacks for Lori, and three dresses for Rosita. The dresses were similar to the dresses the other girls Rosita's age wore. Rosita will look real cute in these dresses, Tim was thinking.

I think I'll stop by Juanita's house when I go through Plainsville and see how Rosita's family is getting along, Tim thought. He was humming a happy tune when he knocked on Juanita's front door an hour later.

Tim heard young footsteps coming to the door. His happiness soon vanished when the door opened and there stood Rosita. For a few seconds, Tim was too surprised to say anything. "Rosita, what are you doing here?" he asked.

"My family came and got me out of that horrible school today," Rosita said. She was laughing at Tim's shocked look.

"Does Lori know where you are?" asked Tim.

"Yes, and there was nothing she could do about it, Bug Eyes!" Rosita screamed.

"Rosita, don't talk to Mr. Jones that way!" Juanita yelled. The heavy set, pretty woman came through the kitchen door into the living room. "Come on in, Mr. Jones, and close the door," Juanita said with a welcome smile.

Tim noticed a young Mexican couple in the kitchen. The woman was holding a baby girl. He thought that Juanita probably just had company. "Why is Rosita here?" Tim asked.

"Carlos's boss had not paid him for quite some time, now. My Carlos, he had to go to the welfare office today and ask for help for our family. They ask how many kids we have. Carlos say twelve. They come tomorrow to count us. Carlos say to get all the kids home before tomorrow," Juanita tried to explain.

"You mean that you have even brought your married, and older kids back to be counted?" Tim asked when he noticed two older girls in the kitchen.

Juanita nodded. "Yes, but things are bad for us right now, Tim, and most of them are living here now, anyway," Juanita answered. She looked at the worn out rug that covered part of the worn out floor. Juanita nervously twisted a dish towel with her hands.

Tim was sorry he had asked Juanita such an embarrassing question. "Rosita, I have a surprise I was bringing home to you tonight," Tim called to Rosita who had returned to the kitchen.

"What is it?" Rosita squealed, She ran back into the room.

"I don't know whether to give them to you or not, since I found you here tonight," Tim said.

"Give it to me anyway!" Rosita shouted.

Tim went to the pickup and returned with two gray plastic bags. Rosita was waiting for him at the door. Tim knew she was only interested in what he had brought her. Her dark eyes sparkled as Tim handed her the packages.

Rosita did not even say "Thank you". She dumped the contents onto the old sofa. Rosita squealed when she saw the dresses. The two older sisters saw the dresses and ran over to the couch. Rosita stepped back to let the sisters take what they wanted. Each sister grabbed the dress they liked best, and held the dresses against their slender bodies. Tim could see that the dresses would fit them.

"Those are Rosita's dresses!" Tim shouted.

The two sisters dropped the dresses and stepped back from the couch.

"If the dresses are mine, then I can do what I want to with them, and I want to give them to my sisters, so there!" Rosita shouted.

"But, Rosita, I bought these dresses for you. You need them to wear to school. Your sisters can go to work and buy dresses like these, but you're too young to do that yet!" Tim yelled. He felt sick. He knew he was losing another battle with Rosita. Tim knew that the minute he was gone, Rosita would give her sisters the dresses.

"What can I do to make you buy me dresses like that?" one of the sisters asked.

Tim ignored the question. "Rosita, aren't you going to live with Lori and me, at least until school is out next spring?" Tim asked.

"Nope," Rosita said. She sounded happy.

Tim looked over to Juanita. "I thought you and Carlos decided that Rosita would be better off finishing this school year with Lori's help. That maybe it would help her catch up in school, and . . ."

Before Tim could finish, the two older girls jumped on Tim's lap and put their arms around his neck. "I'll go home with you and do anything you want me to, if you'll buy me things like you do Rosita," one girl said.

"I'll treat you better than Rosita does," the other girl said. She hugged Tim's neck.

Tim stood up and the girls tumbled to the floor.

"You girls leave Mr. Jones alone, and go back into the kitchen!" Juanita shouted, pointing and shaking her finger at her two older daughters.

"I'm just as good as Rosita!" one of the girls shouted as the young ladies left the room.

"I raise my girls to do right. Now they grow up and don't listen to me," Juanita said. "When Carlos comes in, I'll ask him about Rosita. He might let her go home with you after the count. Come back tomorrow, and we will have answer for you," she said. Juanita stood up as a sign for Tim to leave.

Tim walked toward the front door. He could hear the couple in the kitchen talking in Spanish. He saw them nodding their heads in agreement. Tim had the door open when the Mexican man called to him.

The man picked up his two-year-old daughter from her mother's arms. He brought the baby to Tim. With the same emotionless expression of his ancestors, he lifted the child up for Tim to take. "Take my baby home with you, to be your child forever. We charge you nothing," he said in broken English.

Tim understood. The couple would probably be sent back to Mexico. They wanted their daughter, their first born, to grow up with all the advantages of living in the United States. How much they must love her, Tim was thinking. How bad are conditions in Mexico that would cause this couple to want to give their baby away? Tim wondered.

"You have a lovely child, but we can't take care of one this young as long as my wife is teaching school, and is gone from home every day." Tim said kindly.

The young man stared at Tim with dark brown eyes. He nodded that he understood. Clutching the baby to his body, he took her back and placed her in her mother's arms. The mother showed no more expression than did her husband.

Tim said a quick good-bye and hurried to the pickup. "And, I think I have problems," he said to himself as he started the pickup to drive home.

When Lori came home from school the next evening, Tim picked her up from the bus before the bus turned onto their road. They started their fifty-mile trip back to Juanita's house.

Lori kicked off her high-heeled shoes, and sank deep into the Cadillac's, rose colored, soft cushioned seat. "Tim, don't you think it would be better to just leave Rosita with her folks?" she said. Lori felt so tired.

121

"You're probably right, but I'm afraid for Rosita. I see some things around the Gonzales place that I don't like. I know Rosita isn't protected the way she should be," Tim answered, "I want Rosita to belong to us. Maybe if we can keep her until spring, maybe she will realize what is best for her, and want to stay with us then."

"I hope you're right. It's hard on all of us to be trying to get her back all the time like this," Lori said with a sigh.

Tim and Lori did not get Rosita that evening. Tim made several trips back to Plainsville, but Rosita was still with her family. Lori thought that Tim had given up until the evening she came home from school and Tim said, "Lori, we are going to Juanita's. I just have the feeling that Carlos will let us have Rosita tonight."

"This is the last time I want to make this trip for a long time, Tim. I'm so tired," Lori replied. "Why do you think Carlos will let her come home with us this time?" she asked.

"I just do," Tim answered.

"Carlos and Rosita have gone to the farm to get some more of Rosita's clothes," Juanita explained. "Make her mind," she added.

Tim and Lori had to drive back the forty-eight miles that they could have saved, to pick Rosita up from the farm. Rosita met them at the door with a smile, and several brown paper bags. She hugged Lori and chattered all the way home.

The next evening, Tim felt a special concern for Carlos, Bobby, and Ray. He was standing next to the large pickup when Lori and Rosita got off of the bus. "I can't explain it, but I think we need to go over and check on Carlos," Tim said.

Rosita waited for Lori to climb in beside Tim, before she crawled in beside her.

It had been cloudy all day. "I think this is the coldest day we have had this year," Lori said. The wind was blowing and sand was hitting the outside of the vehicle hard enough to knock off paint.

The heater in the pickup seemed unable to keep them warm. Lori wrapped Rosita up in her long, green, wool coat. The trip seemed to take longer than usual.

"Carlos is gone. Maybe I have just been imagining things," Tim said when they pulled into the old farm yard. It was almost dark and there were no lights on in the old house. He got out and told Lori and Rosita to stay in the pickup, out of the wind, and try to stay warm. Tim banged on the door several times. He started to walk back to the pickup. "I think I'll try just one more time," he told himself. The sand stung his face as he turned around to knock again.

The minute Ray opened the door, Tim knew something was wrong.

"Whatcha doin here?" Ray said through clenched teeth. "Pa ain't here, and you already have Rosita, so why donecha jest go away and leave us alone," Ray shouted above the howling wind.

"I care about the rest of you too?" Tim shouted.

"Jest leave us alone?" Ray shouted back.

Tim turned to leave when he noticed the odor of gasoline and smoke. "What are you boys doing!" Tim yelled above the sound of the wind. Ray tried to close the door, but Tim forced himself past Ray, and into the house.

The house was filled with smoke. Tim rushed into the small living room. Bobby was standing over a trash can. Tim could see that the boys had filled the trash can with rags and paper. They had poured gas in the can and set it on fire. It was still burning.

It was colder in the house than it was outside. Ray and Bobby still had on their school coats, but their skin was blue from the cold.

"Put that fire out before it catches the curtains on fire!" Tim yelled.

Ray did not move, but Bobby ran into another room and brought back a blanket and threw it over the fire. The fire was soon smothered out, but the blanket had a large hole burned in it.

"Why didn't you bring some water to put out the fire rather than ruining this blanket?" Tim asked.

"Because there aint no water!" Ray answered. He sounded bitter.

"You could have killed yourselves by starting a fire. Don't you know that?" Tim asked.

"We were just trying to keep warm the only way we knew how," Bobby tried to explain, shaking from the cold

"If we'd burned up then we wouldn't have to worry about freezing to death!" Ray yelled.

"Why isn't there any heat, water, or lights on over here tonight?" Tim asked.

"Because, the boss wants us to move, so he shut off all the utilities, and took away all the propane," Bobby explained. He showed Tim a note they had found on the kitchen table. It was from Carlos's boss.

"I asked you people to move several weeks ago. I am shutting off all utilities until you move," the note read.

The utilities had been shut off after Carlos had left that day. Ray and Bobby had gotten off the school bus without any warning. After the bus was gone, the boys had done every thing they knew to survive.

"You don't have to kill yourselves trying to keep warm," Tim said. "Either come with us or get under all the blankets you can find. I'll be back as soon as I can with enough propane to keep you warm for a couple of days," he said.

Bobby ran to the bedroom and started pulling the blankets off the beds and putting them in one place. Ray followed Tim to the pickup, and crawled in between Lori and Rosita. They rubbed his hands to help get back the circulation.

Tim quickly drove back home and filled a small propane tank with fuel from the large farmhouse tank. They hurried back to Carlos's place.

"There's papa's car with Becky and Leos in it!" Rosita shouted. Tim parked the pickup beside the empty propane tank.

It seemed like Tim had been gone a long time as Bobby waited under the covers. He finally heard two vehicles next to the house. Bobby's body was so stiff from the cold that it was difficult for him to get up and go to the door.

Carlos helped Tim hook up the two propane tanks. Bobby crawled into the blue Chivy to get warm. Carlos lit the pilot light and turned on the kitchen stove. He showed no emotion of surprise, anger, or worry over what had happened. He did not seem excited about Tim rescuing the boys before they froze to death. Maybe Carlos is just too tired and worried over all of his problems to feel anything, Tim was thinking.

The propane lasted for two days. Carlos and the boys had moved to Plainsville before it ran out.

During the passing weeks, Rosita begin to settle down again. She was passing all her classes. Although she was never close to Tim again, she did show him more respect after Ray and Bobby's rescue.

Tim continually spoiled Rosita by buying her things. Lori tried not to get angry. Maybe she keeps him from missing his own kids so much, she was thinking.

Bobby was the one that jerked Rosita out of school a month later. He told Lori that the older kids were "giving Carlos a bad time for giving his daughter away". "Rosita and I will stop by your house on the way home to pick up her things," Bobby said.

How much will Rosita think is her's? She claims everything, Lori wondered.

Lori had not known that Bobby was coming after Rosita. She and Rosita had ridden the bus that morning, and Lori had no way of following the kids home. It was an hour before school would be out, and at least an hour and twenty minutes before the bus would be leaving. The bus had to stop at each house along the way to let off kids.

Bobby and Rosita had already left. Lori had to think fast. She ran to the school office and tried to call Tim at home. There was no answer. Rosita had her own key to the house, and she knew how to get in through the kitchen window if she could not find her key.

Lori remembered the night Rosita had handed Dano all those paper sacks. Among other things, Tim's expensive leather-tooling set had come up missing. "That was the very night Carlos has asked to borrow a cooking stove," Lori reminded herself.

Lori ran into Mr. Wilson's office. He was not there. She explained her situation to his secretary. "Do you think someone can watch my class, while I go home and check the things that Rosita takes?" Lori asked.

"I think that can be arranged," Mindy answered.

Lori ran into Mrs. Medina's classroom. "Lupe, since you don't have any more students for today, could you take me home right now?" Lori asked. She explained to Lupe what was going on.

"I think we should get there as fast as possible, and I think you need to get your key back," Lupe said. She grabbed her coat and followed Lori out of the building.

Lori and Lupe arrived at the farm in time to help Bobby and Rosita put things into sacks. They searched the house for any of Rosita's things that they might have missed. Rosita told Lori that she had lost her key. Lori helped Rosita look through her purse, and all the sacks. They looked in all the drawers in Rosita's bedroom, but they did not find the missing key.

Rosita hugged Lori good-bye. Lori had made up her mind that she was not going to cry this time. "What will be, will be," she told herself. She watched the Gonzales vehicle until it was out of sight, and locked all the doors again.

Lori and Lupe were back at school in time for Lori to help her last class with their assignment and dismiss them.

Tim was knocking on Juanita's door again the next morning. There was no answer. Tim drove over to the Plainsville School and sit there long enough to know that none of the Gonzales children were in school. "I'm going to talk to the welfare people and tell them that the Gonzales kids are not in school," he told himself.

"Yes, we know," Mrs. Burton said. "I visited there last night. Carlos said he was looking for work somewhere else. He didn't want to put the kids back in school until he knows if they are going to stay here or not," she explained. "I'll let you know if anything develops. I think it is great that you are so concerned over those kids," Mrs. Burton said.

Tim and Lori went back to Juanita's Saturday morning. They were invited into the living room by the oldest daughter. Juanita came into the living room. "My Carlos has gone to south Texas to look for work," she said.

Rosita came in and sit close to her mother. She would not speak to Tim or Lori. After Juanita finished talking, she and Rosita disappeared into another part of the house.

Tim and Lori sit alone for a long time before one of Rosita's sisters came in. "No one will talk to you, but I will," she shouted. "What do you want?" she asked.

"We want Carlos and Juanita to keep their promise. They told us that Rosita could stay with us until school is out this spring," Tim replied.

"You won't take the ones that want to go with you! You won't take me!" the sister shouted. "Why do you want <u>her</u> when she doesn't want to go with you," she asked.

"She has been with us long enough I guess she seems like she is a part of us," Lori answered.

Rosita came back into the room and sit down by Lori. She laid her head on Lori's shoulder. Lori patted her like she had done hundreds of times. Rosita didn't say anything. She finally got up, and she and her sister left the room.

Tim and Lori were alone again. They did not know what to do. They did not know whether to go or to stay.

An hour later, Juaita came back into the room and said, "I'm afraid to let her go now. Carlos sayed for all the kids to be home when he come home. I'm afraid to let her go without asking my Carlos. I know we promise you. When he come back, I will ask him."

Lori had learned to love, and respect, this pretty Mexican woman. She felt like Juanita was doing her best with her children under difficult circumstances. "Thank you, Juanita," Lori said. She followed Tim to the car.

Lori tried to argue, but she ended up going back with Tim the next Saturday. This time Lori noticed some things that Tim had noticed earlier. Rosita was sleeping on the floor with three older brothers. <u>I'm glad I haven't been able to teach her to sleep in anything other than a full set of clothes</u>, Lori was thinking.

Lori also remembered a conversation she had heard the last time they were there. Juanita had been talking to an older sister. "I'm going walking with some friends this evening. Be sure that Rosita sleeps on that small cot in the front bedroom tonight," Juanita had said.

The sister had argued with Juanita. "My Antone is sleeping there, mama," the sister had said.

"Rosita is sleeping there now," Juanita had ordered.

Lori also noticed that the guy that owned the house was always around. He acted like he was part of the family. He was mentally handicapped and hard to understand when he talked, and walked off balance. He watched Rosita continually with a nasty smile on his face.

When Tim and Lori drove into the yard that morning, Rosita and Able were rolling in the grass like a couple of small children. <u>I understand why Tim has worked so hard to get Rosita back</u>, Lori thought.

Juanita invited Tim and Lori into the house to sit and talk. "Carlos is home. He come home sick. He not let anyone in his bedroom to talk to him. I have no chance to tell him you come here for Rosita today. No one go to his room but he ask to see them. He not ask for me yet," Juanita said. She was twisting a dish towel nervously in her hands, again.

Tim and Lori said they understood. They left Plainsville again without their "Sometimes daughter".

Lori did not know that Tim went back to Plainsville on Monday right after she left for school. As soon as Lori got off the bus on Tuesday, Tim said. "Get into the car right now. We're going after Rosita."

Lori protested. "I don't want to argue with them anymore," she said.

"I have a feeling that the arguing is over, and you'll find a surprise waiting for you when we get there tonight," Tim said. "I have a feeling that you're going to have a permanent daughter when we get there tonight," he repeated.

Rosita was standing by the door with her clothes when Tim and Lori got there. "It looks like you have a daughter until spring," Juanita said.

<u>What's going on here, and why have they changed their minds,</u> Lori wondered.

Rosita hugged her mother good-bye. She chattered happily all the way home about her new friends in Plainsville. Rosita went right to bed as soon as they got back to the farm.

Lori came in and prayed with Rosita, kissed her good-night, and turned off the light. She fell into her own bed for another short night's sleep. She was almost asleep when she remembered the events of the evening. She was suddenly wide awake. "Tim, what made them change their minds so fast?" she asked.

"I went to see Carlos yesterday. He told me that the finance company was going to take their new car and newest pickup. He said if he could find a way to save his vehicles, he'd probably let Rosita live with us until school is out," Tim said.

"And?" asked Lori.

"I ask him how much he needed. He said five hundred dollars. I went to the bank today and got the cash and gave it to Juanita tonight," Tim explained.

"You didn't?" Lori exclaimed, sitting up in bed.

"I did," Tim said, proudly.

"Tim, how will we get by with our expenses and make our own car payment this month?" Lori asked in fear.

"We'll get by somehow. Now Rosita is safe with us," Tim said. He pulled Lori close.

"I love the child, but I would never have done that," Lori said.

"You mean you'd have left her in the circumstances she was living?" Tim asked, not expecting an answer. "I just couldn't leave her there. I think by spring, she'll be different, and she will want to stay with us permanently," he said.

"I sure hope so," said Lori.

A few evenings later, he telephone rang. Tim answered it. It was Ray

"I had a fight with pa," Ray said. "I wonder if you guys could come over and pick me up tomorrow so I can live with you, too?" Ray asked.

It was late when they returned home from Plainsville. Lori hurried around the kitchen to fix some supper for her growing family. She soon had some soup and sandwiches on the table.

"This looks good," Ray said. He slid his chair up to the table.

"I'm hungry too," Rosita said, sitting next to Ray.

Lori started to hand Ray a bowl of soup. She saw Ray's hand and let out a terrifying scream. Ray's hands and arms were covered with blood all the way up to his elbows. "Ray, what's wrong with your hands?" Lori asked. She felt like she was going to vomit.

"Nothin," Ray said, sounding embarrassed.

Tim and Rosita were looking at Ray's hands now.

"How come there's blood all over your hands?" Tim asked, feeling sick. "Get up and wash them! Wash them two or three times, with soap, before you come back to the table!" Tim shouted. "Don't you ever come to the table again without washing your hands first! Understand!" Tim yelled.

"Yes sir," Ray answered. He soon returned to the table with clean hands and arms, but no one was hungry by this time.

"Where did all that blood come form?" Tim asked, again.

"I went to the country with pa, after school today. On the way back to town, he shot a rabbit for supper. He told me to skin it and I did," Ray said, simply.

Ray promised that he would stay with Tim and Lori until school was out in the spring. He tried to change and worked harder in school.

Tim bought Ray some nice clothes to wear to school.

Rosita's personality changed, too. She sassed Lori, as well as Tim. Rosita frequently talked to Ray in Spanish while she looked at Tim and Lori and giggled. Rosita was always angry when Tim, or Lori, had to correct Ray. "Ray don't have to mind you! You're not his papa or his mama!" Rosita screamed over and over.

"Your mama and papa told us to make you kids mind," Tim repeated.

CHAPTER XII

ANOTHER TERRIBLE STORM

It was Saturday. It had snowed several inches during the night, and the wind was blowing harder with each passing hour.

<u>Rosita is a good cook. I have seen her fix a delicious, meatless meal for about twenty people at about the cost of a couple of dollars,</u> Lori was thinking. Rosita, would you like to show me how your mother makes her delicious tortillas?" she asked.

"Yes Mam," Rosita answered, proudly.

"We can use those flat pans that are in the east bottom cabinet," Lori said.

Rosita was getting the pans for Lori. Ray was in his bedroom playing some Rock tapes on the tape player Tim had bought Rosita.

"I'm going to check the cattle in the west pasture," Tim called to Ray. "Would like to go with me?" he asked, from Ray's bedroom door.

Ray shook his head "no".

Tim decided to take the small pickup to the west pasture which was closer than the other pastures. He planned to use the four-wheel-drive pickup to check the other pastures that were further away.

Tim came stomping into the kitchen an hour later. He was upset and angry. "Lori, where is Ray?" Tim yelled. He ran through the house looking in each room.

"I don't know," Lori answered. She turned the tortillas over to Rosita. "I thought he was with you," she said.

"Lori, the big pickup is missing, and so is Ray!" Tim yelled. He checked the house one more time.

"Tim, it's snowing so hard that I can't even see the trees next to the driveway by the house," Lori said.

"It's a killer blizzard outside. I know that kid is in the pickup somewhere. I don't know what to do. I almost didn't make it back home a few minutes ago," Tim said.

"My brother is a good driver so you leave him alone, Fatso!" Rosita ordered.

"He might be a good driver, but that is a powerful pickup he has right now. Ray is only thirteen, and he has been told not to start any of the vehicles. I guess I shouldn't have left the keys in it," Tim said. He was disgusted with himself.

Rosita laughed. "Papa keeps all the keys out of our vehicles at home, so it's not Ray's fault!" she shouted.

"Yes it is Ray's fault, so sit down and listen for a change," Lori shouted.

Rosita sit down in a kitchen chair and stared at the flour on her hands.

"We're not as worried about the pickup as we are about Ray," Lori explained. "Sure the pickup cost a lot of money, but it can be replaced. Ray can't. People in the country call a winter storms like this, a killer storm. Sometimes, ranchers that are used to driving get lost in storms like this and have a hard time finding their way back home before freezing to death," Lori said.

Rosita just smiled. Lori decided it was time for another story. "When my mother was about your age, a terrible storm like this blew in across these plains. A little town north of here was trying to have school that day. The superintendent decided to dismiss the students so they could get home before the storm grew worse.

One bus got stuck in a snow drift, and couldn't get the kids home. The snow was blowing so hard outside the bus that they couldn't even see the road, and they didn't know where they were. The storm was just a white monster all around them.

The bus driver ran the bus heater until the bus ran out of gas, and then he ordered the kids to find anything they could to burn. They started a fire in the middle of the bus, hoping that some of the parents would find them before they ran out of fuel" Lori said.

Rosita interrupted Lori. "I bet it was fun to burn all their school books," she said.

Lori ignored the remark and continued her story. "They ran out of things to burn. They were all in a huddle, slowly freezing to death, still hoping that someone might find them.

The bus driver decided that he had to take a chance and walk into the blinding snow in the direction, he thought, a farm house might be. He ordered the kids to stay close together in the bus until he returned.

The next morning the wind had stopped. It was no longer snowing, and the sun was even shining. The parents started looking for their kids. They found them all frozen to death in a huddle in the middle of the bus. They found the bus driver's frozen body in a ditch only a half mile from a farm house," Lori said, finishing her story.

Lori had Rosita's attention, she continued her story telling by saying, "My mother used to tell us about times when it was storming like this, and her mother, my grandmother, tied a rope around her waist when she went out into the storm to feed their livestock. I imagine that they had to tie several ropes together. The kids held the other end of the rope so they could help their mother find her way back through the storm to the house."

"Why didn't your mother's pa feed the livestock?" Rosita asked.

Because he died when the kids were all pretty young," Lori explained. "My mother was only three when he died, and her youngest brother wasn't even born yet," Lori said.

Rosita fell to her knees in front of Tim. "Please go get Ray," she begged.

"I don't have any idea what direction Ray went,. It is usually better to sit and wait for a person to come back rather than for both vehicles to be caught out there," Tim answered.

"The pickup Tim would have to use is not a four-wheel-drive, and it wouldn't make it through the first large snow drift," Lori said. "The pickup Ray has will go through pretty deep snow, if he knows how to drive it in the lower drive," Lori added.

Lori, Rosita, and Tim prayed that Ray would soon be safely home. Lori and Rosita finished the tortillas and fried them. They cleaned up the kitchen and sit down with Tim in the living room. Together, they watched the white monster through the large living room window. They continued to wait.

Rosita became restless and went to the kitchen. She started to watch the storm through the small window in the back door. It was hard to see anything but the blowing snow. Rosita pushed her nose against the cold window. She could feel the cold air touching her face. Her breath bounced back at her from the ice on the window.

Rosita thought she could see Ray trying to force his way through the howling snow. She could see the pickup truck stuck behind him. His face was blistered from the freezing wind and hard snow, and he was going the wrong way.

"Ray, this way!" Rosita shouted.

The storm was making so much noise that she couldn't even hear her own voice. She shook herself. Had she been dreaming or had she really seen something out there?"

"Ray is all right because we prayed for him," Rosita whispered. She looked at the clock on the kitchen stove. They had been waiting for Ray for more than two hours. How do cattle even stay alive on a day like this? Rosita wondered.

Rosita went into the music room where Lori was playing the piano. She sat down by Lori and put her head on Lori's shoulder. Lori patted Rosita and said, "Don't worry, Babe, Ray will be all right."

An hour later, Rosita thought she heard Kato barking above the roar of the storm. She ran to the back door and opened it. The wind caught the door and slammed it against the side of the house.

Rosita strained her eyes to see through the blinding snow. Through the gray haze of twilight, and the storm, she saw her brother walking toward her. It was not her imagination this time. She ran and gave him a big, sisterly hug.

"What's that for?" Ray yelled above the roar of the wind.

"I'm just glad to see you," Rosita shouted.

Ray stomped snow from his boots. He proudly marched into the house to report to Tim. "The cattle four miles north, and two miles west are fine. I broke the ice so they could get a drink," Ray said.

Although Tim was relieved, he grabbed Ray by the collar of his coat and shook him. "Don't you <u>ever</u> do that again!" he yelled.

"Why are you mad at me, when I was just trying to help?" Ray asked.

"Because you were out in a killer storm. You could have been killed or frozen to death! You took the pickup without asking!" Tim shouted. "You are to never, <u>ever</u>, drive a vehicle without me in it, ever again!" Tim yelled.

"I wasn't in any danger," Ray protested. "I just drove slow with my head out of the window, so I could see the side of the road. The truck didn't have no trouble goin through about ten big drifts of snow," He said.

"It's wasn't your good driving that brought you home safely, young man. The Lord protected you!" Lori shouted.

Rosita shook her head to agree with Lori for once.

Ray understood the situation better after Rosita told him the stories that Lori had told her.

They heard later that two ranchers were out checking cattle at the same time as Ray. One of them didn't make it home, but froze to death because his pickup was stuck in a snow drift.

The next Saturday, Tim made Ray go with him to check cattle. They found two small calves that were thin, and almost dead, from the winter storms.

"We'll have to go back to the house and get one of the horse trailers. We need to take these babies, and their mothers, to the house and feed them until the weather gets warmer," Tim said.

Tim backed the pickup under the large goose-neck trailer, trying to slide under the large hitch, when he saw Lee drive into the yard. Tim crawled out of the pickup to visit with his neighbor. He saw Ray slide under the wheel.

"Get back on your side, and don't you move this vehicle one inch!" Tim shouted.

Tim was visiting with Lee a few feet away from the pickup. He heard a loud noise. Tim looked up just in time to see the shiny, new pickup back up and smash into the old, rusty, blue horse trailer.

"Excuse me, Lee, but there's something I have to attend to," Tim said.

"I've got to run, now anyway; be seein ya," Lee said, as he drove away.

Before Tim could reach the pickup, Ray was already in the house. Both back lights were smashed, and one rear bumper was badly damaged. Tim went to the house to find Ray.

"Didn't I tell you not to move that pickup one inch?" Tim yelled through Ray's bedroom door.

Rosita screamed, "You have no right to talk to my brother like that!"

"Yes, he does. He wrecked our new pickup," Lori said, disgustedly. "Ray is in the wrong because he disobeyed and he needs to be punished," Lori added.

"Just take me home," Ray begged.

Saturday would have been a good day to take Ray home. He had torn up so many things that Tim and Lori did not think they could afford to keep him any longer. They did not like the change they had seen in Rosita since Ray had been there, either.

It was too late to take Ray home after Tim had moved the starving calves, and their mothers, to the farm. Tim and Lori decided to take Ray home after church the next day. That way he could be back in school, in Plainsville, by Monday morning.

Ray and Rosita were obnoxious at church the next morning. They would not sit by Tim and Lori during the service. Ray and Rosita were so loud during the preaching, Lori had to move and sit between them, and so the rest of the people could hear the minister's message.

On the way home from church, and during dinner, Ray and Rosita whispered, talked in Spanish, and giggled at Tim and Lori.

When they reached Plainsville that afternoon, Carlos was gone. Juanita apologized for Ray's behavior.

"They're just making up the stories about Ray, mama," Rosita said.

"I believe them," Juanita said, shaking her finger at Rosita.

Rosita was happy, and sweet, after they left Ray and started back to the farm. She became Lori's shadow again. Rosita asked several times if Becky could come and live with them. Lori always reminded Rosita that her mother needed Becky.

Rosita was so good that Lori forgot about her second personality, until it showed itself a few days later.

"Why don't you have Rosita help you more," Tim asked.

"I'm not too busy to handle it, although I do get tired at times," Lori said. "Besides, we don't have her here to work for us. I think she has never had a chance to be a typical child before. She has worked so hard to help her mother and family, that I enjoy watching her do time-killing things that girls her age do," Lori explained.

Lori was fixing supper. Tim started to make a telephone call from the kitchen phone. Rosita was using the telephone in the bedroom. The bedroom door was shut.

When Tim realized that Rosita was using the phone, he started to hang up. The receiver had been off long enough for him to hear something that made him sick at his stomach. He quietly motioned for Lori to come and listen.

"Put that telephone down. It's not polite to listen, and besides, the meat on the stove is ready to turn," Lori protested.

"I'll take care of the meat. You listen to what is going on, because you won't believe it unless you hear it yourself," Tim whispered. He handed the phone to Lori.

Lori took the telephone and put her hand over the receiver and listened. Tim was right. She would have never believed what Rosita was saying unless she had heard it herself.

A young boy's voice said, "Rosita, I have to go now."

"Go where?" Rosita asked in a voice so sultry that Lori hardly recognized it

"I have to go to the bathroom," the boy answered, desperately.

"I wish I was there to go with you. You know what I mean, don't you?" Rosita said. "Please stay and talk to me a little longer," she begged.

Lori felt her face burning. That was her little Rosita saying that. Rosita wouldn't even wear jeans or cut her hair. She told the other girls they were sinful for wearing makeup and slacks. This was the same little girl that had told Lori she always ran and hid when men came to visit her sisters.

Rosita hit boys with her purse if they became too friendly. She had even carried a large knife in her purse for protection. Now Rosita was talking to a high school boy like a whore, when he was trying to hang up the telephone.

Rosita, the little girl that was so determined to be different from her older brothers and sisters, and not hurt her mother like they had. The modest little Rosita that . . . .

Lori heard Rosita say, "I think I'm going to be able to stay all night with your sister tomorrow night. We can be together then, after everyone else has gone to bed."

Lori recognized the boy's voice. It was Jack. His mother was raising him and his younger sister, without a father around. Jack's mother worked in a cafe in the evenings, and was gone from home a lot.

"Look, I have to go," Jack said. There was a click and the phone went dead.

Tim took the meat from the stove, and placed it on the table. "Rosita, come in here, right now!" he yelled.

Rosita thought she was just being called for supper. She came in and sat down at the table in her usual place.

"Rosita, Tim started to use the phone, and heard your conversation with Jack. He made me listen. I would have never believed what you were saying to that boy, if I hadn't heard it, myself," Lori said.

Rosita jumped up from the table. Lori pulled her back into her chair. "I'm glad 'Tim made me listen. I'm afraid that I've believed too many lies you have made up when Tim has told me to watch you closer," Lori said.

Rosita yelled, "I didn't say anything to Jack. I was talking to his sister!"

"Don't make matters worse by telling more lies. We heard everything and we heard Jack trying to get you to hang up. You were making yourself cheap to him!" Lori shouted.

"From now on, you can only use the telephone with permission. You must talk where Tim, or I, can hear the conversation, and there will be no more closed doors, understand!" Lori said.

"You are not permitted to stay all night with Jack's sister, or anyone else. You must have permission ahead of time for anyone to stay all night with you," Lori ordered. "Do you understand?" she asked.

"You need to straighten up your own life before you go around telling Tim, me, or anyone else, how sinful we are. Don't you think?" Lori shouted.

Rosita was sweet and obedient the next few days. At the end of the week, she asked if Jack's sister could stay with her. The girl had been so good that Lori gave her permission.

Tim and Lori were both driving tractors that Saturday. Lori made Rosita and Jane ride with her so she could watch them. The girls rode the twenty-five miles back to the farm with Tim in the large four-wheel-drive tractor.

The girls ate supper and went to Rosita's room to play.

"I don't know why you don't like Tim. He is so nice to you. If you don't want him for a dad, I do," Jane said.

"I don't know why I don't like him, either," Rosita answered.

"Just remember what I said. I'd be happy to come out here to this farm and live anytime you don't want to. I'd like to have a dad like that," Jane repeated.

"I've rented some good farm land twenty miles south of here," Tim said one evening. "Tomorrow, right after school, we are going to the owner's house to sign the leasing papers," he explained.

"Great, where does he live?" Lori asked.

"In Bolus, a town about a hundred miles east of here," Tim answered. "I'll pick you and Rosita up at school so we can get an earlier start," Tim said.

"I forgot. Where did you say we are going tonight?" Rosita asked when she crawled into the car that evening.

"To see a farmer across the state line," Tim answered. "We've been invited to their home for the evening," Tim explained.

Tim, Lori, and Rosita drove into the small town two hours later. The man and his wife were in the front yard, waiting for them. They were standing in front of a beautiful new home. The man invited them inside. They walked past a small music room that was filled with a baby-grand piano. The living room had two large chairs and a curved sectional couch. All the furniture was covered with a white, satin material.

Lori sat next to Tim on the sectional. Rosita snuggled up against Lori the way she always did when she felt bashful. Dean went to the kitchen to fix some ice tea.

Edna sat in one of the chairs and waited for her husband to serve the cold drinks. "Is this your daughter?" she asked.

"Our daughter for a little while," Lori answered. "I wish we could keep her until she is grown, but we'll be returning her to her parents as soon as school is out this spring," Lori explained.

"I have two children, that have children of their own that are almost grown," Edna said. "Thirteen years ago, we adopted a boy," she added.

"That's great," Lori commented.

Our son is only thirteen, but he is over six-feet-tall. Most people think he's at least eighteen," Edna said. "He has grown up fast. He has a girl friend that comes over almost every night to watch TV with him in the family room downstairs. The kids are so quiet that we almost forget that they are down stairs," She said.

After the cold drinks were served, Dean asked Tim to go to town with him. "I have some business I need to take care of. We'll be back in about thirty minutes," Dean said.

"I own a flower shop down town. That is where the men are going to pick up some papers," Edna explained.

"The only thing I have ever done is teach school," Lori said.

"I'm one of her students," said Rosita proudly.

"You certainly have a beautiful home," Lori commented.

"We like this house. We have just moved in from one of our farms, because of my husband's health. He has brain cancer, you know," Edna explained.

"We didn't know. I'm terribly sorry," Lori replied.

"Would you like to see the rest of the house while the men are gone?" Edna asked.

"Sure. I always like to look at houses," Lori answered. She and Rosita followed Edna from one room to another.

Edna showed the upstairs, and then she led her guests down the stairs into a large family room. Edna pointed to her husband's office through a side door. They crossed the family room where Edna opened another door.

"This is our son's room. Wait a minute, and I'll see if it's presentable before I ask you in," Edna said, laughing. "It looks better than usual, so come on in," she said.

Lori walked into the room with Rosita right behind her. Lori did not notice the lovely furniture, because the large pictures on each wall caught her attention first. The pictures were mounted in expensive frames. They were pictures of nude women standing in seductive positions. One picture was of a blonde model, one was a brunette, and two models were redheads.

<u>Wow! These pictures wouldn't even be allowed in Playboy magazine, and here they are decorating a thirteen year old's bedroom!</u> Lori thought.

Lori and Rosita were embarrassed, but they didn't say anything as they followed Edna into the next room.

Dean and Tim were now in the office going over some papers. "I think we should go down town for a steak when you guys are through," Edna said. "There's a nice small restaurant we like, and the meal will be on us," she explained.

"That's sounds like a great idea, but let's wait until Samuel gets home so he can go with us," Dean said.

"I told him to be home by dark because we were having company," Edna replied. "Even if we do wait on him, he probably won't want to go with us anyway," she added.

"He always gets angry when we ask him to go out and eat with us. I guess he thinks he's too old for that," Dean explained.

It was after dark when Samuel stomped into the house. He was angry. "I don't know why I have to be home so early. You guys ruined my evening!" he yelled, showing no respect for his parents, or their guests.

Samuel looked old enough to be out of high-school. Lori was wondering if maybe the adoption papers had been mixed up and he was really older than his parents thought he was.

Samuel's mood changed the minute he saw Rosita. He smiled and started talking to her in a soft tone.

Samuel was tall, handsome, and rich. Rosita was spellbound by his attention.

"We're getting ready to go downtown for a steak," Edna explained. "Would you like to go with us?" she asked with apprehension.

"Sounds good to me. When do we go?" Samuel replied, winking at Rosita.

"That's nice of you, son, to want to go with us this time," Dean remarked.

"I think it'll be a lot of fun," Samuel said. He winked at Rosita again.

Samuel ushered Rosita to the back seat of their new, expensive van. Rosita giggled at everything Samuel said, all the way to the Restaurant. The young people sit in a booth by themselves during the meal. They were having a lot of fun. They are having too much fun, Tim was thinking. He made sure he was back in the van before Samuel and Rosita got there.

Although it was getting late, Edna wanted to stop and show Lori her flower shop. Lori followed Edna around the shop while Dean was showing Tim some new kinds of plants they had just had shipped in. Samuel showed Rosita some novelties they had just received for their coming sale.

Edna gave Lori two small palm trees to take home for house plants.

Tim suddenly realized that Samuel and Rosita had already gone back to the van. He rushed out to chaperon them. He was angry because Dean wasn't watching Samuel.

The kids were in the back seat when Tim crawled into the van. They jumped up and moved away from each other when they heard the door open.

Rosita was angry over the intrusion, but she tried to act nice in front of Samuel.

"I guess your husband is in a hurry," Edna said.

"It is getting late, and we have a long way to go tonight," Lori explained.

Rosita and Samuel giggled all the way back to the house.

"Why not come in for a cup of coffee before you start home?" Dean suggested.

Lori had always wanted to play a baby-grand piano. She mustered up enough courage to ask Edna if she could play it.

"Sure. We'd enjoy listening to you because neither of us can play," Edna said.

Lori played some church songs. The keys felt like satin, and the instrument was very easy to play. "Will you sing a song with me, Tim?" Lori asked.

They sung a song about God's healing power. "That song was to give you hope, Dean, and we will be praying for you, too," Lori said.

"Thank you. I guess that's all the hope I have left, and I do believe," Dean replied.

Tim jumped up from his chair. "Where are the kids?" he shouted.

"I think they're in the kitchen," Edna said.

Tim ran into the kitchen. "They're not here!" Tim shouted.

"My goodness, it's nothing to get excited about. They have probably just gone downstairs to the family room to watch TV," Edna said.

Tim ran downstairs to look for Rosita. Lori played another song that Dean and Edna had requested.

Lori heard Rosita screaming and doors slamming. Tim ran into the room. "You better go check your girl!" Tim yelled.

"What's the matter with you?" Lori asked.

"I went downstairs to look for Rosita. I heard giggling coming from the bedroom. I jerked the door open. The kids were on the bed. Rosita pulled down her dress, and Samuel jumped under the covers. He didn't have on anything but his socks!" Tim yelled. "I jerked Rosita off the bed, and pulled her out of the room. I told her never to go into a place like that again!" he shouted.

"Where is she now?" Lori asked.

"She ran past me and up the stairs. She jumped into the car and locked the doors. See if you can get her out of there and check her!" Tim screamed. He pushed Lori toward the front door.

Lori felt numb, and sick. She looked over at Edna and Dean. They looked disgusted. "Aren't you going to do anything?" Lori asked.

"It's not Samuel's fault. That girl is nothing but a dirty, cheap, little Mexican! It's all her fault!" Edna shouted.

Rosita saw Lori coming with her car keys. She jumped out of the other side of the car and ran into the house. Rosita ran across the house and into the bathroom.

Lori ran after Rosita as fast as she could run. She heard the bathroom door lock just as she reached it. "Rosita let me in, please," Lori called.

"No!" Rosita screamed.

"Then, we will just have to call the police to come and unlock the door and get you out. That will be even more embarrassing for you then than it is now," Lori called softly through the bathroom door.

A few seconds passed. Lori heard the door unlock, and quickly slipped through the door and closed it.

Rosita jumped into the empty bath tub, and crouched into the furthest corner. She looked like a trapped animal. Her face was buried in her dress between her knees. She was crying uncontrollably.

Lori could feel, and taste, the hot, salty tears running down her own face. Her eyes were stinging from a mixture of tears and makeup. I guess no matter what she does, I'll always love her, Lori thought. She knelt down on her knees in front of the bath tub. Lori parted the masses of long, silky, black hair until she could see Rosita's tear-swollen face.

Rosita stopped wailing. She started to sob so deeply that each sob shook her slender bod

"Rosita, we still love you. Let's go home now. I know it was more Samuel's fault than yours. I know that you are terribly embarrassed, but be glad Tim found you when he did, and that it didn't go any further," Lori whispered. It took all her strength to lift Rosita up into her arms.

"Check her and see how far it went!" Tim was yelling through the door.

Lori looked at the crying child in her arms. I just can't embarrass her any farther. I will just hope and pray that she is still a virgin, Lori was thinking.

"Rosita, I know you don't want to face the people outside the door. Put your head into my shoulder, and I will lead you past Tim, Edna, and Dean, out of the house, and into the car. This way you won't have to look at anyone. It will be dark in the car," Lori said. "Are you ready?" she asked.

Rosita shook her head. She buried her face into Lori's shoulder. Lori put her coat and arm around Rosita's trembling body and head. They walked through the door, down the hall, past three angry people standing in the lovely living room, and out of the house. Rosita did not raise her head until Lori opened the car door with her free hand.

Rosita jumped into the back seat of the car and crawled under a blanket.

Dean and Edna said an angry good-bye. They did not invite their guests to come back. "We'll talk about our contract, later, on the telephone," Dean said.

When they reached the main highway, Tim asked. "Did you check her?"

"I'm sorry, Tim, I just couldn't," Lori answered, as Rosita started crying again. "Tim, it's really cold in here. Please turn on the heater," Lori said.

"I have the heater on as high as it will go. It's only blowing out cold air. There must be something wrong with it," Tim explained. He stopped the car at a gas station.

"The heating element is out. There is no one here that can fix it, even if we did have the parts," the station attendant said.

Lori persuaded Rosita to crawl up into the front seat so they could share the blanket and coats. By the time they drove up to their own house, they were all so cold that their hands and feet hurt. Rosita was still sobbing. It had been a night they would never forget.

Rosita was up and ready for school without being called. The incident was never discussed.

Lori and Tim thought the trouble was over until Lori found a letter that Rosita had written to Samuel. Rosita didn't have Samuel's address, so she couldn't mail it.

The letter said: I love you Samuel. I want to come and live with you, my love. I'll meet you anywhere. I love you and I know you love me. I will love you forever, and in all ways. Love, Rosita.

Lori destroyed the letter and hoped that Rosita would not figure out a way to get Samuel's address. That poor girl. She thinks she is in love with that boy. I'm sure he has no feelings for her at all. His folks probably didn't even punish him, or blame him for what happened. Now Rosita is captured by a girlish dream, Lori was thinking.

Rosita came into the house from riding Lori's bike. "Rosita, please sit down here beside me. I need to talk to you," Lori said.

Rosita sit close to Lori on the black leather couch in the music room.

"Rosita, I found the letter you wrote to Samuel, and I read it," Lori said.

"You had no right to do that!" Rosita screamed. She jumped up from the couch, ready to run, but Lori grabbed her by the skirt and pulled her back down onto the couch. Lori held Rosita's head up, so she could look into the girl's eyes. "I wish I didn't have to do things like this. I don't like to bust the bubbles of your dreams, but you know we have to watch you close, and take good care of you," Lori said.

"Rosita, Babe, Samuel doesn't love you. You were just another plaything for him. He has other girl friends. He was only wanting your body. Don't make a fool of yourself for a guy like that," Lori said.

"I know he loves me. I'm going to run away with him someday, and you can't stop me!" Rosita screamed.

"If I can't stop you, then maybe your mother can. I am willing to sacrifice losing you back to your mother rather than have you be used and hurt by a guy like that," Lori explained. "I've been thinking. Maybe it's time for you to go home, for a little while at least. Maybe you can go home for Easter vacation next week," she said.

Rosita did not answer. Lori did not know if she wanted to go home or not. "I think you still love your mother enough that you won't run away from her and try to meet Samuel, right?" Lori asked.

Rosita dropped her head.

"Your mother and I will try to decide where you should be after Easter vacation," Lori explained.

"You don't like me anymore, do you?" Rosita asked, almost in a whisper.

Lori replied, "Yes Babe, I even love you, and I want you to grow up to be a good Christian lady. I pray that God will give us the wisdom to know what's best for you."

Lori and Rosita hugged each other and cried. Lori felt Rosita's hot tears rolling down her arm. What kind of child is this that can change personalities so quickly? One minute, she is acting like a hardened woman of the streets. The next minute, she is acting like an innocent, lovable, small child, Lori was thinking.

CHAPTER XIII

THE OTHER ROSITA

The next week, Tim announced, "We're going to Wilmington this weekend to get a tractor part fixed. Since it's at the foot of the mountains, maybe we can take a drive into the mountains while we're there."

"That sounds like fun," Lori replied.

"Rosita, have you ever been to the mountains?" asked Tim.

"Not that I can remember," Rosita answered. "I don't know if it would be any fun or not," she said.

Friday morning Lori and Rosita packed their clothes before they left for school. Tim was waiting for them when they came out of the school building.

"Where's the tractor part?" Lori asked, as she and Rosita crawled into the car. "I thought we would be going in the pickup to carry the part in the back," she said.

Tim laughed. "It's a tiny part for a large implement, and it's in the trunk," he explained.

The journey took five hours. Lori and Tim visited, while Rosita slept in the back seat almost all the way.

"Where do you guys want to eat supper, and what do you want to do this evening in the big city?" Tim asked after he had left the part at the repair shop.

"I don't care," Lori and Rosita said at the same time.

Tim drove around until he found a nice looking motel close to a skating rink. "Let's get a room here, eat some pizza down the street, then we can take Rosita roller skating," Tim suggested. "I haven't been skating for a long time," he said.

"That would be fun!" Rosita squealed.

Lori suddenly felt terribly tired and depressed. <u>It must be ovary trouble</u>, Lori thought. "I just want to go to bed. You two can go skating if you want to," she said.

"We won't go without you," Tim said. Rosita nodded her head to agree.

Tim rented a room and carried in their suitcases. Lori lay down on the bed. Tim and Rosita sit down on each side of her.

"I just want to be left alone for awhile," Lori pleaded.

"I won't leave you here alone," Tim argued.

"I need some time alone, so please go skating without me!" Lori shouted. She felt herself starting to cry. Lori could not remember the last time she had some time alone. She felt stuffy and caged in. Lori ran into the bathroom and slammed the door. She was so desperate to be alone that she crawled under the counter that held the bathroom sink.

"I don't want you to stay here because of me, so please go on!" Lori yelled through the door. "I just want to be alone for a little while," she repeated. Lori sat on the floor and cried.

It seemed that all the stress of the last few months had caught up with her. "Why do I have to go with you? I want you two to go, but I don't want to go with you. What's so terrible about that?" Lori screamed.

Lori's ears were ringing. She felt like she was going to faint. <u>Fainting will be such a relief from the way I'm feeling right now</u>, Lori was thinking. <u>It must be my age</u>, she thought.

The bathroom door slowly opened, and Rosita slipped inside. She knelt down beside Lori's crouched body and started patting her on the shoulder "Please don't cry, Lori. I love you, and if you don't feel like going skating, then I don't either," Rosita said. She was crying too. "Wash your face with cold water, so we can go out and eat," Rosita ordered as she helped Lori up off the floor.

Lori obeyed, although she felt shaky. She ate supper with her family. Later, they went back to the room and watched TV.

"If it doesn't storm tonight, we'll show you the mountains tomorrow, Rosita," Tim said just before he turned off the light.

Tim and Lori took Rosita to the highest suspension bridge in the world. The bridge was over a deep canyon, between two mountains. It was too cold that day for many tourists to be there. Lori wanted to drive the car across the bridge, but Tim and Rosita were afraid to ride with her. She finally talked Rosita into just walking across the bridge, and back, with her.

Tim waited in the car and tried to keep warm.

Rosita looked down between the boards of the bridge. She could see a river and railroad track at the bottom of the canyon. The bridge was so high that the river and track looked like tiny pencil lines.

As they started across, Rosita screamed and grabbed Lori's arm. She hung on as though she thought that the bridge was going to fall into the massive canyon, and Lori would not fall with it.

As soon as they reached the other side, Rosita was ready to hurry back to the car. She pulled Lori back onto the bridge in the direction of the car. They were close to the middle of the bridge when the wind started blowing harder. The bridge started to sway back and forth.

"Did you feel the bridge move?" Lori asked.

"No I didn't!" Rosita shouted.

Lori was laughing so hard that she could hardly walk against the wind. "It did move, and no matter what you say, you can't change the fact that the bridge moved," Lori said, still laughing.

Rosita and Lori were cold when they finally reached the car. Lori was still laughing. Tim wanted to know what was so funny. He laughed, too, when Lori told him what Rosita had said.

They left the beautiful, snowy mountains in time for Tim to pick up the tractor part, before the repair shop closed. Tim, Lori, and Rosita had fun eating out again, and started back to the flat, dusty plains early the next morning.

It was the last day of school before Easter vacation. Lori decided it would be closer to take Rosita home directly from school rather than going home first, and then driving to the Gonzales's.

"Be sure you check everything Rosita puts into her sacks," Tim said before Lori left for work.

"She is a sweet, changed, little girl, now, and I don't think we have anything to worry about anymore. She won't steal from us now," Lori said, protesting.

"Check her sacks anyway," Tim ordered.

"I hate to invade her privacy," Lori replied.

"Remember how she used her privacy on the telephone?" Tim said.

Rosita came into the kitchen and gave Lori a morning hug. "Can I ride the bus so I can visit with my friends, maybe for the last time?" Rosita asked.

"That would be all right, but be sure you load everything before you get on the school bus," Lori answered.

Lori had not planned to check the sacks, but Rosita acted strange when she put her sacks in the car. Lori saw a changed expression on Rosita's face as quickly as she walked out of the house with the first sacks. Her expression changed from a soft smile to a mean look. She almost looked like two different people.

Lori watched Rosita load more sacks. Each time the expressions were repeated. When the last sacks were loaded in the back seat of the car, Rosita locked both doors. Lori saw her expression change into a soft smile again as she bounced into the house to help her clean up the kitchen.

"I'm going to leave early, Babe, so I can do some work in my room before the bell rings. Be sure the doors are locked before you get on the bus," Lori said.

Lori arrived at school fifteen minutes early. She started to hurry into the school building, and then she stopped. Maybe I better check her sacks as much as I hate to, Lori thought. She quickly returned to the car and started going through the things Rosita had packed.

In the bottom of one sack, Lori found some new pillow cases and games that had been taken from the bedroom closet. Maybe they need them worse than we do, but it's not right for Rosita to take them without asking, Lori was thinking.

Lori ran her hands through each sack until she could feel the bottom of the sack. She felt something in one sack that made shivers go up and down her spine. Lori pulled the object out of the sack. It was Tim's small pistol. She found two boxes of bullets in another sack.

Lori was so upset over the gun that she hardly noticed the jewelry, and other things, that Rosita had taken. She was shaking so badly that it was hard to hold onto the gun and bullets long enough to drop them into the trunk of the car and close the lid. Lori had just closed the lid when Rosita's bus pulled up behind her and into the unloading area of the school playground.

Three weeks earlier, Carlos had found a job and moved his family to a nicer farm close to Plainsville. I wonder if I will have any trouble finding the Gonzales place this evening? Lori was thinking, as she walked to her room. She did not talk to Rosita about the stolen articles until they were on their way to Plainsville.

Rosita seemed happy to be going home that evening. She was chattering beside Lori the way she always did when she was happy.

Lori waited until they were out of town before she asked, "Rosita, why do you steal from us, and why did you steal Tim's gun?"

"I didn't steal from you. I love you. I don't even like guns. I don't steal, and I don't know why you accuse me of things like that!" Rosita said.

She sounds so convincing that if I hadn't seen the articles myself, I would believe her, Lori thought.

"Why do people always blame me for things I don't do? Lori I don't do bad things," Rosita said. She started to cry.

"Rosita, I found the things you took, including the gun and bullets. I took them out of your sacks and put them in the trunk. You can't deny that you did it," Lori said. "But, why did you do it, Rosita, why?" she asked.

"I don't know!" Rosita screamed, still crying.

"I don't want that dumb answer!" Lori shouted.

Rosita stopped crying, and dropped her head down toward her lap. "Lori, I <u>don't</u> really know. I can't even remember doing it," Rosita whispered.

Lori was too angry to notice the confused look on Rosita's face. "The welfare lady told us to be careful when we took you home with us. She said that the kids in your family steal. We thought she was just picking on you because you are Mexicans. You took a lot of things today that aren't yours, and you have stolen money out of my purse," Lori said.

"I have taught a lot of Mexican kids, and not one student ever stole from me in all my years of teaching," Lori added.

"Among other things, you stole Tim's expensive leather-working tools and gave them to Dano that night. You lied and said the sacks contained your school work. You stole from us at the very time your father was asking Tim for a cooking stove. You have lied to us so many times, that I have lost count. We love you, and we are trying to help you," Lori said. "Why do you do these things to us?" she asked.

"I don't think I did, but if I did, Lori, I don't know why," Rosita said, sobbing.

Lori did not know what else to say, or what to do about the situation.

Lori did not have any trouble following Juanita's directions to their new place. Juanita was glad to see Lori, as well as Rosita. The house was one of the nicest that they had ever lived in, and Juanita showed Lori through the house with pride. It had an upstairs, and a basement. The house was furnished with the old, worn-out furniture, but it was clean and neat.

Rosita ran outside to play with Becky, without even telling her mother hello.

Juanita gave Lori a hug. She asked Lori to sit down on one of the kitchen chairs. Juanita poured two cups of hot coffee, and sit down across the table from Lori.

Lori looked at the pretty woman across the table from her. She thought about all the problems Juanita bravely shouldered each day, even besides her epilepsy that had caused her to lose three babies.

One of the babies, Rosita had told her about, was only three months old. The Gonzaleses had gone to town. Juanita was sitting in the car, with all her children, proudly holding her new baby when the baby had an epileptic attack. Juanita had sent one of the older kids into the Drug Store to get Carlos. By the time Carlos got to the car, the baby was dead.

Two of Juanita's daughters had run away before they were fourteen. Neither one had returned and Juanita had never heard from one of them. She didn't know if the girl was dead or alive.

<u>And, I have to tell her more bad news</u>, Lori was thinking. Lori told Juanita about the trouble they had with Rosita. She told her about the stealing, the lies, about the gun, and about Jack and Samuel.

Juanita looked sadly at Lori and said, "I teach my children to do right, but they do what is wrong."

"Maybe Rosita will behave for you better than she has for us," Lori said. "We thought we could help her when we worked so hard to get her. Now, I don't know. I don't know if I should come back after her when vacation is over or not," she said.

"We promise you her until school is out. Maybe you come back after her," Juanita replied.

"Have you seen some tiny, sharp looking tools around your house?" Lori asked.

"Yes. Dano gave them to Becky and Leos to play with. I didn't know where they come from," Juanita answered.

"I understand. I must go home now, so I can fix Tim's supper," Lori said, getting up from the table.

The two women hugged each other, and said good-bye. Lori looked around to tell Rosita good-bye, but she didn't see her anywhere.

The car was too quiet without Rosita chattering and bouncing beside Lori. <u>I was so mad at her such a short time ago, and now I miss</u>

her so much, Lori thought. "Maybe Tim and I are getting to old to raise another child," Lori told herself.

Tim and Lori didn't expect to ever see Rosita again. It was the last day of Easter vacation week when the telephone rang. Tim answered it the way he always did, when he was home.

"Rosita, she want to go back. She promise to be a good girl," Juanita said.

"Great!" Tim said.

"Can you come and get her now so she can start to school with Lori, tomorrow?" Juanita asked.

"Sure!" Tim answered. He forgot he had any other obligations. He and Lori made another trip that evening to pick up their "sometimes" daughter.

Rosita behaved so well after her return from vacation that Tim and Lori almost forgot that she had another personality. There were two very serious incidents that reminded them that the child was not like other children.

Tim needed some extra help with the farm-work again. It was time to start the planting and cultivating. It was also time to move all the cattle to summer pastures. Lori was busy with her Saturday house cleaning, washing clothes, and baking. "I'm going to town to see if I can hire some help," Tim told Lori before he left.

Tim came home that afternoon with two women that he had hired.

"They can't be as strong as men, and they probably don't even know as much about farming and ranching as I do!" Lori protested.

"They are both divorced and have young children to support. They are willing to work long hours and learn. The only men I could find want to work short hours and be paid high wages.

I've learned, from experience, that women take their jobs more seriously, and they do what they are told to do. If they can't be to work on time, they'll find a way to let you know. Sometimes men won't let you know at all when they are not coming to work," Tim tried to explain.

"I guess you're right about the men you've hired so far to work out here. With most of them, I felt more like we were working for them instead of them working for us," Lori said, having to agree with Tim.

"I don't know what else to do right now. We can't afford to pay high wages," Tim said. He walked out of the house and spent the rest of the afternoon showing the women how to run the two tractors he had ready to take to the field. They made a few practice rounds in the field next to the house. It was after dark when the two women finally left.

It had been a dry year. Tim had been unable to rent pasture close to the farm due to a mix up of communication that caused him to have to rent some pasture land that was located over a hundred miles west. They had separated the cows and calves into two trucks to find out the usual land had been rented to another party. The cows and calves were still on the trucks. The land they found was located between two mountain ranges.

"Would you and Rosita like to go with me to look at the pasture land?" Tim asked Lori. "It is so far that you'll have to miss one day of school, but you haven't missed any school yet this year. I think the break from our work will do us all good," he added. "I need to look at the land quickly to get the cows and calves off the trucks," Tim explained.

That day at school Rosita caught a group of girls in the rest-room at school. "Keep the door shut. I have something to tell you, if you can keep a secret," Rosita whispered.

The girls held the door shut and gave Rosita their undivided attention.

"I sure feel sorry for Mrs. Jones," said Rosita.

"Why?" the girls all asked.

"Because," Rosita said slowly, enjoying the attention. "Mr. Jones came home drunk last night. He had six young women with him. He even went to bed with one of them. Mrs. Jones was so angry that she took me and we went over to her aunt's house. We stayed all night there last night.

Mrs. Jones told me that she is leaving Mr. Jones. She said we're going to move to a new place where she'll look for another teaching job tomorrow," Rosita said, finishing her story.

The girls looked at one another. "I don't believe it," one of the girls said. "Mrs. Jones doesn't seem upset today, and she would let the school know if she was planning on leaving," she explained.

"Yeah, I don't believe it either. I think you just made this up just to see what we would say," another girl said.

"Okay, then don't believe me, but you'll know that I'm telling the truth when we aren't in school tomorrow. Mrs. Jones and me will be looking for a new place to live," Rosita said. "Then you'll see that I am telling the truth," she added.

During the noon recess the girls discussed what Rosita had told them. They watched Lori for the rest of the day to see if she showed any signs of being upset. The girls didn't believe Rosita's story until Lori and Rosita did not show up at school the next morning. They looked at each other and nodded their heads in agreement when the substitute teacher walked into class.

Dr. David's daughter, Bonnie, went home to eat dinner during the noon break. "Mom, have you heard what happened to our teacher, Mrs. Jones?"

"I haven't heard anything about her lately," Bonnie's mother answered.

"She said that Mr. Jones came home drunk with six young women and, he even went to bed with one of them. Mrs. Jones is leaving Mr. Jones, and she's going somewhere else to teach," Bonnie said.

"That's hard to believe," the mother replied.

"We didn't believe it either, but Mrs. Jones isn't in school today, and she hardly ever misses," Bonnie said, before she hurried back to school.

Later, when Dr. David came home for lunch, Bonnie's mother told him the story about Lori. "I can't imagine Lori talking about things like that in class," Dr. David replied. "I'll ask Stacy, when I get back to the office, and see if she knows anything about it," he said.

"I haven't heard anything, but I'll see what I can find out," Stacy said. She picked up the telephone and called Lori and Tim's house. There was no answer. Stacy begain to worry. <u>If Lori is sick, she would either be home or here at the clinic</u>, Stacy was thinking. Stacy called Mitch to see if he knew where his mother was.

"I haven't talked to mom for several days," Mitch said.

Stacy did not tell Mitch what she had heard. She called Lori's house every hour for the rest of the day, and late into the night. There was still no answer.

Meanwhile, other students told their parents about the Joneses. The gossip spread like wildfire.

Tim, Lori, and Rosita picked up the land owner's brother to show them the pasture land. Kent was a nice fellow and the four-hour trip was a pleasant one.

"What's happened here!" Kent moaned when Tim stopped the car in front of an uninhabited house on the ranch. Tim also felt sick as he looked out over the pasture land. It had been dry in the valley, too. What was supposed to be green grass was only bare ground.

"I know what happened," Ken said in anger. "My brother rented some of the pasture to a rodeo stocker. He was supposed to bring in only a few horses and bucking bulls. It looks like he has brought in a lot of animals and let them run all over the ranch. He didn't take the animals off when his contract expired, or even when the grass ran out. The grass has been eaten into the ground, and much of the ground has even been blowing. Look at the piles of sand. There was beautiful grass there last fall!" Kent exclaimed.

There was still a herd of horses running on the east side of the bare land.

"It will be a long time before this land can be pastured again, and my cattle have to be moved off the government pasture tomorrow!" Tim exclaimed.

"This pasture can't help you. I'm sorry," Kent replied. "By the way, this is the time to be moving cattle <u>on</u>, not <u>off</u> of government pastures. How come you have to be moving your cattle <u>off</u>?" he asked.

"That's a long story," Tim started to explain. "I thought I had everything set up to pasture some of my cattle on the same pasture that I have used for years. The land owner and I had sort of a standing agreement, so I didn't call him to tell him I would be using the pasture land again.

The land owner heard I was going broke, and out of business. He rented the land to someone else.

I took a load of cows in one truck, and their calves in another truck, to one of his pastures. I started to unload them when I noticed there were several head of cattle already there. I rushed to town and called the owner.

He said he had rented the land to someone else and that they already had their cattle on it. He said he couldn't do anything about it now.

The cows are still on one truck and the calves on the other truck. The calves will die if I don't get them with their mothers to nurse by tomorrow," Tim explained. "And the truckers have people waiting on them to move their cattle, and the trucks are costing us by the hour right now," Tim said.

"You <u>do</u> have an emergency," Kent agreed. "We don't have any more unused land, but if we did, I would almost give it to you for all the trouble you're going through," he said.

Stress always made Tim hungry. Let's go eat dinner, and try to decide what to do next," he said.

"The least I can do is pay for your dinners," Kent replied.

They ate at a nice Mexican restaurant, where Kent had eaten before.

"I'm going to stop by the office of a lawyer I know, and see if we can sue the people that ruined our land," Kent said. "Maybe he'll know about some available pasture land around here," he added.

"All the pasture land around here, for miles, is already taken," the lawyer said.

"We'll have to rush home and take those cows to the farm so they can feed their calves," Tim moaned. "I don't know what we will do after that," he said.

"I'm going to pray and believe that we'll find pasture before we get back to the trucks," Lori said.

"I wish I could believe that. You just don't know how hard it is going to be to find pasture land, since it has been so dry all over the state," Tim replied.

They were half way home, when they traveled over a small mountain pass. Rosita was talking about the beautiful mountains. At the bottom of the pass was another small town.

"I have a strong feeling we should stop at the real estate office over there and ask about pasture," Tim said, pointing across the street.

"Then, that's what you should do, no matter how hopeless it looks," Kent agreed.

Tim parked the car in a parking lot next to a grocery store. Rosita went into the store to buy some ice cream. The others went into the real estate office across the street.

"I know this is a dumb question, but do you know where there is any un-rented pasture land," Tim asked the pretty lady at the desk.

"We don't have any but I think the people that own the real estate office across the street have some pasture land left," the young secretary said.

"Praise the Lord!" Lori shouted.

Kent looked at her like she was from some other planet.

Tim thanked the lady three times. He rushed into the second real estate office, with Lori and Kent right behind him. He repeated his question to the secretary.

"I'm not sure, but my boss is here and you can talk to him," the secretary said. She led them into a large inner office where a young man was setting behind a dark, wooden desk. These people are looking for some pasture land," she explained before she went back to her own desk.

"Yes, I know where there is some land. It belongs to my dad. He has decided, at the last minute, not to run any of his own cattle on it this summer. It is available to lease," the man said.

This time, Tim said, "Praise the Lord!"

"Amen! You sound like my kind of people," the real estate broker said with a broad smile.

Tim shook hands with the man and explained their emergency. The agent put together a set of papers for Tim to sign. They were soon on the road again.

Tim dropped Kent off where he had left his car that morning. The others rushed on to the farm for a little sleep before daybreak. After only three hours of rest, the three of them were half way to the trucks by sunrise.

The emergency loads were soon on their way to new pastures. Tim went back to the farm to call more trucks to pick up the rest of the cattle.

Tim, and one of the hired women, worked on horseback to move the scattered cattle from the old pastures to the portable pens they had set up in one corner of a pasture. Lori and the other hired hand used the two pickups to help round up the cattle and get them into the pens for loading.

Everyone worked two, long, hard days, rounding up the cattle, separating the cattle into mother and baby pairs, and putting the pairs on the trucks.

Lori was beginning to change her mind about female help, and even Rosita jumped out of the pickup several times to turn back an animal running the wrong way.

The last day they worked was Mother's Day. Stacy had planned dinner to honor Lori, and her own mother. She had even gone to the farm to look for Lori. Stacy noticed that several vehicles, including the car, were gone. Poor Lori, I wish she would have told me that she and Tim were having trouble instead of just leaving, she was thinking as she drove back to town.

Lori had packed lunches for the first day of cattle loading. Tim had sent one of the women to town after fried chicken the second day of loading. Lori did not have to go home and cook. There had been no one on the farm all week end except for a few hours in the middle of the night.

Stacy had given up on reaching them.

Late Sunday evening, the last cattle truck drove up to the loading shoot. The driver had a blue-healer, cow-dog in his truck. "This dog belonged to my dad. He got mad at her this morning, when she was helping him load some cattle. He told me to take her with me and shoot her somewhere along the way," the driver explained.

Tim patted the speckled dog on the head. "I think we might have room for another dog on our farm," he said.

"You're lucky I came along to rescue you," Tim said to the dog. "I guess we'll just call you, Lucky,"

Lucky jumped into the pickup with Tim and waited for another ride.

I feel bad because I didn't get to spend today with my kids," Lori said while they were eating a midnight sandwich. "I know we would have had to hire someone else to take my place this weekend if I hadn't helped. As soon as we get caught up with this work, I'm going to spend some time with my family," Lori said, almost to herself.

Rosita and Tim both gave a tired nod to agree with her.

"I guess you guys didn't get to be with your mothers today, either," Lori said.

Lori wondered why Mr. Wilson was so surprised to see her when she came into the school building the next morning. <u>I have only missed one day of school, and he knew I would be back today</u>, Lori thought. She had just started her first class when Stacy ran into her room. She was crying.

"Why don't you let people know where you are?" Stacy asked.

"What's the matter, Stacy?" Lori asked.

"I need to talk to you right away," Stacy said.

"Read this page, and I'll ask questions over it when I return," Lori instructed her students. She followed Stacy into the hall.

"Are you and Tim separated?" Stacy asked.

"Heavens no! We've had a lot of arguments, but we're not separated," Lori answered. "Why?" she asked.

"Do you know what the talk is all over town?" asked Stacy.

"No, I haven't been around town the last three days," Lori answered.

"They say that you told your class that Tim came home drunk. He had some women with him, and he even went to bed with one of them. They say that you have left Tim and that you have been looking for a teaching job somewhere else," Stacy explained. "I haven't been able to reach you, so I didn't know what to believe," she said.

Lori fell back against the wall. "I'm afraid I know where the gossip came from. If it is all over town, I better inform the school board that it isn't true before I lose my job. I can't believe anyone would believe that I would talk about things like that in front of my students, anyway," Lori said.

"You can go by Dr. David's after school and explain it to him. He can tell the rest of the school board," Stacy said. "By the way, I fixed a Mother's Day dinner for you yesterday, and everyone was there but you," she said.

"I'm sorry. I do appreciate you," Lori said as she squeezed Staci's hand. "I will try to keep you more informed on our whereabouts in the future,"

Lori was glad she had brought the car to school. She stopped by Dr. David's house on her way home.

"When Bonnie told us, 'she said', we thought 'she' was talking about you instead of 'Rosita'," Dr. David explained.

"When Bonnie said' she said', we thought she meant you, and she was really talking about Rosita," Dr. David's wife explained again.

"Tim doesn't even drink!" Lori exclaimed.

Dr. David started laughing.

"What's so funny?" Lori asked. "This gossip has hurt my family, and almost cost me my job. It hurts me to think that people actually thought that I would talk about such things to may class, even if the story had been true," she said.

"I didn't think you would," Dr. David said. "The reason I was laughing is because I was thinking about the way some people will believe anything they hear. I heard a rumor last week that my dad, who is sixty-five year old, dedicated to the practicing of medicine, loves his family, and is a dedicated Christian, is running around on my mother," he explained.

"That's pretty far out, all right," Lori agreed, laughing.

Lori went to the car after Rosita. Rosita was questioned about telling the stories. She denied it, even in front of Bonnie. Rosita was almost convincing enough for the group to believe that it was Bonnie who was lying and not her.

"The sad part of this whole mess it that some people wait for things like this to get started. They like to run and tell their neighbors what they have heard. I found that out when Hollis and I were going through our divorce," Lori said.

"I'll tell the rest of the school board, so you won't have to worry about losing your job," Dr. David said.

"Thank you. I'll try to keep Rosita from starting any more horrible stores," Lori replied.

On the way home, Lori said, "Rosita, do you know my family got hurt over the lies you told."

"But, I didn't tell the lies," Rosita said. "I love you, and I wouldn't do anything to hurt you," "Please believe me," Rosita begged.

Lori had the feeling that Rosita really did not remember telling the stories. She sounded so innocent.

"Lori, will you please help me find those papers on the new bulls?" Tim asked one evening. "I know I put them somewhere, and I just can't find them. I've looked through all the drawers in both desks," he said.

"I don't know where else to look except through the dresser drawers where we keep our jewelry," Lori answered. She looked through some papers that she had put at the front of a drawer.

Lori picked up a facial tissue. She tore it up to throw into the trash can. I wonder what this tissue is doing in this drawer? Lori was thinking. Now I remember. I put my wedding rings in it when the diamond came out. I didn't want to loose it, Lori thought.

Lori shook the tissue. The eight hundred dollar, diamond, and the rings were not in the tissue. Lori searched the drawer, again.

164

"My wedding rings and diamond are gone!" Lori screamed. She dumped the contents out of the drawer and onto the bed. She checked each article again. Lori started crying. "My wedding rings are gone," she sobbed.

Tim heard Lori crying and came into the bedroom. "What's the matter?" he asked.

"My wedding rings and diamond are missing?" Lori sobbed.

"What were they doing in the drawer?" Tim asked.

"I haven't worn them since the diamond fell out. You remember I told you about it. I had chased the cattle back on our land one evening. The next morning my diamond fell out right on my desk at school. Praise the Lord, it didn't fall out while I was chasing the cattle. It would have been impossible to have found it in the drifts of sand where I was chasing the cattle.

I took off my rings off, and put the diamond inside the rings. I wrapped scotch tape around them so I wouldn't lose the diamond, and now they are all gone," Lori said.

Lori's grief soon turned to anger. She ran into Rosita's room and turned on the light. "Rosita, where are my wedding rings?" Lori screamed.

"I don't know, Lori, but I'll help you look for them," Rosita answered. She put her arms around Lori and patted her on the back.

"Rosita, did you take my rings?" Lori asked, sobbing.

"No, I wouldn't take your rings. They must be in your bedroom somewhere. I'll help you look for them," Rosita answered. She followed Lori into the other bedroom. They looked through every drawer, and everywhere else they could think of.

Lori felt like she was having a nightmare. She knew Rosita had taken the rings. Yet, as she watched the girl innocently helping her, she couldn't believe that the child could have done such a thing.

"The lady that cleaned house for me this week must have taken them," Lori moaned. "She seemed like such a nice person, and she really needed the job," Lori added.

"It probably was her," Rosita agreed.

"Rosita, you took my rings," Lori screamed. "Now tell me where you put them!" Lori shouted.

Rosita looked straight into Lori's eyes. She had that lost expression on her face again. "Lori, I don't know if I took them or not. If I did, I don't know where they are," Rosita whispered. "Will you help me look for them in my room?" the girl asked, in desperation.

"You did take them, didn't you?" Lori asked again.

"I really don't know," Rosita replied.

Lori followed Rosita to her room. She started dumping all of Rosita's things out of her sacks onto the bed. Rosita was looking through drawers. She was looking as earnestly as Lori. They did not find the rings.

"Dear Lord, let the rings still be in the house somewhere. Let the diamond still be with the rings," Lori prayed.

Rosita started looking through her school things.

Lori picked up an open folder. She saw the report Rosita had written about her for an English assignment. As she thumbed through the report, a tiny object fell out into her lap. There were the rings with the diamond still taped in the middle.

"Rosita, you took my rings to school?" Lori asked. "Praise the Lord that you didn't lose them!" she shouted. She was crying out of happiness now.

Rosita put her arms around Lori and started to cry too. "I didn't know I took them. I didn't mean to hurt you, Lori," she whispered between sobs. Rosita slowly walked back to her bedroom and crawled into bed.

Lori followed Rosita into the bedroom. "Rosita, you are two different people. One of you is a sweet, religious, thoughtful, innocent, little girl. The other you can't be trusted around boys, lies, cheats, and steals." Lori said. "Would you like for me to pray, and in the name of Jesus, demand that the bad you will go away forever?" Lori asked.

"Please help me, Lori," Rosita whimpered. "I feel like I am being torn apart on the inside," she said.

"Tim, please come in here and help me pray for Rosita," Lori called.

"She has stolen all of my good jewelry, including my expensive tie pen," Tim yelled back. "I'm not in the right frame of mind to pray for her right now!" he shouted.

Rosita looked so pale and helpless, lying back on the large white pillows. "Please help me, Lori," she begged.

Lori prayed, "Bad spirit, I'm talking to you and not Rosita. I am a Christian, so I can pray in the name of Jesus. In the name of Jesus, I demand that you come out of this child and bother her no more, in the name of Jesus!"

"Thank you, Lori," Rosita said. She put her arms around Lori's neck and held her tight for a long time.

Lori kissed Rosita goodnight, turned off the light, and closed the door. She was, more than ready, for a good night's rest.

The next morning when Rosita sat down at the table for breakfast, Tim shouted, "Rosita, when I get home from work tonight, all my things better be back in the drawers right where they belong. Understand!"

Rosita looked down at her plate and did not answer.

Tim checked the drawers as soon as he came in from work that night every article was put back exactly where it had been before Rosita took them.

Tim and Lori

First Rosita

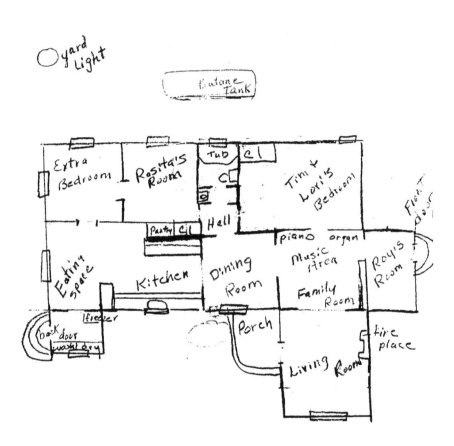

Tim and Lori's Farmhouse

The Robber

CHAPTER XIV

THE LIE

The students, as well as the teachers, were busy the last week of school before summer vacation. Lori was giving test, figuring grades, and filling out report cards. Books and supplies were boxed and stored. Everything had to be put out of the way for the janitors to shampoo the classroom carpets, and do other summer cleaning.

Pete was Rita's grandson was one of Lori's sixth grade students. He had an accident on his three-wheeler motorcycle. Pete's leg was broken, and he missed the last week of school.

On Wednesday, the fifth and sixth graders went to Plainsville for their last "last day of school" parties. The fifth graders went swimming, and then on a picnic. Lori's sixth grade went on a picnic first, and then they went swimming. This separated the classes to make more room at the swimming pool. It also made it more fun for the students.

Rosita borrowed Lori's camera. She took pictures of her classmates and teachers.

After the other students had gone home, Rosita asked, "Lori, can we take these extra refreshments to Pete?" "Maybe we can stop by the Drug Store downtown and buy him a 'Get-Well' card and a small present," she said.

"I think that's a great idea," Lori replied.

Rosita picked out a man' cologne, and had it gift wrapped. She bought a funny card that she thought Pete would like.

Pete lived three miles east of the farm. Lori and Rosita took a different road home, and went by Pete's house first. Pete's parents were divorced and he was living with his grandparents until he finished High-School. Lori parked the car in front of the new farm house that Pete's grandparents had just built. The house was pretty, although it was not completely finished on the outside. Lori rung the door bell and Pete's grandmother, Rita, open the door.

Rita invited Lori and Rosita into the large living room. The large room had a dining area, and a large kitchen in the north end. Lori noticed beautiful cabinets and woodwork every where. The furniture was new and complimented the newness of the room. Pete was lying on a couch with his broken leg elevated up on a chair.

Pete was excited about his card and gift. He enjoyed eating the cupcakes and candy that Rosita had brought him. "Would you like to see the pictures of horses that I have been drawing, then maybe I can scoot over to the table and we can play some table games," Pete said.

Lori enjoyed visiting with her old college friend. "Are you planning to go back into teaching, again," Lori asked.

"I've decided to wait until Pete is out of high-school before going back. We are raising him you know," Rita answered.

"That sounds like a good idea, if you can afford to do that," Lori replied. She looked across the large living room to the table where Pete and Rosita were laughing and having fun with their game. "I'll miss Rosita when she goes back to her parents, and Tim is fond of her too," Lori said.

Lori waited for the kids to finish their game. "It's time to go home now, Rosita," she called.

"Thanks for remembering me," Pete said.

"I would like for you to come over and visit us, although we don't have a new house," Lori said.

"Pete is better at visiting the neighbors than I am," Rita replied. "He rides his bicycle, or three-wheeler, all over this area to visit people, although it will be at least three months before he can ride again," Rita explained.

"Yes, I know. Pete has been to our place a couple of times. He and Rosita have had fun jumping on the trampoline together," Lori replied.

The next evening Lori and Rosita went to visit Lori's boys. Lori had been surprised by the way her two sons, and the rest of the family, had accepted Rosita. No one seemed to notice her dark skin. Rosita felt like she was a part of Lori's family, too.

Rosita taught Mitch some sign language so he could communicate with a deaf person he worked with at the gasohol plant. Rosita loved Bryan, and enjoyed watching him do toddler things.

Friday was Lori's birthday. Rosita baked her three cakes. She decorated each one and wrote Lori's age in large numbers on the top of each cake. One cake was left at home for them to eat. Rosita took one cake to school, and the other cake was to share with Lori's mother and Arthur.

The students teased Lori about her age, since they had finally found out how old she was. Rosita cut the "school" cake in small enough pieces that every fifth and sixth grader could have a piece.

That Sunday, Lori, Tim, and Rosita met Lori's folks at a small cafe after church. After eating dinner, the whole family traveled fifty miles to the Nursing Home. It was Rosita's last day to spend with Elizabeth, Arthur, Sarah, and Daddy Andy.

Tim was driving, and thinking, <u>I wish there was a way to keep Rosita. Our families couldn't love her more if she was really ours. She can make dad laugh when no one else can. We need her more than her family does.</u> Arthur said something and brought Tim out of his daydreaming.

Tim saw his mother's yellow sedan in front of the Nursing Home, and parked beside it. The five visitors entered the large building that had become the permanent, and last, home for over eighty senior citizens. There was the usual smell of urine as they walked down the hall to Daddy Andy's room.

The two families visited an hour when Sarah said, "The people are waiting in the Tumble Weed Room to hear you all sing. We better go in there and get started."

Lori played the piano and Arthur played the guitar. The elderly people were singing too. One lady in a wheel chair was waving her hands in time with the music. Daddy Andy could not sing, but he shouted, "Praise the Lord!" a few times. "Praise the Lord" was one of the few things he could still say.

It was supper time and the old people were walked, or pushed in wheel-chairs, to the large dining room. The family told Daddy Andy good-bye and left the Nursing Home. Sarah ate with the rest of them at a restaurant, before they took her back to the long, tan mobile home. Everyone said good-bye, and started the hour trip back home.

"This day sure has gone fast," Tim said, as he headed the car west again. The others agreed.

Rosita laid her head in Lori's lap, curled up like a small child, and went to sleep. She looked so pretty and innocent lying on Lori's light-blue dress. Her black hair lay in soft curls around her young face.

"I wish we could keep her," Lori whispered. "I wonder what her life will be like when she returns to her other world with her own people," Lori said.

Elizabeth tenderly patted Rosita's dark head. "I don't know, but I know that she will never be the same since she has lived with you and Tim," she said. "You and Tim will never be the same, either, since she has lived with you. I know that some good will come out of her stay with you," Elizabeth added.

On Monday, Lori was going from teacher to teacher collecting grades for her report cards. Each teacher had a positive report about Rosita. They all mentioned how much she had changed. "I think it would be great if you could keep her," Most of them said.

Tuesday morning, the teachers finished the grade cards. The students came that afternoon to pick them up. Rosita told all of her friends "good-bye". I know she would enjoy coming back next year and going through sixth grade with them, Lori was thinking.

With Rosita's help, Lori was soon finished at school. She took a last look at her room to be sure everything was done. Lori and Rosita returned to the farm to rest and enjoy a beautiful summer evening.

Lori waited for Rosita to ask to go home. Rosita acted like she had not even thought about it. Tim came home from work. They ate supper and watched TV just like they would always be together.

Lori was washing clothes and cleaning house the next morning. Rosita was helping. She looked happy and satisfied.

The telephone rang. Rosita ran to answer it. Her happy expression turned sober. "It's my sister," Rosita said. She handed Lori the telephone.

"Yes, this is Lori," Lori answered.

"Rosita must come home right now because mama is sick again," the sister said. "I am sick. There is no one to take care of the little ones," she added.

"Are you coming after her?" Lori asked.

"No! You must bring her home to the house in Plainsville, right now!" the sister ordered.

"All right. That <u>was</u> our agreement. You will have to give us time to pack her clothes and drive the fifty miles to get there," Lori replied.

"We will look for you in two hours!" the woman shouted.

Lori and Rosita put all of Rosita's things into paper sacks once again. They were soon on the road to Plainsville.

Rosita did not seem happy about going home. <u>Is it because she loves us, or is it because she is dreading to go back to all that hard work</u>, Lori wondered.

Lori had her answer when Rosita snuggled up to her and tightly held her hand. Lori felt a lump in her throat as she looked down at the two interlocking hands. One hand was young and dark, and the other hand was wrinkled and white.

"Rosita, you are going into your different world again. I want to tell you something, and I want you to listen carefully," Lori begain. "You are different now. When the devil tempts you to do wrong things, you must tell him, in the name of Jesus, to leave you alone," Lori explained. "Do you understand what I am trying to tell you?" Lori asked.

Rosita squeezed Lori's hand and said, "Yes, I know."

"It is important for you to remember because the devil wants you to do those wrong things again. Jesus is your only hope to be the person that you want to be," Lori explained.

Rosita nodded her head that she understood. She held Lori's hand tightly all the way to Plainsville.

How can I think so much of this child that has caused us so many problems? Lori was thinking. The lump was still in her throat. It hurt when she tried to swallow.

Lori and Rosita reached Plainsville a little early. Lori stopped the car at a drive-in, and ordered two ice cream cones. They ate the ice cream slowly, enjoying their last time together.

Lori drove the car to the little house where Juanita used to live. One of Rosita's sisters was living there now. Juanita and the sister came out of the house to greet them, followed by several younger children. Juanita seemed surprised to see them, and no one was sick.

Lori visited with Juanita. She told Rosita good-bye, and started home. "I won't let this upset me, even if I never see her again," Lori told herself.

Tim and Lori were so busy that summer they hardly had time to think about Rosita. The two women Tim had hired decided they had to drive too far to work, and found jobs in town. It seemed like as soon as Tim had someone trained to where they could be a lot of help, they found another job, or just quit and went on government welfare.

Lori gladly changed her school clothes for field ones. Tim showed her how to pull the sixty-foot implements with a large four-wheel-drive tractor they called "Brute". Tim tried to take care of the rest of the farming and cattle while Lori spent long hours every day on Brute.

Two weeks after the female help left, Tim hired Lonny, a tall, slender, blonde, high-school boy. Lonny begin driving the other four-wheel-drive tractor they called "Whity". The sixteen-year-old knew more about farming than most adults.

Tim felt free to leave Lonny with his rig and concentrate on other things that needed to be done.

Lonny knew machinery, and knew how to fix it when it broke down. He even took broken parts to his folk's farm and welded them. Lonny lost very little time from breakdowns.

The land where Lonny was working was next to a river. The river was usually dry. There were a lot of shrubs between the sandy hills, and a large number of rabbits, hawks, snakes, and coyotes on the land. "I'm going to bring my rifle with me tomorrow and shoot some rabbits for my dogs to eat," Lonny said above the noise of the large tractor.

It was 4:15 a.m. Lonny's alarm clock sounded like a train coming through his upstairs bedroom. He enjoyed farming so it wasn't hard for him to get up this early and get dressed. Lonny bounced down the stairs where his mother had his usual breakfast ready for him.

"I'm glad when you are working and not wanting to go to town all the time," his mother said with a smile.

"Oh mom, you worry too much," Lonny replied. He enjoyed the early mornings when he and his mother could visit alone while his dad and two younger sisters were still asleep. Lonny wished he got along with his dad as well as he did with his mother.

Lonny ate hardily. He went back to his room after his rifle. He smiled as he picked up the weapon. He had always liked guns. Lonny loaded the gun and took an extra box of shells. He was soon on his way to the field in his small, red sports car.

I'll be glad when dad lets me drive one of the old pickups to work. I hate to take this baby to the field over these rough roads, and where sand blows into her. I'm afraid I'm going to tear her up, Lonny was thinking. He was climbing into Whitey by daylight.

Lori's rig, across the field to the west, was already moving. Lonny knew Tim was in a field east. The fields were in the middle of the four-mile piece of land that Tim had rented from Dean, Samuel's dad.

Lonny started Whitey. While the tractor was warming up, he went back to the car for his gun, extra shells, and lunch. As he walked back to the tractor over the freshly turned earth, he thought about how good the early summer morning felt and smelled. Lonny carefully placed the rifle on a ledge behind the seat of the tractor. "It will be easy to grab from here when I see a rabbit," he told himself.

The tractor lunged forward, pulling the plow blades deep into the ground. "Nothing smells as good as fresh dirt. It smells like fresh rain," Lonny said. He took several deep breaths.

Lonny worked a couple of hours. He knew he was covering a lot of land. He stopped once, and shot a rabbit. Throwing it across the back of the tractor's hitch, he started plowing again.

The tractor hit a large clump of hard dirt just as Lonny started to make the turn at the end of the field. The gun slid across the metal ledge, bumped the side of the tractor, and was falling to the floor when Lonny heard the rifle discharge. At the same time, he felt a numbing sensation in the back of his right leg.

Lonny stopped the tractor with his left foot because he could not move his right foot. He felt terrible pain shooting through his leg, then through his whole body. At the same time, Lonny felt something hot running down his leg and into his boot.

"Oh God! I'm shot!" Lonny exclaimed.

I hope I don't bleed to death before I can get help!" Lonny shouted through clenched teeth. He tried twisting his body to see how badly he was wounded. The wound was in the back of his leg and he could not see it.

By the amount of blood Lonny felt filling his boot, he knew he was bleeding badly. He grabbed a grease rag off the dusty tractor floor, and tried to tie it tightly around his leg, just below his knee, to slow down the bleeding. When he sat back up in the seat, he felt like his head was spinning.

Lonny gripped the back of the seat with one hand, and the bottom of the steering wheel with the other hand. He gritted his teeth and slid his body onto the platform just outside the cab of the large tractor.

Lonny used his left hand to reach back into the cab and turn the key to the "off" position. Whitey sputtered and died.

Holding his leg stiff, Lonny slid down the ladder leading down from the tractors platform. He grabbed every place on the machine he could hold on to, to keep his body from falling until he reached the soft, freshly over-turned earth. <u>I didn't know it was so hard to get out of this rig</u>, Lonny thought as he remembered that he usually got on, or off, the tractor with two or three bounces.

Lonny lay in the dirt to give the world a chance to stop spinning. How long he was there, he did not know. Lonny had not been conscious all the time. He opened his eyes and pushed himself into a sitting position. The old grease rag was now bright red. Lonny looked at his watch and realized that he had laid there in the dirt for at least thirty minutes. "I have to get help fast," he said.

"This finishes football for me this year," Lonny shouted. He was now angry at himself. Then he thought <u>I might not live to even see another football season.</u>

Lonny could not stand up. He started crawling toward the car on his hands and one good knee. He crawled as far as he could, and then rested. He did not dare lye down, and take a chance of passing out again.

Feeling much weaker now, Lonny held his head as high as he could to see how close he was to the car. The tiny red speck in the distance was not much larger than it had been when he first left the tractor.

Lonny started crawling again. He counted each stride, and made them into a rhyme, like he was exercising, to keep up his strength and determination. By concentrating on counting, he didn't think so much about the horrible pain. It helped to keep him from fainting again.

It seemed like an eternity before Lonny reached the car. He was tall enough to reach the door handle without standing up on his knees. With a painful scream, Lonny pulled himself into the front seat of the vehicle.

Lonny sit up and became terribly nauseated. He held his head out of the car, and lost all his breakfast. Vomiting seemed to lessen the pain in his stomach. His body did not feel so tense. Lonny closed the door and started toward Lori's field.

Brute was not moving. Lonny's vision was still hazy, but he could see that Lori's old red and white pickup was gone. <u>Lori must have had a breakdown</u>, Lonny thought. He knew he didn't have much time left, so he slowly made a wide turn in Lori's field, and started toward Tim's field.

"Oh God, what can I do now!" Lonny shouted as he saw that no one was in Tim's field, either. Tim's tractor was sitting close to the road. The field was deserted. <u>One of them must have broken down and they both went to town after parts</u>, Lonny was thinking. "I've wasted a lot of time. I've got to try to get home," Lonny said.

Lonny could not see well enough to drive fast. It took him an hour to drive to his folk's place. He was honking the horn as he turned into the driveway. <u>The worst is over</u>, Lonny thought in relief. Now his folks could take care of him and take him to the hospital. Lonny honked the horn for several minutes before he realized that his folks were not home.

"Oh God, I don't know if I can make it the thirty miles into town or not. I know I'm too weak to make it into the house to use the phone. I should have gone the other way from the field for help," Lonny moaned. <u>If I had gone straight to town instead of coming by here first, I would be in Dr. David's office by now</u>, he thought.

The grease rag on his leg felt a little stiff. "Maybe my blood has started to clot around the wound," Lonny said, trying to encourage himself. He made a large turn in the farmyard, and started the thirty miles to town.

Lonny had to stop several times until his head stopped spinning, and he could see the narrow, dusty road again. He finally reached the pavement nine miles south of town. "You're almost there, Old Boy," Lonny told himself loudly.

There was usually some traffic on the main road, but Lonny did not see one car that he could stop for help.

Lonny always enjoyed going to town, but he had never been so glad to see the two, tall, white grain elevators rising up from the flat prairie. They looked like a floating moorage. It seemed like a long time before

Lonny drove up to the emergency entrance of the community hospital. It had taken him an hour, and a half, to get to town. Lonny fell across the horn of his car and fainted again.

"Welcome back," a kind voice said.

Lonny opened his eyes. He was no longer lying in a dusty field, or hot car, but in a clean white bed. I must have had a bad dream, he thought. Lonny tried to move his leg. He felt stitches and bandages. Lonny looked down at his hospital gown. He wondered how long he had been unconscious.

"Welcome back, I said," the voice came again.

Lonny looked up and saw Nickie. She had graduated from high-school two years ago, and was now working in the hospital as a nurse's aid. "Hello Nickie," Lonny said, weakly. He felt an I.V. needle resting in his wrist.

"Why wouldn't you talk to me when we went out to get you from your car?" Nickie asked, teasingly. "Why did you shoot yourself in the leg, or did someone else do it?" she asked.

"I did," Lonny said. He felt embarrassed.

"Couldn't you find anything else to do in your spare time?" Nickie asked.

Dr. David came into the room. "We have contacted your mother. She is in town and on her way here," Dr. David said. He sat down in a chair and faced Lonny. "We weren't able to remove the bullet from your leg. It is so deep that it might cause more damage to dig it out than to just let it stay there," Dr. David explained.

Lonny nodded his head to show he understood.

Dr. David continued. "I know you are crazy over football, and this isn't going to help with practice only two months away," Dr. David said.

"You mean it will take that long for my leg to heal?" Lonny said, moaning.

"Listen, young man, you're lucky to be alive as much blood as you lost before you got here," Dr. David said. "In answer to your question, it might take even longer than just two months for you leg to heal," the doctor explained.

"Oh no, and this my junior year!" Lonny whaled.

"I know, and if the bullet starts to bother you, you might want to go to a specialist and have it taken out. That will take even longer," Dr. David explained.

"I guess you're right. I'm just lucky to be alive," Lonny said, falling back on the pillow.

Lori and Tim came in late that night. The telephone rang. It was Lonny's mother. "Lonny has been in a shooting accident," she said.

"Oh, dear Lord, how bad is he hurt?" Lori asked.

"Thank goodness!" Lori exclaimed after she found out that Lonny was going to be all right. "How did it happen?" she asked, thinking that it probably happened at home.

"It happened in the field. He couldn't find either you, or Tim, when he needed your help. It was a bad time for both of you to be out of the field," Lonny's mother said. She sounded like she thought the accident had been her and Tim's fault.

"We were in the field. Tim and I have been on the tractors since five o'clock this morning except when we took time to chase some cattle back into our pasture. We were gone away from our tractors less than an hour," Lori explained.

The bullet had gone through the fatty part of the leg so Lonny was soon able to walk again. He was too weak to go back to work and lay around his folk's house for three weeks. Lonny ate well and tried to get his strength back. When Lonny finally did return to work, he could only work a little at a time.

Lori drove Whitey after she finished her own field. She was thinking about the ledge behind her where Lonny had laid his rifle. The ledge was about even with her neck. How did that gun keep from shooting Lonny in the neck or back, Lori wondered. "Thank you Lord, for another miracle," she shouted above the noise of the tractor.

Lonny's personality completely changed. He lost all interest in farming. Lonny's younger cousin, Kenny, started coming to work with him. Kenny was supposed to be Lonny's "legs" when Lonny needed tools, or needed to fill the tractor with gas.

Lonny's parents were separated. Lonny's mother took the three children and moved to town. Kenny's parents were divorced, and Kenny was staying with Lonny's family for the summer.

Kenny was accustomed to roaming around town, and he grew restless riding in the tractor with Lonny all day. When Lonny moved Whitey to the field close to the farmhouse, Kenny spent his time roaming around the farm. Lori and Tim were still working on the land twenty miles away. Kenny was at the farm unsupervised.

One evening Tim and Lori came in late. They were tired and dirty. As the pickup lights lit up the yard, Tim said, "Lori, look. All the windows in my old pickup have been knocked out."

Lori nodded her tired head.

Tim was getting everything ready to go back to the field early the next morning. Lori cleaned up the kitchen and was fixing their lunches. Everywhere Tim looked, he saw more smashed glass, and missing windows. All the windows on the place were smashed except the house, and the three newest vehicles. The hen house had all the windows missing, and the building had been heavily vandalized.

Tim was angry. He stomped back into the house and told Lori what he had found. "Lonny and Kenny must know something about this," Tim said.

"And to think, we were ready to open our home to Kenny because his folks are divorced. We thought he would be better off out here in the country, than he is roaming the streets in town," Lori replied.

"I know it will make us late getting to the field, but we're going to stay around here until the boys come to work. We're going to find out what is going on before more things happen," Tim said.

Lonny had been getting to work later each morning. Tim knew that the family separation was one reason Lonny was late. It was ten o'clock before the boys drove in.

Tim called to the boys from the back door. "You boys come inside the house so I can talk to you," he ordered.

The boys shrugged their shoulders and came inside. Lori said good morning and fixed two extra cups of hot coffee. She placed the coffee on the kitchen table and motioned for the boys to sit down.

"What do you boys know about broken windows around this place?" Tim asked.

"Nothing. What broken windows?" Kenny answered. He started to laugh.

"Yeah, what broken windows," Lonny said. He started laughing too.

"I know you boys are guilty. We need to get this straightened out, or we won't get any farming done today, so let's start telling the truth!" Tim shouted.

Lonny looked over at Kenny. "We might as well tell him," he said with a giggle.

"Yeah, I did it. I like to smash glass," Kenny said. He started to laugh again. "Whatcha gonna do about it?" he asked.

"First of all, I think you owe us an apology for destroying our property. The windows will be expensive to replace," Tim shouted.

"I apologize," Kenny said with a giggle.

"Now I think you should work for us, free, until you have worked long enough to pay for the damage you have done," Tim said.

"I'll be glad to drive a tractor for you," Kenny replied.

"You're only twelve and too young to drive a tractor," Tim shouted. He sat quietly in his chair for awhile. The boys were growing restless. "What I want you to do is clean up this farm by pulling weeds, picking up trash, and things like that," Tim ordered.

"I'm just a kid, and you can't make me work that hard!" Kenny exclaimed.

"I guess I'll just have to turn it over to the sheriff," Tim said. He picked up the telephone and started to dial.

"Okay, I'll work for you," Kenny said. He covered up his mouth as he snickered.

<u>We would have really had our hand's full if we had ended up keeping Kenny and sending him to school</u>, Lori was thinking.

Lonny and Kenny came to work only two days after that. Tim called Lonny's mother to inquire about the boys. "Lonny says his leg bothers him too much to work anymore," Lonny's mother said.

"I'm not surprised," Tim replied. "He acts so different since his accident, and by the way he walks, I can tell that his leg must be pretty stiff. Kenny needs to come out here and work a few more days to pay for all the glass he broke, though," Tim explained.

"Kenny has gone back to live with his mother. His mother told me that you worked him so hard that she should turn you in for child abuse," Lonny's mother said.

"May I have her telephone number so I can talk to her?" Tim asked. He wrote down the number and made the call.

"Kenny is innocent. He didn't break the glass at your place. He told me so himself. His hands are blistered from pulling weeds. I should turn you over to the authorities for making a boy work like a man!" Kenny's mother shouted.

Tim hung up the telephone. "I guess it will be easier to forget, and pay for, the vandalism, rather than to take it to court and be out more money," he said.

Tim and Lori discovered more damage. The windshield in the new pickup had been hit by something larger than a rock. There were two broken window panes in the living room, too.

Lori helped Tim put heavy cardboard in the windows of the hen house. They added boards across the places where the walls had been broken out.

Tim hired an older man to work for a few days. On Saturday, Sam was helping Tim and Lori load cattle to take to a different pasture. He fell off the loading chute and broke his ankle.

Tim carried Sam to the pickup. He and Lori finished loading the cattle. "Do you think you can take Sam to the hospital while I drive the truck to the new pasture?" Tim asked.

"Yes, but I can't carry him to the door of the hospital like you just carried him to the pickup," Lori replied.

"I can get to the hospital door if you can just get me to the hospital," Sam said. He moaned from the pain all the way to the hospital.

Lori pulled into the emergency drive of the hospital and ran to the door for help.

Nickie came to the door. She looked past Lori and started laughing.

Lori turned around and laughed too. Sam was crawling on his hands, and one knee. He had his hurt foot sticking straight up in the air. He was hopping like a crippled rabbit.

Lori left the hospital knowing that she and Tim had a lot of work left to do.

Tim and Lori finished farming their four sections of land without any more help. The air conditioner in Brute would not work and it was over a hundred degrees inside the tractor day after day. Lori lost thirty pounds, and her complexion was prettier than she could ever remember. She had never felt healthier. "I have my own personal health SPA called Brute," Lori told her friends and family.

The only scary time was the hottest day in Brute. Lori started feeling dizzy and cold. She stopped the tractor, got out, and laid on the ground. Tim knew something was wrong and hurried to Lori's field. He put Lori in the new pickup and turned on the air conditioner. Lori felt like she had the flu, and Tim would not let her work until the next day. "You almost had a sun stroke," Tim explained.

Farming was a pleasant change from the busy classroom. Lori loved the outdoors. It was great to be alone with her thoughts of life and God. She enjoyed getting up before sunup, and driving to the field for a long day. Lori enjoyed the smell of the freshly turned soil that smelled like spring rain. She enjoyed watching the wild animals of the prairie. I know why daddy loved farming so much, she often thought.

Tim was working with the large land-leveling implement across the road from where Lori was farming with Brute. "I got a little spooky driving Whitey today," Tim said one evening.

"Why?" Lori asked.

"While I was flattening that land and soap-weeds, I stirred up several dens of young rattle snakes. One of the rattlers even chased me back on the tractor while I was moving some old wire," Tim explained. He shivered as a cold chill went up and down his spine. "I just hate snakes," he added.

The next day the shanks of the large implement Brute was pulling became clogged with tall weeds and dirt. It took Lori two hours to clean away the debris so she could start planting milo again.

Lori had driven the planter down one side of the field when she noticed that her arm was hurting, and feeling numb. She stopped the tractor and pulled up her shirt sleeve. Lori's arm was terribly swollen. There was a red lump on her arm right below two matching punctures in her skin.

"Dear Lord, Paul in the Bible didn't die from the bite of a poison snake, and I claim the same kind of healing he had," Lori prayed.

Gradually Lori's arms stopped hurting. Then she felt the swelling going down. Her arm looked normal by quitting time. Lori told Tim about what had happened. "I probably wouldn't have had enough faith for healing if I had actually seen the snake," Lori said.

"Sorry, but I don't believe you," Tim replied and walked out of the room.

The summer was not easy for Tim. The heat of the summer work, and financial problems, caused his blood-pressure to go dangerously high. Tim had to get off the tractor several times a day because of dizziness. Sometimes he was so sick that he had to go to the house and lay down in front of the air cooler.

Prices were dropping on the sale of crops and cattle. The farm was losing thousands of dollars a day. The cattle that had survived last winter's storms, and falling into an oil-slush pit, were poor, and most of their calves were born dead.

The land was so dry that much of the crop was blowing out almost as soon as Lori planted it.

"Wheat is selling for the same price it was at the end of World War II when a farmer could buy a combine for $5,000. I had to pay $100,000 for my last combine," Tim explained to Lori one evening.

Tim was visiting with one of his neighbors that had stopped by at the end of the field. "You know, Tim, my wife and I inherited twenty-nine irrigation circles, free and clear, three years ago. Me and my boys have done the farming so we haven't been out no money on hired help. Because the cost of farming, and natural gas for our irrigation pumps, is so high, almost all the circles have been mortgaged so we can have enough money just to operate. I don't know what is going to happen to the farmer if things don't change around, quick," the neighbor said.

"I know what you mean," Tim agreed. "It takes all of Lori's monthly teaching check to run the tractors for a day and a half," Tim explained.

While Tim finished up some planting, Lori took the combine and tried to find wheat tall enough to harvest. There were a few patches in some low places. She had to run the combine header so low that it was easy to run it into the ground when she hit a bump or the slightest incline. Lori had to always be ready to jerk the header up to keep it out of the dirt.

"Why don't you give up?" Tim asked.

"Let me try again tomorrow. Maybe I can find a little more wheat close to the river basin," Lori explained. "After that, I'll give up.".

It was Tuesday night during the last week of summer vacation. "Tomorrow is my last day to work, Tim. I have a teacher's meeting day after tomorrow. School will start the day after that," Lori explained.

"I don't know how I can get everything done without your help," Tim answered.

"I know, but I just have to keep my job. That is our only dependable income," Lori replied.

Tim nodded his head in agreement. The telephone rang. Tim answered it as usual. He talked for a minute. He looked surprised, and then he smiled.

CHAPTER XV

"Hi Tim, this is Rosita. My mother wants to talk to you," the voice on the telephone said.

Then, Tim heard Juanita say, "My Rosita, she wants to come and visit you. I have been in hospital for many days. My Rosita shares my food with me here. Sometimes, I know not where she is. My Rosita wants to come and stay with you. She will treat you nice, Tim, real nice. Can you come after her tomorrow?"

"Are you sure she want to come back?" Tim asked.

"Let her tell you," Juanita answered.

Rosita took the telephone and repeated everything Juanita had said. "Can you come and get me,?" Rosita asked.

"Just a minute. You better talk to Lori," Tim said. He handed Lori the phone.

Rosita and Juanita told Lori exactly what they had told Tim. "I have a teacher's meeting tomorrow. Rosita can go with me on Friday, but not Thursday," Lori tried to explain.

"That's all right. You come and get her tomorrow morning. Pick her up here at the hospital," Juanita said.

"Okay. See you in the morning," Lori said, and hung up.

Lori left for Plainsville early the next morning. An hour later, she walked into Juanita's hospital room. Rosita was waiting for her. She ran to the door and hugged Lori. Lori hardly recognized the girl.

Rosita's beautiful hair was cut short. It was dirty and tangled. Rosita was taller and more slender. She was wearing tight jeans, and a tan T-shirt. Her clothes were dirty and wrinkled.

Lori hugged Rosita and Juanita. She shook hands with an older sister who was there.

"You look nice and skinny. What's your secret?" the sister asked Lori.

"Just diet, hard work, and a hot tractor to work in," Lori answered with a grin. "How long has your mother been in the hospital?" she asked.

"About a month," the sister answered. "She fell during one of her seizures, and injured her skull and back. She is scheduled for two surgeries next week as soon as we can find a way to get her to the city," the sister explained.

Lori visited a few minutes. "I will pray that everything will turn out all right," Lori promised. "I must hurry to the field. Rosita get your clothes," she said.

"This is all I have," Rosita answered.

"I guess I can wash them for you tonight," Lori said. She and Rosita said good-bye and walked from the hospital, arm in arm.

Rosita bounced her way to the car, but she was unusually quiet all the way to the field. Rosita's personality had completely changed, although she was happy to be with Lori again. "Tim will be glad to see you too," Lori said.

"I'll be glad to see him," Rosita said with a smile.

Lori drove by Tim's field first. He was working on his tractor when they drove up. Tim came around to Lori's side of the car and said, "I'm glad to see you, Rosita."

"I don't think I can go through with this," Rosita whispered. She slid behind Lori and acted bashful again.

Tim and Lori had no idea what Rosita was talking about. They looked at each other a shrugged their shoulders in bewilderment. "See you later," Lori said as they left for the wheat field where she was still looking for wheat to cut.

Rosita crawled into the combine, laid down on the metal ledge behind Lori's head, and went to sleep. The loud noise of the combine dumping the wheat into the truck bed did not even wake her up.

I wonder how long it has been since Rosita has had a good night's sleep? Lori was thinking. She finished cutting the last wheat she could find, tall enough to be caught by the combine header, and emptied the bin for the last time. Lori had to shake Rosita to awaken her. "I thought I was going to have to carry you to the car," Lori said, teasingly.

Tim came home at about the same time as Lori and Rosita. Rosita was glad to be home again. She ran to her bedroom, pulled off her shoes, and plopped down on the bed. She was soon asleep again.

"Why don't you start doing the things you need to do to get ready for school tomorrow? I'll fix us some supper," Tim said.

"Thanks. I think I will. Maybe I won't be so late getting to bed tonight that way," Lori replied. She had her hair washed and curled before Tim called her to supper.

It was difficult to wake up Rosita. She ate a good meal and went back to bed. Lori had to wake her up later and persuade her to put on one of Lori's old one-piece slack suits, so she could wash Rosita's clothes.

Rosita argued.

"You'll be conformable in this. See, it has a high neck, and long sleeves. I can have your clothes clean before I leave for school in the morning," Lori said.

Lori left the room and waited for Rosita to change. She went back into the room and prayed with Rosita. Lori kissed her "sometimes daughter" goodnight, and picked up the dirty clothes and put them in the washer.

Lori was up early enough the next morning to put Rosita's clothes into the dryer, so they could be drying while she fixed breakfast.

"Are you going to wake up Rosita for breakfast?" Tim asked.

"No. I think I'll just let her rest. She seems to be so tired. I told her last night that her clean clothes would be ready for her before I left for work," Lori explained.

Tim finished eating breakfast, kissed Lori goodbye and left to work in the field close to the house.

Lori took Rosita's clothes out of the dryer and folded them. She put them in Rosita's room just before she left. Rosita was still asleep when Lori closed the bedroom door.

Lori drove the car upon the main road in front of the farm and turned north. She waved at Tim as she passed the field. The dust was swirling around the tractor. Lori doubted that Tim could even see the car go by. A rain would be so nice, Lori was thinking.

After the house had been quiet for several minutes, Rosita jumped out of bed and checked every room. She looked out of every window to be sure she was on the farm alone. Rosita ran to the telephone in the kitchen. I can watch the road better from here, she thought.

Rosita picked up the telephone book and went down the names until she found the name of a church. She dialed the number and a kind voice answered.

"My name is Rosita Gonzales. We are very poor and we need money, food, and some clothes. Can you help us please," Rosita said.

"Of course we'll help you," the kind voice answered. "Do you need the things delivered, or can you pick them up at the church?" the lady asked.

"I'll let you know later this afternoon," Rosita said. She hung up, and then dialed another church in town, repeating her story. Rosita worked until she had reached almost every church in town.

Lori was in the school library. She was taking notes about new rules for the coming school year, as Mr. Wilson was explaining them in the teacher's meeting. Lori looked up and saw the school secretary motioning to her. She quietly slipped out of the library, and walked over to the Principal's office.

"You're wanted on the telephone," the secretary said. She pointed to the telephone on the front desk that had a blinking light.

Lori pushed down the blinking light and said, "Hello. This is Mrs. Jones."

"Mrs. Jones, this is Jenny," a young voice said.

Jenny had been in Lori's fifth grade class the year before. <u>I wonder if Jenny is going to start to school late this year too, because she is taking care of her little brothers and sisters while her parents work in the field like she did last year,</u> Lori was thinking. "Yes, Jenny, Is something wrong?" she asked.

"Rosita just called me. She said she was afraid because someone is walking around the outside of the house and the dogs are barking," Jenny said, with a Spanish accent.

"Why didn't Rosita call me, if she is afraid?" Lori asked.

"She said she didn't want to bother you. She said she just needed someone to talk to until she got over being scared. I just thought you ought to know," Jenny explained.

"Thanks Jenny. I'll call her right now," Lori said.

The telephone rang several times before Rosita answered. She told Lori the same story she had told Jenny.

"Rosita, Babe, it's not necessary for you to be afraid. Just be sure all the doors are locked, and don't go outside. Tim is farming close to the house, and he will notice if anyone is messing around there," Lori explained.

"Okay," Rosita said. She did not sound frightened now.

Lori hurried back to her meeting.

"This is the way we'll do that this year," Mr. Wilson was explaining.

<u>I wish I knew what he is talking about, Lori</u> thought. During the lunch break, Lori borrowed another teacher's notes and copied down the information she had missed in the morning meeting. Lori started working on some bright-colored bulletin boards in her classroom. She used some things she had used when school started the year before. She made some new things to make the bulletin boards look a little different.

Lori finished one bulletin board. It had a figure of Charley Brown with a puzzled look on his face. Snoopy was telling Charley, "You have a brand new chance again this year, Charley Brown. Don't blow it!" Snoopy was handing Charley a blank report card.

I hope each student will make the most of their new chances this year by acting correctly and getting good grades, Lori was thinking.

Rosita hung up the telephone and ran to check all the door-locks again. She peaked out of the living room window. Both Lucky and Kato were on the road in front of the house. They were barking, jumping around, and looking down the road. The dogs soon came back toward the house. Maybe whoever, or whatever, it was is leaving now, Rosita thought.

Rosita ran back to the telephone and called two churches located further away. The preachers told her to contact the local Welfare Office over at the county seat. She finally reached one church that said they would help the family immediately.

It was almost noon. Rosita ran to her bedroom and closed the door. She changed clothes and hung the one-piece slack suit in the closet. She ran into the kitchen. "Maybe, if I fix Tim a sandwich and a bowl of soup for lunch, he won't find out what I have been doing," Rosita told herself. She had two large sandwiches, and bowls of soup, on the table when Tim came in.

"What a pleasant surprise," Tim said. He went into the bathroom to wash his hands.

Rosita poured some ice tea, and sit down at the opposite end of the table. Tim returned, sat down, and asked the blessing. They begin to enjoy their lunch.

"How was your morning?" Tim asked.

"Fine . . . I slept late," Rosita answered. "The dogs woke me up. I think someone was walking around outside and the dogs were barking at them. I locked all the doors until they left," she said.

"I sure didn't see anyone," Tim replied. "I imagine they were barking at a rabbit or skunk," he said.

"I think it was a person, and I'm not going outside today," Rosita replied.

"That's not a bad idea," Tim said. He finished his lunch and went into the bedroom to make a telephone call. After he completed his call, he thanked Rosita for the meal, and went back to the field.

Rosita straightened up the kitchen and ran back to the telephone to visit freely, with some of her friends.

Lori was in the afternoon teacher's meeting. Mr. Wilson explained some more new rules. He passed out the new student lists. "Mrs. Jones will have all the sixth grade students. I'll help her with field trips, parties, and anything else she needs," he said.

"I'll remember that," Lori said with a smile. The secretary was motioning to her again. She pointed to a lady standing next to her in the hall that was open to the library. "Yes?" Lori asked when she walked up to the lady.

"I just wanted to tell you that I'll have the food and clothes ready for you to pick up as soon as you leave school this evening," the lady said proudly.

"What?" Lori asked.

"The food and clothes for the poor Gonzales family," the lady explained.

"Oh. Thank you," Lori said. She shook hands with the older lady. Carlos has a good job now, as good a job as a lot of people around here, Lori was thinking. "I'll be by as soon as I finish here," Lori said.

"I think the child would rather have had money, but our church feels that, with food and clothes, the children are getting what they need," the lady explained.

Lori borrowed notes from another teacher to catch up on the part of the meeting she had missed. She stopped by the lady's house after school. Together, they loaded the back seat and trunk with supplies of food and clothing for the Gonzales family.

"I think it's wonderful the way you and Tim have helped this poor family," the lady said.

"We try to do what we can," Lori said, and waved good-bye. She relaxed, and enjoyed the drive home. It was a beautiful evening. For once, the wind was not blowing. Lori met two other vehicles with their jet streams of dust behind them. The streams were blinding for a few seconds, and Lori had to drive slower until she could see the road again.

Lori saw a large army jet flying low across the flat prairie. <u>They look like</u> <u>huge, graceful sharks in a big friendly, blue sky</u>, Lori was thinking.

Rosita ran out of the house and met Lori at the car. She gave her a big hug. "I have some things for your family," Lori said with a frown.

"Oh, goody," Rosita said, and helped Lori carry the boxes into the house.

"Rosita, why didn't you tell me what you were going to do today?" Lori asked.

Rosita ignored the question. She acted as happy as Lori could ever remember. "I fixed Tim some dinner, and I also fixed some supper. You can rest and not worry about cooking," Rosita said. She was jumping up and down with happiness.

"Rosita, did you come back to live with us just so you could get things for you family?" Lori asked.

"Come and see how nice the house looks," Rosita said. She pulled Lori's arm toward the dining room.

The house was neat and clean. Rosita had opened some canned soup and added some ingredients of her own. It had delicious Mexican taste. Lori gave Rosita a hug before she went to change her clothes and gather the eggs. Rosita followed her to the hen house. She was still bouncing and chattering.

"I was surprised when I came in at noon and had a good meal waiting for me," Tim said that evening. He winked at Rosita. "I came in about three o'clock for a cold drink, and Rosita was still busy in the kitchen. I tried to flip her on the seat, but she swatted me with your big wooden spoon," Tim said with a smile.

After supper Rosita insisted that Lori rest while she cleaned up the kitchen. They watched a little TV before they went to bed. Lori went to Rosita's room to pray with her and kiss her goodnight.

Tim carefully stepped into the room long enough to thank Rosita for the meals and tell her goodnight.

After Lori had turned off the light and closed the door, Rosita ran her fingers over the soft bed. It felt good to be in her old bedroom again. The yard light gave the room a moonlit glow. <u>It's good to be back, even</u>

though I miss my family. I wish I could live in both places at once, Rosita was thinking.

Lori found a few clothes in the boxes from the church that fit Rosita. She pressed them so Rosita would look a little more presentable at school.

Rosita went to school with Lori the next morning. Lori told Mr. Wilson that Rosita might be in school here again this year.

Rosita was happy to see all her old friends. The students came to school long enough to enroll and pick up their books. Rosita was happy helping Lori with her room, and other duties.

The kids had gone home for the day when Tim stopped by. "I'm going over to Camfield to get some tractor parts. I wondered if Rosita would like to go with me," Tim said.

Rosita stomped her feet and yelled, "I'm not going with you because I want to stay here with Lori!"

Mr. Wilson was walking down the hall. It was an embarrassing situation. He pretended that he did not hear, and looked the other way as he walked passed Lori, Rosita, and Tim.

Tim could not believe the change in Rosita from the day before. He shrugged his shoulders in bewilderment, and left.

Lori did not feel like she could afford to go to the beauty shop anymore. She and Rosita went to Aunt Martha's after school, and Lori's aunt gave Lori a permanent.

Richard, Aunt Martha's grandson was staying with her. He was twenty-one years old. Richard had been in Special Education all through school, and could neither read nor write. He started to flirt with Rosita immediately.

Rosita enjoyed Richard's attention.

Lori and Aunt Martha thought the kids were getting too friendly, and watched them closely.

Aunt Martha was one of Lori's closest friends. She had been left a widow when her three children were small. She had also been divorced twice. Aunt Martha knew what heartache was. She always had a "shoulder for Lori to cry on".

Rosita and Richard exchanged addresses. Lori and Rosita left for the farm as soon as the permanent was finished.

Rosita went to the field with Lori on Saturday.

Lori took Rosita, the food, and clothes back to her mother's room at the hospital early Sunday morning. Lori could not tell if Juanita was surprised over the supplies or not. "I suppose this is the last time I'll see you," Lori said once more, and told Rosita good-bye.

Rosita did not answer.

Lori wished she could go on to church, but she hurried to the field instead. She and Tim did not get home until almost ten o'clock that night. They could hear the telephone ringing as they unlocked the back door.

"Will you come and get my Rosita, and put her in Lori's school?" Juanita asked.

"I guess so," Tim replied.

"Good. Her papa is taking her to the new farm right now to gather up her clothes. They will be ready for you when you get here," Juanita said. She sounded contented.

"I can't possibly go with you, Tim," Lori said. "I have to wash the dirt out of my hair, and get ready to start teaching tomorrow. It will be midnight by the time you get back. I'll just stay here and wait for you," she explained.

"I wish you could go, but I know you have a lot to do," Tim replied. He was soon showered, and on his way to get their "sometimes" daughter, again.

Lori watched the vehicle lights going east for a few minutes. She took a bath and washed the field dirt out of her hair from the spout above the tub. Lori curled her hair and sit under her old hair dryer. She went to sleep several times while her hair was drying.

It was very late when Lori heard them come in. She heard Tim, Rosita, and <u>Ray</u>! Lori threw on her robe and walked into the dining room. Tim and Ray were laughing, but Rosita had the countenance that Lori had only seen a few times. She did not like the personality that went with it. "I thought you just went after one," Lori said with a sigh. She was so tired, but she tried to sound happy.

"I came back with two, though," Tim said, proudly.

"Where shall I sleep?" Ray asked with a big yawn.

"I want you to have the bedroom next to mine this time," Rosita said.

"I guess that will be okay. All the beds have clean sheets," Lori replied.

Tim and Lori had difficulty getting the kids to bed. They made so much noise after going to bed, that Tim and Lori had to threaten to punish them if they did not be quiet. Rosita was extra sassy.

"What happened?" Lori asked, as she and Tim crawled into bed.

"When I picked up Rosita, Ray looked like he would give anything to come along with us too," Tim started to explain. "I asked Carlos about Ray. He told me that Ray was nothing but trouble. Carlos said that the only way he could handle Ray was with a two-by-four foot board.

Carlos told me that Ray stole his pickup, and ran over a lot of his boss's irrigation pipe. Ray drove over some trash and busted a hole in the radiator, and tore up the pickup. After that he stole a new John Deere tractor. Ray drove it so far and fast that he burned up that engine, too. When the tractor quit running, he beat it up and knocked all the windows out of it.

Carlos said that Ray had caught a ride to Plainsville, and stole a gun from one man, and two-hundred dollars from another man. It took the police two weeks to find him," Tim said, finishing his story.

"And you brought him here, anyway!" Lori exclaimed with a sigh.

Tim continued. "I asked Carlos if I could take the boy and try to do something with him. Carlos said that he hadn't asked us to take Ray, only Rosita. He said if I took Ray, he would not be responsible for anything Ray did. And not to come to him with the problems Ray might cause us," Tim explained.

"You took Ray under those conditions!" Lori exclaimed again.

"Yes, I told him we would take Ray and see if we could help him. Then I told Ray to run and get his clothes. He was really happy," Tim answered.

"Did the kids bring back any of the clothes we bought them last spring?" Lori asked.

"I asked them that on the way back. They both said that their older brothers and sisters needed the clothes," Tim answered.

"Just as I thought. We'll have to buy them a lot of clothes so they'll look half decent at school," Lori said with a moan.

"Tim, I'm scared. I guess I should have enough faith to believe that we can help these kids, but I'm just plain scared, especially since we are so broke, ourselves," Lori whispered.

"Lori, you were the one who wanted to help Ray a year ago, remember?" Tim asked. "Now is your chance," he said.

"I hope it isn't too late," Lori said, wearily.

"Ray told me on the way home tonight that his dad got so mad at him once that he grabbed him by the back of his shirt, and the seat of his pants, and banged his head into the side of a pickup until his nose bled. He said he had a headache for days. Of course, Rosita said that it wasn't true," Tim said.

"I'm glad that Carlos doesn't know that Ray told you that," Lori said.

"There's only one thing that worries me right now," Tim said.

"What, on earth, is that <u>one</u> thing?" Lori asked.

"Rosita was so excited about coming home with me until she found out that Ray was coming too. Then, she became angry," Tim explained.

"Yes, I noticed that as soon as you guys came in tonight," Lori said. "I can't understand it. She seems to think a lot of Ray. It looks like she would be glad to have him here," she added.

"I'm sure that everything will turn out all right," Tim replied.

"Then you can start by making them stop giggling right now, and making them go to sleep!" Lori shouted.

Tim yelled at Ray and Rosita to be quiet and go to sleep. The kids still giggled.

Lori got up, and quietly walked across the hall to Rosita's room. The kids were still giggling. She quietly opened the door, turned on the light, and said, "This is the last time we are going to tell you to be quiet and go to sleep." "If you don't mind us, there will be some sort of punishment!" Lori yelled.

Ray jumped out of Rosita's bed and ran into his own room. Tim and Lori thought that Ray had been in his own bed all the time. "Ray, get your clothes. You are going to sleep in the bedroom next to ours from now on!" Lori shouted.

"No, he isn't! He's sleeping next to mine!" Rosita screamed.

"He is sleeping where I tell him to," Lori shouted. "I will <u>not</u> give him another chance to sneak into your bedroom and get into your bed again!" Lori yelled. "Ray, get in here this minute!" Lori shouted.

Lori could hear activity in the adjoining bedroom. Ray soon came through Rosita's room with his roll of clothes. He did not say a word, or even look at Lori. Ray went to his old bedroom, and closed the door.

Lori closed Rosita's door and went to bed. She did not hear any more noises. It seemed like she had just drifted off to sleep when the alarm clock sounded. It was time for a new day, and a new school year, ready or not. Lori was shaking from fatigue, and stress, as she dressed for school.

Lori left early with Rosita and Ray, so she could enroll them into school before her first class started. She talked to Mr. Wilson first.

"I'm sorry Lori, but I refuse to let Ray be enrolled here in the Elementary School," Mr. Wilson said. "The other boys are afraid of him and he needs to be with boys closer to his own age, and size," he explained.

"I understand," Lori said. She went over to the building where the Junior Hi and High School were located, to see if she could enroll Ray there. Rosita and Ray followed Lori into the High-school counselor's office.

"I need to enroll Ray in school, today," Lori told her old friend. "Can you fill out the papers right away so I can get back to class?" Lori asked.

The counselor smiled. "I can enroll Ray in all of his classes. If I need any information, I'll be over to see you during your break this morning," Mrs. Randall said. "So, go on, and get ready for our first full day of school," she said with a smile.

"Thank you," Lori said. She pushed Rosita out the door so they could hurry back to the elementary school.

Rosita plopped into the front seat and slammed the car door as hard as she could. "Ray and me have been in the same grade for a long, long time. It ain't fair for him to be a grade ahead of me. I'm a better student in school than he is! If you don't put me in the seventh grade with Ray, and my old friends, I'll run away!" Rosita screamed, kicking her feet against the dash of the car.

"Rosita, Ray has to be in special classes. If I put you in the sixth grade, you can pass without any Special Ed. help. You're right, Ray couldn't. I don't want you in Special Ed. classes because you don't need them," Lori tried to explain.

"I don't care!" Rosita shouted, still kicking.

The school secretary took over Rosita's enrollment, so Lori could get to her first class.

During mid-morning break, Mrs. Randall caught Lori in the teacher's work room. "I think Ray is all set up in school, now. If it's all right with you and Tim, I have some papers for you to sign so he can play football," Mrs. Randall said. "The coach talked to him this morning, and Ray is real excited about it. We think it will help him try harder in his classes, and it might help him to get along with his peers. The coach is excited because Ray is larger than the other boys on the team," Mr. Randall explained.

"I know Tim isn't too crazy over sports, but we think it would help Ray. The boys practice during school, so you and Tim won't have to make any extra trips to town, except for the games," she said.

"I think it's a great idea, Carol," Lori replied. "I think I can talk Tim into liking the idea," she said. "What about his grades, and being eligible to play?" Lori asked.

"The teachers will give Ray special help, and most of his classes are in Special Education, anyway," Mrs. Randall answered. "If it's all right with you and Tim, Ray needs a physical examination from Dr. David this evening, so he can start practice tomorrow," she said.

"Lori, do you know how much responsibility you and Tim have taken on, by taking these kids?" Mrs. Randall asked.

"Yes dear, we do. We know they are children that can't be left alone five minutes without some sort of supervision," Lori answered.

"I admire what you and Tim are trying to do. I hope everything goes okay," Carol Randall said. "If there's anything I can do to help, Lori, please let me know," she added.

"Thanks. I think football will keep Ray busy, and boost his self-esteem," Lori replied.

"By the way, could you talk to Rosita?" Lori asked. "She was angry when Tim brought Ray back last night, and she's really angry about Ray being a grade ahead of her in school," Lori explained. "If you can help these kids here at school, Tim and I will help them all we can at home." she said.

"I remember when our kids were in sports. They were too tired after practice to get into any mischief," Mrs. Randall said. "Ray will need shorts, and a shirt, for practice. He will also need cleats, plenty of heavy socks, and . . ." Mrs. Randall said. She stopped talking and laughed. "I guess you know what he needs," she added.

After school, Ray ran all the way to Lori's room. All he could talk about was football.

"Ray, you need to hurry on over to Dr. David's office for your physical. Rosita and I will pick you up when I finish working here," Lori said.

"I want to go with him!" Rosita shouted.

"No. You'll have to stay here and wait for me," Lori said, ignoring Rosita's hateful attitude. "How was your day?" she asked Rosita after Ray left.

"Terrible, if it's any of your business!" Rosita shouted.

Lori still ignored Rosita's nasty attitude. She finished her work while Rosita sit in a student desk and pouted. Rosita drug her feet as she followed Lori out of the school building to pick up Ray.

There was a long line of students still waiting for their physicals. Ray was in about the middle of the line.

"Ray, it looks like you will be here for awhile. We're going to go down town and shop. If you get through before we get back, please wait right here for us," Lori instructed.

"Okay, mom," Ray answered, looking very important.

"I want to stay!" Rosita shouted.

"No. You must go with me. The office is already over-crowded," Lori answered.

Rosita stomped out of the Dr. David's office like a spoiled child. She sat in the car and pouted while Lori shopped. Ray had just finished with his physical when they returned to Dr. David's office. Lori crawled into the car, under the steering wheel. Rosita sit in the middle of the front seat, and Ray sat next to Rosita.

"I almost got into a fight today," Ray was saying on the way home. "I remembered that things are different now. I was mad, but I turned around and walked off," he said.

"I'm proud of you, Ray," Lori replied.

"You mean you were too chicken to fight!" Rosita shouted.

"I just didn't want to," Ray said, proudly. "That's the way it's supposed to be, isn't it Mom?" he asked. Ray leaned over and kissed Lori right on the mouth, before she could protest.

"She isn't our mom!" Rosita shouted, pushing Ray back into his place.

Lori and Ray told Tim about football.

"You need to take the car to school again tomorrow, and buy Ray the best football shoes you can find, and the best of everything else he needs," Tim said. "I want him to look as good as the other boys," he explained.

"Thanks, pop," Ray said. He slapped Tim on the back.

"Just be sure you do your best in school for us," Tim ordered.

"Yes Sir, Pop," Ray said.

"He's not your pop!" Rosita screamed.

Although Rosita was usually hateful, she and Lori helped Ray with homework for at least two hours every night. Ray tried at first, and then he became so frustrated that he lost interest. If Lori didn't watch the kids, Rosita would just do Ray's work for him.

Ray was even having a hard time in his Special Ed. classes. His attention span was short. He could not read any of his lessons. Writing was even harder for him. It took him a long time to write anything. Success seemed next to impossible.

Rosita was well-mannered at school, but hateful at home. She complained constantly about being in the sixth grade. She often threatened to run away. "After all, I'm helping Ray with his seventh grade work," Rosita screamed at Lori, almost every evening.

The only problem Lori had with Ray was that he wanted to kiss her on the mouth when he was extra happy. Lori tried to stop him each time, but Ray was much larger than she was.

Rosita continually whispered to Ray in Spanish and laughed. Lori often felt like they were making fun of her and Tim. Ray never acted rude unless Rosita led him into it.

The day before the scrimmage game, Ray brought his football helmet home so he could clean and shine it. The white helmet had a lot of different colored scars on it left by head-on-collisions with players of other teams.

"Mom, what can I use to get the paint off of this helmet?" Ray asked. He was scrubbing the helmet with soap he had found under the kitchen sink.

"I can't remember what my boys used," Lori answered. "Let's call Mitch to see if he remembers what he used on his helmet when he was in high school," she said. Lori dialed the number and handed Ray the telephone.

Ray talked to Mitch, and then listened. He nodded his head a few times to show that he understood, although Mitch could not see him. "Mitch wants to talk to you now, mom," Ray said. He handed the telephone back to Lori.

Lori and Mitch were still talking when Ray and Rosita started making strange noises over the telephone in the music room. Lori asked the kids to be quiet several times. She finally had to yell, "I'll talk to you later, Mitch."

Lori hung up the telephone and walked into the bedroom where Tim was sitting on the corner of the large, red velvet bed. Lori plopped down in the large lounge chair, next to the bed, and yelled, "Ray, Rosita, you kids come in here right now!"

There was no response. Lori called again. The house was still quiet. She called again.

By this time, Tim was angry. He jumped to his feet and went stomping into the other part of the house to find the kids. Ray and Rosita were under the bed in the farthest bedroom. They were laughing uncontrollably.

Rosita saw Tim. She jumped out from under the bed on the opposite side, and grabbed Ray's leg and tried to pull him from his hiding place.

Tim ran around the end of the bed and grabbed Rosita's arm, then he grabbed Ray's leg and jerked him out from under the bed. He grabbed Ray's arm, stood him to his feet, and marched the two young people into the bedroom where Lori was waiting. Rosita was hitting Tim as hard as she could, and Ray was trying to get away, as they came through the bedroom door.

Tim shoved Rosita into the red velvet bean-bag chair, and he shoved Ray onto the edge of the bed. He sat down beside Ray. "Lori has something to say to you, so sit down and listen, and you better come the next time you're called!" Tim shouted.

"I want you two to know, right now, that if we're going to live together, we're going to live like a family. That means respecting each other's rights," Lori said.

Ray jumped up from the bed and started to run. Tim grabbed him, and pushed him back down on the bed.

Rosita jumped up from her chair and grabbed Tim's arm, and tried to slap him. "You're not our boss!" she screamed.

Tim pushed Rosita back into the chair.

Ray leaped up on Tim's back. He was pounding and cursing. Tim grabbed Ray's thick, curly hair, jerked him to his feet, jerked his hair again, and told him to sit down and listen to Lori.

Ray started to get up again.

Tim jerked Ray's hair so hard, it brought tears to Ray's eyes.

Ray looked at Tim with hate. "Yes, sir!" he shouted and sit back on the corner of the bed.

Lori talked softly to the kids about their rudeness. "I was so embarrassed when I had to stop talking to Mitch and hang up the phone, because you would not be quiet enough for us to talk," Lori explained. "I don't ever expect you kids to do anything that rude again, understand?" she said.

Ray and Rosita relaxed a little. They were still mad at Tim. They looked at Lori and nodded their heads in agreement.

"I think you both owe Lori an apology," Tim said.

"We're sorry, Lori," Rosita and Ray, each said, seriously.

The kids were polite the rest of the evening. Tim and Lori thought the incident was over.

The next day Rosita was talking to four of her friends in the hall between classes. "Mr. Jones has started beating on Ray and me for no reason at all," Rosita whispered.

"That's hard to believe, and I don't see any marks on you," one girl said.

"Of course not. He hits me where it doesn't show with my clothes on. If it wasn't so embarrassing, I would show you. I had to put makeup on Ray's eyes so he wouldn't look too terrible to go to school this morning," Rosita said.

Rosita limped a little, and told the PE teacher she didn't feel like she could do any exercising for two days. The other girls begin to wonder if Rosita was really telling the truth about the beatings.

Lori hurried into the kitchen as soon as she came in from school. She whipped together some ingredients, and put the cake into the oven to bake. Lori seasoned a beef roast and put it into the microwave oven. "We're going to a sheriff's posse pot-luck supper tonight," Lori told Ray and Rosita.

"We don't like pigs, and we won't eat with them," Rosita said.

"They don't like us either," Ray added.

"Law officers are for our protection. They are not pigs!" Lori exclaimed. "Lawmen are good people who are willing to put their own lives in danger to make our lives safer," Lori explained.

"Is it safer to round up whole families, including little kids, and put them into trucks like animals, and send them back to Mexico, where they can't make any money, and take care of their families?" Rosita asked with bitterness.

"But, those people sneak into our country illegally. They take jobs that should belong to the people that live in this country," Lori said.

"If Mexicans did not work harder, they wouldn't get those jobs," Rosita said.

"I can't argue that, but if we let all the people into the United States, there won't be any work, or room, for the rest of us," Lori replied.

"But, other people have a right to be here, too," Rosita said.

"I can understand how you feel," Lori replied. "My daddy told me about a time when he was farming. He saw a bunch of Mexicans farming by hand in the field next to his. He saw some helicopters hovering over the field. The people and their kids tried to hide under the skinny broomcorn stalks. My dad said that later that day, he saw trucks come into the field. The people were herded into the trucks like cattle. It really upset him because women, and little kids, were treated like animals. There was nothing he could do, so he just tried to forget about it," Lori said, finishing her story.

"See," Ray said.

"We can't solve all the world's problems, but we're going to have supper with some mighty nice people tonight. You two are going as our kids. You're going to have a lot of fun, so you might as well plan on it," Lori ordered with a smile.

Tim came home early. The food was done by the time everyone had their baths and was clean and neat. It took them forty-five minutes to drive to the county seat, where the party had already started. Rosita and Ray pouted all the way, and Tim had to make them get out of the car.

The large building had several offices, including the sheriff's office, on the main floor. The large basement was the location of the jail, kitchen, and some other meeting rooms.

Rosita saw a lady with two small children. She soon had the children on her lap. Rosita asked if she could take the children outside to enjoy the warm summer evening. The lady nodded yes, and with a sigh of relief, went to the kitchen to help the other women prepare the meal.

Ray found two younger boys that he could be "Macho" with, and was soon having a lot of fun.

At seven o'clock, one hundred people passed between two tables that were covered with food. Rosita and Ray ate like they were starved.

The kids went back outside to play after they finished eating. The women cleaned up the kitchen while the men prepared for the meeting. It was time for the initiation of the new members into the sheriff's posses. The men decided to initiate the guests too.

The posse members lined everyone up in front of the door of a large, dark, room. The door was closed. The people waited. One by one, the people were ushered into the dark room. After a few minutes, a terrible scream was heard. No one came back out of the room.

The kids ran back into the building to see what the screaming was all about. No one came back out of the room to tell what was going on behind the closed door. The only way to find out what was happening was to get into the line of people that were disappearing into the dark room.

Lori was standing in line between two other women. "I just started to work for the sheriff's department this week, and I hope those guys remember that I have to work tomorrow," the lady in front of Lori said.

"I don't think they'll hurt us," Lori said. She shuddered as she heard another piercing scream.

"I guess I don't either, but it sounds like people are being murdered in there," the lady said, trying to laugh.

The lady standing behind Lori said, "My friend just moved to a large city in Georgia, to work for a police department there, and she had a shocking experience. She lives alone. There is so much crime in the city that she bought a Doberman Pincher for protection. One day my friend came home for a couple of hours sleep. She was working a double, split shift at the police station. When she opened her front door, her dog met her. The dog's mouth was full of blood.

My friend took the dog to the nearest vet, and left him. She had to hurry back home and get ready to go to work. The vet called my friend as soon as she got back home. He told my friend to stop what she was doing and get back to his office immediately. My friend called the police station to tell them she would be a few minutes late for work. She returned to the vet's clinic, thinking her dog was dying, or dead.

The vet had my friend to sit down. He showed her the dark finger from a man's hand that he had taken out of the dog's mouth. He had already called the police that were patrolling the district where my friend lives, and ordered them to search my friend's apartment.

The police called and reported that they had found a man, laying in shock, and bleeding to death, in my friend's closet. He was missing a finger."

There was another scream from the dark room.

"I'm not going to scream when I go in there, no matter what happens," one lady in line said. She entered the room, and a few minutes later, she screamed as loudly as anyone else.

"This reminds me of what the Bible says about what will happen in the last days when people will be beheaded for their faith," Lori said with a shudder. She was shaking as she walked into the dark room, and the door was closed.

A small flashlight was turned on so Lori could barely see. Someone told Lori to sit in a certain chair. Lori did what she was told. A man dressed like he was from India came in and sit down in the opposite chair. The man was bare from the waist up, and had a turban wrapped around his head.

"You must do exactly what I do," the man ordered. The man chanted and clapped his hands in an Eastern rhythm.

Lori recognized the voice of the sheriff. "Yes Sir," she said, trying not to laugh.

Sheriff Wade chanted as he waved his hands around his head, swung one hand out in front of him, while he waved the other hand behind him.

Lori tried to imitate his every move.

The sheriff stood up, waved his arms around his head, and sat down very hard and straight.

Lori tried to do exactly what the sheriff did. When she sat down hard in her chair, she felt a sharp pain, and screamed, just like everyone else had done. Someone had placed a large sponge full of ice water in her chair. Lori caught her breath, and started to laugh.

Sheriff Wade laughed and said, "This is something as silly as what your sixth graders would do, isn't it?"

"That's all right. Everyone is having a great time, and that's what is important," Lori replied. It's nice to have a Christian sheriff that you know is always trying to do what's right, Lori was thinking. She followed Sheriff Wade into a dark corner and joined the crowd of people waiting to watch the next person to be initiated.

Ray was the last one to go through the ritual. After he was good and wet, the lights were turned back on and everyone started to help clean up the mess.

Ray grabbed the wet sponge and squeezed it out on top of the "Arabian's" head.

Sheriff Wade ran after Ray and dumped a bowl of ice water on Ray's head.

Ray grabbed a pitcher of water and poured it on the "Arabian's" head.

The sheriff started chasing Ray. Ray ran out of the building, and into the dark, with the sheriff right behind him. Ray and the sheriff returned a few minutes later. They were both soaking wet from a water hose fight, and laughing.

Tim asked Lori to drive home because his eyes were bothering him.

Ray was still laughing when he said, "I sure did get that Arabian guy, didn't I?"

"Don't you think that you were a little rough on him?" Tim asked.

"Naw. I just got him a little wet," Ray said with a giggle.

"Do you know who that guy was?" Tim asked.

"No. Just some old guy at the party," Ray answered, still laughing.

"That, Ray my boy, that was our county sheriff that you were throwing all that water on," Tim said.

"Oh my God!" Ray exclaimed. He slid down into the floor of the car. "I didn't know that pigs ever did anything, but be mean to people," Ray said.

"They're not pigs, and don't you ever call them that again!" Tim exclaimed.

Everyone was quiet. Thirty minutes later, Tim turned around and looked in the back seat. "What are you kids doing?" he asked.

"Nothin," Ray and Rosita both said.

"Ray, get over to your side of the car, and stay there!" Tim shouted.

"Yes sir," Ray said, hatefully.

Tim rode the rest of the way facing the back seat.

"What was the matter with you on the way home tonight?" Lori asked Tim as they all walked into the house.

"I'm not sure of what I saw, but I hope I didn't see what I thought I saw, is all I have to say," Tim answered.

CHAPTER XVI

Tim and Lori were adjusting to their "ready made" family. Ray was enjoying football practice and looking forward to his first big game. Tim had trusted Ray enough to teach him how to drive Whitey and pull different implements in the field.

Each evening, after school, Ray and Lori changed into their field clothes, and were on the tractors as soon as possible. They worked in the field until dark. Rosita either worked around the house, or rode the tractor with Lori.

When Ray was finished driving Whitey, he started driving a smaller tractor, and pulling a "one-way" implement.

"Never turn the tractor the wrong way, or the one-way will run up on the tractor tires and cut them to pieces. When the one-way gets full of weeds, you stop the tractor, and clean it out by hand. Remember never turn the tractor the wrong way. That is why this implement is called a one-way. Just keep turning the tractor in the direction I have started for you," Tim had explained over and over.

At the last minute Friday evening, Rosita decided that she was going to the field with Ray and Lori. She jumped into the car just as they were leaving.

"You didn't change from your school clothes, Rosita, so you'll have to stay in the car. I don't want you to ruin you new school dress," Lori said on the way to the field.

"Lori, I want to work real hard for you and Tim, and I don't want any pay, either," Ray said.

"That's real thoughtful of you, Ray," Lori replied. "Why do you feel that way?" she asked.

"Because, you and Tim are the only ones that have ever given me a chance to be somebody. My old man would never have let me play football. I have a lot of friends now. I don't have to fight anymore to prove how tough I am because I can do that on the football field. This is the first time I've had a chance to somebody important, at least somebody good," Ray said. He sounded like he was almost to cry. "Thanks mom," Ray said, and kissed Lori.

Lori glanced at the handsome, curly-headed, brown-skinned, guy sitting next to Rosita. "You're welcome," she managed to say. "Tim can use your help. Most kids never consider how much is spent on them, and we appreciate your thoughtfulness."

Rosita tried to take over the conversation by talking in Spanish, then giggling.

It was long after dark by the time they all got home. Lori fixed some soup. Everyone went right to bed after eating.

"I need for you to go to Plainsville and get a fuel filter for my old pickup," Tim said early Saturday morning. "I'm going over to one of the west fields and get the other one-way. That way, we will have two one-ways going. I can pull it to the field with the four-wheel drive pickup," Tim explained. He wrote down the part number on a piece of paper and gave it Lori. "I should meet you at the south fields about noon," Tim said. "We'll ask the kids which one of us they want to go with, today," he added.

Lori had to wake Rosita, but Ray was already up and dressed in his field clothes.

During breakfast the kids were asked what they wanted to do.

"I want to stay home today," Rosita said.

"You can stay home for a couple of hours, and I can pick you up on my way to the field," Tim answered.

"If you're going to do that, maybe it would be a good idea if Ray went with me," Lori said. "He might be a lot of help if the pickup breaks down before we get the new fuel filter on it. If we get to the field before you do, we can start farming," Lori added.

Lori and Ray had a good visit on their way to Plainsville. They were in town trying to find the right part when the pickup started dying. Once it died right in the middle of Main Street. A farmer pulled them into a gas station with a larger pickup truck. The gas station attendant helped them to get the pickup started again.

By the time Tim had gathered all the old tires he could find for the one-way, he was already thirty minutes behind schedule. When he drove past the house to go after the one-way, Rosita came out of the house and wanted go to with him. Tim was surprised, but delighted. He did not try to start a conversation because he did not know what kind of mood Rosita might be in.

The old one-way was so covered with sand that Tim would not have found it, if he had not known exactly where he had left it two years before. It took a long time to dig away the sand enough to put on all the tires. Then he had a hard time attaching the old rusty hitch to the pickup. When Tim finally crawled back into the pickup, Rosita was angry.

"It's about time you're ready to go. I'm tired of waiting for you, Bug Eyes!" Rosita shouted.

"I changed the tires as fast as I could," Tim said.

Rosita folded her arms. "I wish I'd stayed at the house," she said.

The tires kept blowing out. It took two hours to pull the one-way six miles to the house.

"I'm going to the house," Rosita said as soon as they pulled into the yard.

"That's a good idea. It will take me quite awhile to patch up some of these old tires. You can fix something to eat, or what ever you want to do," Tim said without looking at Rosita.

It took two more hours for Tim to fix the tires. He went to the house for a cold drink and to check on Rosita. Rosita had fixed some Mexican macaroni, baked some sugar cookies, straightened up the house, set the table, and packed a lunch, for everyone, to take to the field.

"A grown woman couldn't work this fast," Tim said.

Rosita giggled, but did not say anything. They ate their lunch and were soon on their way to the south fields.

The first parts-man tried to sell Lori a fuel filter with a different number on it. She tried two other stores. The pickup was getting low on fuel, and Lori didn't have enough money to buy any gas. She was afraid to turn off the pickup while she checked the different stores, because she was afraid it would not start again.

Lori found a filter in the fourth store. The fuel gage of the pickup was setting on empty when they started their twenty mile journey to the field. "We will just have to pray and believe that we will make it to the field where the gas tank is," Lori said.

Lori watched the gas gage as much as she did the bumpy, dirt road she was driving over. It seemed to take an extra long time to get to the field. "Praise the Lord! I think we've been running on angel power," Lori exclaimed as they drove into their field next to the tractors.

Ray grinned. "We even beat Tim and Rosita," he said.

Lori knew they were late. She could not believe that Tim and Rosita were not already there. "Something must have gone wrong, but there's nothing we can do about it," Lori said. "The fuel in the big tank is diesel for the tractors. The pickup fuel is in the gas tank on the back of Tim's pickup. We probably don't have enough fuel to even get back out of the field," she said. "We'll just have to wait," she added.

"Can I start my tractor?" Ray asked.

They walked across the field together. It was a nice, warm, fall day, and the wind wasn't blowing. The fresh dirt smelled refreshing. "You know, Ray, this would be a pretty country if it wasn't for the wind," Lori said.

Ray shook his head to agree, and climbed up into the tractor. He sat tall and straight in the tractor's seat. It reminded him of the times of playing "king of the mountain" at school.

Lori crawled up onto the platform and helped Ray start the tractor. Ray was anxious to get moving. "Be careful!" Lori yelled above the noise of the huge machine. She climbed down the ladder and watched the tractor pull away. The rig moved a little jerky, so Lori watched until Ray was moving the one-way more smoothly.

Lori's smaller tractor was not a diesel. It was low on fuel. Lori could not do any work until Tim got there with the other fuel tank. She walked through the soft dirt back to the pickup. Lori ate an apple she had stored in her purse. It was nice to rest and enjoy the quietness around her. There were two hawks floating above a certain spot in the distance. Lori wondered if they were watching a baby rabbit, wanting a meal.

Lori checked her watch again. They had been back to the field for over an hour. She started to worry again. "All I can do is pray and wait, and watch Ray in case he has trouble," Lori reminded herself.

Lori took a small Gideon New Testament out of her purse and read some scriptures. Her eyes grew tired from reading in the bright sunlight. She rested her eyes by looking at the hilly country around her again.

The small hills gradually sloped toward the dry, winding river bed, a little to the north. The river never had enough water in it to support trees, but there were several areas of small shrubs in the low places.

It was getting late. Lori had vain imaginations of everything from vehicle trouble to an accident. Just as she was turning the key, and praying that the pickup would start, she saw a swirl of dust on the field road. It eventually became a small speck headed toward their field. It had to be Tim and Rosita. "Thank you Lord," Lori whispered.

As the maroon and white Dodge pickup approached the field, Lori walked across the fresh dirt once more and greeted Tim and Rosita.

Rosita bounced out of the pickup. Her hair was shining, and she had on a good dress. "Where is Ray?" she asked.

"He is over there," Lori said, pointing toward the right field.

Rosita jumped upon the back of the pickup where she could see Ray's tractor. She jumped back down and started running around in the weeds in search of some small, wild animal.

"You look nice, Rosita, but this isn't a very good place to wear your good school dresses," Lori said.

"I had a lot of trouble getting this old one-way ready to travel," Tim explained. "I had to stop several times and change tires on it," he said.

"I wondered what took you so long," Lori replied.

It's a good feeling to be running this equipment, Ray was thinking. Tim will be proud of me for covering so much ground, he thought. Ray felt the one-way starting to pull harder. He looked behind him. The one-way was filled with weeds and dirt. "I don't want to take time to clean out the disks right now," Ray told himself. He pulled the tractor, just a tiny bit, the wrong direction. The one-way swung over a little, and bounced over the mound, shaking off some of the weeds and dirt.

"Good," Ray said a loud. "I can go over that pile of dirt on my next round, and Tim will never know the difference," he said.

On the next round, Ray was thinking about his first football game. He hit the pile of dirt, forgetting to swerve. Ray looked behind him. The one-way was pulling so much dirt that it looked like a road grader.

Ray was angry with himself. He crawled down from the tractor to take a look at his mess. Getting down on his hands and knees, he started to dig into the soft, damp sand and weeds, in an effort to uncover the buried one-way disks.

"Look what you've done now," Ray kept telling himself. He was not making any progress in uncovering the one-way. It was buried too deep. Ray had an idea. He was able to get rid of the dirt before by turning the wrong way just a little. Maybe that will work again, Ray was thinking.

Ray backed the tractor up a tiny bit, and turned the machine the wrong way. The tractor lunged forward. Before Ray could hit the brakes, he saw the one-way jump up and land on the tractor tires. He tried going forward, but the one-way went even higher. It looked like a lion attacking a deer.

Ray climbed out of the tractor. He tried to shovel the dirt away with a broken-handled shovel he had found in the tractor cab. Everything he did made the situation worse. What will Tim do to me for this? Ray wondered.

Ray remembered how angry his old man had been when he destroyed things. He remembered how he had been punished. "There is only one thing left to do," Ray told himself. "I must run away before Tim sees what I have done," he said.

"Lori, would you please get me the fuel filter so I can put it on the pickup," Tim asked.

Lori handed Tim the tiny piece of metal.

"You got the wrong part!" Tim exclaimed' Lori felt disappointed because she had tried her best to get the right part.

"Lori, its taking Ray too long to come around the field this time. He must be having trouble. Take the pickup and see if you can help him, then you can go back to town after the right part while I work on this one-way," Tim said.

Tim pulled the end-gate of the pickup down and started laying out the right tools to work with. Lori started the old pickup and rushed across the field to check on Ray.

Ray's tractor was not moving. "O no!" Lori exclaimed when she saw the one-way slashed across the tractor tires. She could not see Ray anywhere. Lori crawled up on the top of the tractor cab, and looked in every direction. She knew that Ray had made a bigger mess than he could handle, and that he had ran off in state of panic.

The tall, white grain elevators in Plainsville were visible to the east, although they were more than twenty miles away. There was not much Ray could hide behind to the south and west. Then Lori spotted the ugly oil-slush pit north of the field.

"Oh dear Lord, he wouldn't jump in that pit and drown himself, would he?" Lori asked herself. She drove over to the pit and checked for tracks. She was thankful that she didn't find any. Lori drove around the whole area and had started back to Tim's pickup when she remembered the pickup she was driving was still out of gas.

"Tim, I can't find Ray anywhere! He has turned the one-way the wrong way, and has things in a mess! I'm afraid he has run away!" Lori shouted.

"I'm sure he has gone toward the elevators in Plainsville. That's where he ran off to before," Tim said. "We'll have to look for him in your pickup because I have all my tools laid out on the end-gate of this one," Tim explained.

Tim filled the pickup full of gas from the large fuel tank in the back of the Dodge. Lori climbed in beside Tim, and Rosita climbed in next to her. Tim took a few minutes to check the damage Ray had done, before they headed toward Plainsville.

Ray ran through the soft dirt until his sides begin to ache. He fell into a clump of weeds and looked back toward the tractor. Ray watched Lori's pickup driving over to his rig. He laid flat on his stomach so Lori could not see him, if she happened to look in his direction.

"Maybe Tim won't be mad at me, and I should go back and tell him that I'm sorry for the mess I made," Ray told himself. Then he remembered how angry Tim had been when he had pulled his hair a few days ago.

Ray lay in the weeds and dug his fingers into the cool sand under the weeds. Fear was in control as he watched the red and white pickup leave the field. He lay quietly for a long time, trying to decide what to do. He was seized with more fear when he saw the red and white pickup return to his rig. He knew Tim was looking at what he had done. Ray raised his head up just enough to see the pickup leave the field and drive east toward Plainsville.

Ray lay on the ground until he felt sure that Tim and Lori were not coming back. He stood up and started to run again. He stopped and looked back. There was the new Dodge pickup still in the field.

I can use the four-wheel-drive pickup to get the one-way down and then Tim won't be mad at me when he comes back, Ray thought. He ran back across the field. As Ray walked toward the pickup, he remembered that Tim had said that he would <u>never</u> leave the keys in any of his vehicles again. He was almost afraid to look. Sliding into the pickup, Ray smiled as he felt the keys still hanging in the ignition.

Ray drove to his own field in a swirl of dust. He tried to push the tractor with the pickup. He heard a terrible noise. Ray jumped out and looked at his rig. The one-way's teeth were even deeper into the tractors back tires now than they had been before. The front wheels of the tractor were pointing in opposite directions.

"I <u>must</u> run away, now," Ray said. He jumped back into the pickup and spun the wheels, making his own whirlwind as he left the field.

Ray was soon speeding down the main country road which led to the farm, and town. The faster the pickup went, the more important Ray felt. <u>This is fun</u>, he thought. Ray forgot about the jog in the road ahead, and made the turn on two wheels. He felt a little shaky, but soon had control of the vehicle again, and was speeding even faster than before.

Tim, Lori, and Rosita were speeding in the opposite direction. They stopped by a two-story, Spanish-looking, farm house to see if the people had seen Ray. It was about the only farm and house between the field and Plainsville. While Tim was knocking on the door, Lori crawled on top of the pickup and looked in every direction.

The people were not home, and they were soon on their way again.

Tim and Lori had been too occupied to notice that Rosita was angry until she started kicking the dash of the pickup.

"What's the matter with you?" Lori asked.

"Ray and me decided to run away this week and he <u>did</u>, but he left me behind!" Rosita screamed. She was pounding on the pickup door now.

"I think that idea was your idea rather than Ray's. He wasn't about to leave with his first real football game coming up this Thursday. He wasn't about to miss that," Lori said.

When they reached Plainsville, Rosita slid down in the seat of the pickup.

"What are you doing that for?" Lori asked.

"Because I don't want to be seen with you and Tim, because you are so dirty," Rosita said, smugly.

"Do you think Ray might have caught a ride with someone and gone to his sister's house where Juanita used to live?" Tim asked Lori.

"I think we should look there first," Lori answered.

Tim parked the pickup in front of Rosita's sister's house. "I'll check to see if Ray is here," Rosita said. She jumped out of the pickup and ran into the house before Lori could stop her.

Lori and Tim waited for thirty minutes before they decided that Rosita was not coming back. Tim was getting out of the pickup when Dano came out of the house, walking toward them. He was holding his head high like he owned the world. "I haven't seen Ray, and I'm going to keep Rosita," he said with a sound of authority.

"No you're not!" Tim shouted. "Carlos asked us to keep her, and we aren't turning her over to anyone but him!" he exclaimed.

"I just called him, and he is on his way over here to pick her up!" Dano shouted. Then his tone changed. "While you guys are waiting for the old man to get here, would you like to see the fire we had last night?" he asked.

Lori and Tim followed Dano to the west side of the house. They both gasped when they saw the hole in the side of the house. It was large enough for an elephant to walk through. There was also terrible smoke damage inside.

"I was readin by candlelight after I came in late last night. I guess I went to sleep. The candle caught the curtains on fire. Leos and Becky were sleeping in here too. They didn't know anything was gong on until the fire truck woke them up," Dano said, laughing. "They thought it was real exciting," he added. Dano was still laughing as he walked back into the house.

Tim and Lori continued to wait in the pickup for Carlos. Sometime later, Dano and his new girlfriend, Leos, Becky, Rosita, and some other young people, came out of the house. They marched, arm in arm, down the street and out of sight. Rosita looked at Lori and Tim, smiled with a sneer, and threw her head back. Lori could almost hear her say, "And there's not a thing you guys can do about it, so there!"

"How dumb can we be?" Lori said.

"What now?" asked Tim.

"There is no telephone in that house, remember? The Gonzaleses always had to go somewhere else and borrow a telephone to call us!" Lori exclaimed.

"You're right. They couldn't have called Carlos. We have been waiting here all this time for nothing," Tim said. "There is just one thing left to do. We'll have to go to the police station and see if they can help us get in touch with Carlos, and find Ray," Tim explained.

They entered the police station and were greeted by a pretty, but very fat, blonde dispatcher. After Tim explained their problem, the dispatcher contacted the deputy on the intercom. The deputy came out of a door from a back office.

"Please have a chair and start from the beginning," the deputy said. He pointed to two comfortable looking chairs beside a desk piled high with papers.

"I know the Gonzaleses," the deputy said. "They keep this place pretty busy, sometimes. I know them all. It looks like those kids blew a pretty good deal, seein that ya all were willing to give them a good home and all. Maybe it's too late to do anything with them anyway," he exclaimed.

Tim stopped talking when a tall, huge man, with black hair, and black western clothes, came in and sat down in the extra chair. He looked like he had just stepped out of a Western band.

"It's all right to talk in front of him. He volunteers his help around here, and he can be trusted," the deputy said.

After Tim finished talking, Lori told the deputy, "I <u>will not</u> leave Rosita here, especially with Dano.

"That's no problem," the deputy said. He picked up the telephone and called the town of Bear Creek. "That person you were looking for, I think we can deliver him to you tonight," he said, and hung up. "The police in Bear Creek have a warrant out for Dano's arrest. He's been writen bad checks over there," the deputy explained.

"I knew that he got out of jail last week in Huntsdale, but I didn't know he was in trouble anywhere else," Lori said.

The big guy spoke for the first time. "I seen um at Harley's house just a few minutes ago. Ya want me to get the other deputy and go get um?" the guy asked.

"Tim, do you remember what Dano told us once about Harley?" Lori asked.

"I sure do. He said the guy was sex crazy. He said that Harley was his friend, but he was going to keep Rosita away from him, even though Harley was his best friend," Tim answered.

"You're rights about Harley," the big guy said as he left the police station.

A few minutes later, the CB radio began to flash. "We are on our way with said suspect. Some came out of the house and called us pigs, but we didn't see the girl," the other deputy reported.

The officer at the desk called Carlos's number several times. There was still no answer. "I can't understand it. Carlos is almost always home this late in the evenings," the deputy said.

Tim jumped out of his chair. "Lori, maybe we better hurry back to the field. There is a possibility that Ray could have doubled back. If he did, the other pickup is there for him to run away in!" Tim exclaimed.

"You surely didn't leave the keys in it, did you?" Lori asked.

"We left in such a hurry that I forgot to grab them. All my good tools are in the back and the end gate is down," Tim said.

There was still no answer at Carlos's. "I've put out a missing persons report on Ray, and I'll keep trying to call Carlos. I'll call you as soon as I know something, and you call me if you find Ray," the deputy said.

It was past midnight by the time Tim and Lori got back to the field. Ray had used the pickup to push the one-way, trying to fix the mess he had made. It looked worse than before. "And the new pickup is gone," Tim moaned.

Ray had taken the next turn in the road a little slower. He felt important driving such a new and powerful vehicle. Ray spun into the McCormick's yard in another swirl of dust. The two little girls were playing in the yard. Judy came to the door when Ray honked the horn. "Is Lee here?" Ray shouted.

"No, Ray, he isn't here," Judy replied. "He and Kathy went to a horse sale, and they will be getting home late," Judy explained

"I want to talk to Lee!" Ray shouted.

"Ray, Lee isn't here," Judy repeated.

Ray spun the pickup around in the yard causing a fog of more dust. He looked up and saw Kathy's two little sisters. They were screaming and running from the wild vehicle. "Oh, God! No!" Ray said as he remembered Sita.

The terrified girls ran into Judy's arms. They were both crying. "What makes Ray act like that mommy?" one of them asked.

"I don't know, but thank God you're both okay," Judy answered. "I can't believe that Tim would let Ray drive that pickup alone," Judy said, more to herself.

Ray sped toward the Jones's farm without looking back. He drove into the yard and started to get out of the pickup. "Wait, I need to get some friends to ride around with me before Tim and Lori get home," Ray said to himself. He put the vehicle into reverse and slid back onto the road.

Ray spun into Pete's place in another swirl of dust. He pounded on the front door.

Pete answered the door.

"Hey, Pete, wouldja like to go for a ride with me?" Ray asked.

"Grandma, can I go riding with Ray?" Pete asked. He was excited about the idea.

"Absolutely not!" Rita shouted. "Ray shouldn't even be driving, and besides, it's dark!"

"Can I show him around the place while he's here?" Pete asked. He was excited to have company, even though it was Ray.

"Be sure that's all you do," Rita snapped. "You better be back in the house in fifteen minutes," she shouted. "The nerve of Tim Jones to let that kid drive his pickup."

Pete grabbed a large flashlight and showed Ray the different animals and buildings. They were followed by Pete's large white dog.

In one building, Ray noticed Pete's three-wheeler motorcycle, and a new bicycle. <u>Those could come in handy</u>, Ray thought.

"I have to go back in," Pete said.

Ray had not been invited in. He was soon on his way to the next neighbor's house.

There were no lights on in the next house. Ray pointed the bright lights of the pickup at the front door. "Dan, come out here. I want to talk to you?" Ray yelled after honking the horn.

Mr. Johnson came to the door and yelled at Ray. "Dan is in bed. He can't come out. If you don't leave immediately, I'll call the police. You have no business driving at your age, and you are disturbing the peace!" he shouted. "I can't believe Tim is letting you drive, and at this time of night, too.'

Ray tried to throw as much dirt as possible as he turned the pickup around. He quickly drove back to the Joneses.

The house was still dark. Tim and Lori were not home yet. Ray found that all three doors of the house were locked. He had a tough time squeezing through the kitchen window, but he was awfully hungry. He had not eaten since breakfast. Ray started to eat some of Rosita's cookies, and relax. Then he remembered the trouble he was in. "What will Tim do to me when he finds out I ruined his tractor?" Ray asked himself, again. <u>I must hide, again</u>, he thought.

Ray left the house. He made sure that he locked the door as he left. Ray jumped into the large pickup once more. He parked it on the main road to town, right next to the turn off going to the Joneses. "Now they'll think that I caught a ride to town with someone, and quit looking for me. Then I can run the other direction, tomorrow," Ray said to himself.

Ray walked back to the farm. He was annoyed by Kato's barking. Ray saw the little white Luv pickup. "I think I'll drive this for awhile," he said. But, the keys were not in the vehicle.

Tired, hungry, frightened, and cold, Ray found one of Lori's old coats and curled up in it in the seat of the Luv pickup. Ray waited, not knowing what to do next. He saw one of Lori's Christian books laying on the dash of the Luv. The title of the book was <u>Move Ahead with Possibility Thinking</u>, by Robert Schuler. Ray could not read the title. He took the book, and in desperation, used his pocket knife to scratch the words, "if yu luv me, placez hel me" on the back of the hard cover.

Tim and Lori picked up some of Tim's good tools in the field where the large pickup had been parked. They stopped several times on the way to the farm to pick up more tools as they saw them shining in the pickup lights. "Oh, dear Lord, help me find all my tools," Tim said more than once. They found the purple and white pickup next to the main road in front of the farm.

Tim started the pickup and noticed that it still had gas in it. "Ray must have caught a ride to town with someone," Lori said. Tim agreed.

Ray looked into two bright flashlights. He could not see who was holding the lights, but he heard a gruff voice say, "All right kid. Come out of there with your hands up over your head."

Ray was shaking from the cold, but he did what he was told. He heard his old man's voice say, "I'm not gonna help you this time, boy. You're on you own."

Ray felt the cold metal of handcuffs, and heard them snap over his wrists. He was shoved into the back seat of a car with a "cherry" on top.

One officer drove while the other officer sat next to Ray. He was holding a gun pointing in Ray's direction. It seemed like a long time before they stopped, and he was jerked out of the car and marched into a cold cell.

Ray saw a small sink and a bed with no covers. He heard the door slam shut, and the key locking it. Ray was shaking as he lay down on the small, bare bed. He was uncomfortable, hungry, and <u>very</u> cold.

<u>I wish Kato would stop barking, but what is Kato doing here in the</u> <u>jail?</u> Ray thought. He shook his head and was soon awake. "Thank God, it was just a dream," Ray said aloud.

The pickup lights flashed across the yard as Tim turned toward the house. Ray slid down out of sight. "Kato, shut up," he told the dog barking beside his pickup.

The dog only barked louder.

Ray raised his head up just far enough above the dash to see Tim park the large pickup in the dirt driveway beside the house. Then he watched Lori park the other pickup in behind Tim. Ray watched Lori and Tim go into the house. <u>Where is Rosita?</u> he wondered.

Ray waited a few minutes before crawling up to the house. He looked through the window of Rosita's room. The window was slightly open. Ray heard Tim talking to Carlos on the telephone in the bedroom across the hall.

"Do you know where Ray is?" Tim asked.

Carlos sounded tired and sad. "I know not what goes on. Bobby, he call me and says you beat my kids up. He sayed that Ray has black eye. I rush to town. I get to the house, and Bobby say, we not call you. We not know where Ray and Rosita are," Carlos explained. "My kids not respect me," he added. "What's going on Tim?" Carlos asked.

Tim told Carlos everything that had happened. "Dano hid Rosita somewhere before the police picked him up," Tim explained.

"I'll let you know if I find Rosita, or Ray," Carlos said, and hung up.

Tim called the police station in Plainsville.

The deputy said, "I reached Carlos's place after you left. Someone else answered the phone and said that Carlos had gone to town to pick up Rosita, then on to your place to pick up Ray. I thought that everything was all right."

"We'll keep in touch," Tim said, and hung up.

Tim was crawling into bed when Lori ask, "Tim, don't you think you should alert the police in this area to watch for Ray?"

"Lori, I'm sure he is over in the other county by now," Tim answered. "I'll call them in the morning if we haven't found him by then," Tim said just before he went to sleep.

Ray crawled back into the little Luv pickup and wrapped Lori's coat around his cold body. He was as cold as the night that he and Bobby almost burned down the house. He was shaking as he finally went to sleep.

The first rays of the morning sun were shining in Ray's face. His legs cramped from sleeping in such a terrible position and from the cold. He had to rub them before he could walk.

Ray's first thought was to start running again. He checked each vehicle to find one with a key in it. Tim had learned his lesson. Ray could not find any keys in the pickups or car. "Pete's three-wheeler," Ray said to himself. "Kato, shut up," he whispered to the barking dog.

Ray started running toward Pete's place. He started to feel a little warmer. Ray was thinking about all the times Pete had gotten him into trouble at school, and on the bus. Pete is a little punk that is just too big for his britches. He talks big, but is too little to back it up and he always has to tattle to an adult. He has everything. Now is my chance to get even., Ray thought with a smile.

Ray slid into the small building. He was disappointed because the keys were not in the three wheeled motorcycle. In desperation, Ray pushed Pete's new bicycle to the door of the building.

Pete's large, white dog starting barking from the yard close to the house.

Ray stepped back into the shadows of the metal building and stood still until the dog stopped barking. He quietly pushed the bike some distance from the farm before he jumped on it and peddled as fast as he could. He went south a mile, then turned west for two miles. He did not know where he was going.

"I must get something to eat," Ray said when he heard his stomach growl. It had been almost twenty-four hours since he had eaten anything except for two cookies. Ray turned the bicycle into the next farm. The place was small but neat. All of the buildings had recently been painted white. They looked bright in the early morning sunshine. Ray knocked on the front door.

An elderly man answered the door. He looked puzzled when Ray asked, "Could you please feed a poor, hungry kid?"

An elderly woman came to the door. "I'm sure we have plenty. Come on in and join us for breakfast," she said. "Where did you come from?" the woman asked as she closed the front door behind Ray.

Ray did not answer. He followed the couple to a table covered with a white table cloth and pretty dishes. His mouth started to water as he smelled the bacon, eggs, and toast cooking. Ray remembered the manners Tim had taught him and asked where the bathroom was located. "I need to wash my hands," he told the couple. Ray tried to act proper, but it was difficult to eat slowly because he was so hungry.

Ray was enjoying his meal until the woman asked, "Haven't I seen you a time or two when I drove passed Tim Jones's place?"

"I work for Mr. Jones. He won't pay me. He is mean to me," Ray answered. "He loves my sister, though, and he even <u>bought</u> her," he added out of fear that they would call Tim.

"I see," the lady said. She tried to hide the shock she was feeling. "What did you say your name was?" she asked.

"Ray Gonzales," Ray answered proudly.

"Ray that looks like the neighbor boy's bike you rode in on. He rides it over here sometimes to visit us," the lady said.

"It is. I was visiting with him yesterday, and he let me borrow it," Ray answered.

"That was nice of him. He seems to be a pretty nice young fellow," the elderly man said.

Ray finished eating. He thanked the couple for the food and headed the bike in a new direction.

The lady called Rita immediately. "There was a Mexican boy here on Pete's bike a few minutes ago. He said he had borrowed it. I thought I better check it out," she said.

"Stole it you mean!" Rita screamed. "The Joneses need to take better control of those criminals they have brought back into our neighborhood. That boy was terrorizing the whole area in the Jones's pickup last night!" she exclaimed. "I'm going to call the sheriff right now and report them," Rita said.

"The boy told us that Tim Jones is in love with his sister and that he even <u>bought</u> her," the neighbor said.

"That does it!" Rita shouted. "I reported months ago that I thought that Tim Jones was using that little girl. Our sorry sheriff's department didn't do a thing about it. Just wait until I call them now," she said.

Rita called the sheriff's number immediately. She wasted no words as she told the deputy how sorry the department was. "You let criminals run loose that put the whole neighborhood in danger, and let men <u>use</u> innocent little girls," Rita shouted. "What are you going to do about it now!" she shouted over the phone.

Two lawmen left the jail immediately. They went to Pete's place first to get a description of the stolen bike, and then they started looking for Ray.

After Ray traveled several miles from the place he had eaten breakfast, he noticed a farm up ahead. As he peddled closer, he recognized it. It was his papa's former boss's place. The farm was used mostly for equipment because Mr. Shipman had a nice house in Plainsville. Mr. Shipman stayed in the old farm house sometimes when he was busy farming or working with cattle.

"I'm hungry again. It must be about noon," Ray told himself. "I think I'll stop and see if Mr. Shipman is here. Maybe he will give me something to eat," he said. Ray rode the bike into the drive. He was glad to see Mr. Shipman's car beside the old house.

As Ray waited for Mr. Shipman to answer the door, he looked around him. Mr. Shipman had made the house from remodeling what had once been an old gas station and store. The old gas pumps were still standing in front of the building as a reminder of earlier days. Fat, black and white cattle were grazing on a pasture north of the house.

Mr. Shipman looked surprised when he answered the door and saw Ray. "I thought you guys had moved out of the area," he said.

Ray was reminded of the time Mr. Shipman had turned off the utilities, and he and Bobby almost froze to death. "My family moved, but I've come back to work for Tim Jones, and go to school here," Ray explained. "Could you fix me a couple of sandwiches?" he asked.

"Doesn't Mr. Jones feed you!" Mr. Shipman exclaimed.

"I rode my bike further away from the farm than I intended to. It'll take too long to get back. I'm awfully hungry," Ray stuttered, trying to think of answers quickly.

"I suppose I can rake up enough vitals for a couple of sandwiches," Mr. Shipman said. "Come on in while you wait," he added.

Ray was soon back on the bike with two sandwiches in a sack. "I must be getting back," he said as he headed east.

"Hey, wait a minute!" Mr. Shipman yelled. "The Jones's place is that way," he shouted, pointing in the opposite direction.

"Oh yeah thanks!" Ray yelled and turned the bike around. He peddled west until Mr. Shipman went back into the house. Ray stopped and waited a few minutes before he started east again. He rode past Mr. Shipman's place as fast as he could, hoping that Mr. Shipman was not looking out of one of the windows. Ray did not slow down until he was far enough away to feel safe from being spotted.

There were very few places to hide on the flat, barren prairie. Ray was looking for a place to pull of the road and eat his sandwiches without being seen. He saw a large culvert under the road up ahead. "I can hide in there and enjoy my lunch," Ray told himself. The bike was too tall to hide, so he laid it over in a pile of weeds in the ditch.

Ray was eating his sandwiches when he saw a lawman standing at the opening of the culvert. He turned to run out of the other opening, and saw another lawman there. This time it was not a dream. He was trapped like a wild animal.

"Okay kid, come on out with your hands up," a voice shouted.

Ray knew he could not escape. He did as he was told. He crawled out of the culvert and surrendered. The two men searched him to see if he had any secret weapons and took his large pocket knife. Ray was pushed into the back seat of a black car with a red light on top. The bike was loaded into the trunk of the police car. "We can leave the bike at Pete's place on our way to the Jones's," the under sheriff said.

After the bike was returned, and the two officers received a "tongue lashing" from Rita, they went to Tim and Lori's to pick up Rosita.

"They have found Ray," Lori said when she saw the sheriff's black, shiny Ford pull into the drive way. She opened the door almost as soon as Deputy Robert knocked. "Where did you find Ray?" Lori asked with relief.

Deputy Robert did not answer Lori's question. He almost pushed her over as he stomped into the kitchen where Tim was waiting. "Where's the girl?" Deputy Robert shouted.

"We don't know except her brother Dano hid her somewhere in Plainsville last night," Tim answered. He wondered why his friend was so rude.

"I'll see for myself!" Deputy Robert shouted. He pushed Tim aside and checked every room and closet in the house. He returned to the kitchen only when he was sure that Rosita was not there.

"May I talk to Ray?" Lori asked.

"I guess, but it won't do any good. We're taking him in," Deputy Robert answered rudely.

Lori walked out to the black car that had "SHERIFF" written in gold letters on each front door. She greeted the other officer, who was also a friend. Deputy John crawled out of the car and let Lori slide into the back seat beside Ray.

"Ray, don't you want to come back and live with us?" Lori whispered.

Ray did not answer. He bent over and put his head between his knees, trying to hide.

Lori felt hot tears on her cheeks again. She looked at the dusty curls on the head of the dark-skinned child. She gently patted Ray's bent, dusty shoulders.

"Ray, I know you're terribly embarrassed by what you have done," Lori said. "We know you ran away because you were afraid. The mess you made in the field is not as bad as it looks. It can be fixed. Tim is not mad," Lori explained.

"Ray, you didn't break the law like you did the last time you ran away. See, you're getting better. With football and everything, you will continue to get better," Lori said.

Ray did not move. His body felt as stiff as a board.

"Ray, I believe one reason you don't want to stay with us is because you are afraid of what you will do the next time you panic. You don't want to cause us anymore trouble, but we can face this thing together," Lori said, pleading with the boy.

Lori saw tears falling on Ray's dirty arms that were wrapped around his knees. "Please Ray, try living with us again, and let us help you," Lori said with a sob.

Deputy Robert was now shuffling his feet impatiently outside the car. Lori felt his stare going through her back. "What will you do with him?" she asked.

"We'll find a foster home for him to stay in this evening, and decide what should be done with him tomorrow," Deputy Robert said loudly. "He <u>did</u> break the law by stealing Pete's bike. I think he has a bad enough record in Plainsville to put him away for awhile," he said.

"Please let us know when you find Rosita," Tim said more than once.

The sheriff's car was driving out of sight when the telephone rang. Tim ran into the house to answer. It was Carlos. Tim quickly explained what had happened to Ray. "Have you found Rosita yet?" he asked.

"Rosita, she come home this morning while I was in field. She won't tell me who bring her home," Carlos said.

"Let me talk to her," Lori said.

Tim handed Lori the telephone while Carlos gave Rosita his end of the line.

"Rosita, where were you last night, and who took you home today?" Lori asked. "I think your father has a right to know what is going on," she added.

"I don't know," Rosita said. "When are you going to bring me my things?" she asked, hatefully.

Lori was angry and out of control. "We have made dozens of trips for you. We have bought you many things. We have helped you to be respected by you friends. We have loved you and spoiled you rotten. All we have gotten in return is a kick in the face!" Lori shouted. "You think you are too good for us now. What do you want to do, grow up like Dano?" Lori screamed.

"I want to grow up just like Dano," Rosita screamed back. "If it wasn't for you turning him in, I'd be with him right now!" she shouted.

"We didn't turn him in, Rosita," Lori argued.

"Yes you did! I hate you for it!" Rosita screamed. "I'll get even with you for that. You just wait and see!" she shouted. "When are you going to bring me my things?" Rosita asked again.

"As far as I'm concerned never!" Lori shouted. "You can come and get them yourself! You'll never be welcome in our house again. Ray is, but you're not! Every time you decide to come back, it's so you can use us again. This is the final good-bye!" Lori yelled.

Lori hung up the telephone and started to cry from anger as well as sorrow. "I wonder if she has any feeling for us at all?" Lori whispered.

Lori cried a few minutes, before gaining control of her emotions. She washed her face with cold water. Tim watched, not knowing what to do or say.

"How could I have talked to her like that?" Lori asked herself as well as Tim.

"She deserved it because she was sassing you," Tim said.

"I'm the one who is supposed to act like an adult. She is only a child. I acted as much like a child as she did," Lori stammered. She tried to steady her hands as she called Rita to apologize for Ray.

"I'm sorry Ray stole Pete's bicycle, and I hope he didn't damage it," Lori said meekly.

"My grandson's bike is ruined!" Rita shouted over the phone. "You should be forced out of the community for letting Ray terrorize the area in your pickup last night. He even tried to get Pete to go with him. Ray tried to run over the two little McCormick girls, and he tore up their yard by spinning the pickup around in it. He terrorized the Johnson's last night too, and demanded that Dan go with him.

All of your neighbors look down on you, Lori, for bringing those criminals back into the community!" Rita shouted. "Lori, are you still there?" Rita asked, not giving Lori a chance to answer.

Lori tried to apologize again. Rita would not stop yelling long enough for Lori to say anything. Lori finally hung up.

Lori threw herself across Tim's shoulders and started to sob.

CHAPTER XVII

SCHOOL AND PROBLEMS

It had been two weeks since Ray's arrest. Tim called the sheriff's department to ask about Ray. He was told that Ray had been tested by a Psychologist and needed psychiatric help. The boy had been put in a foster home in a city in another state where he could receive treatment twice a week.

Tim thanked the deputy for the information. "Please call if you need to contact me for anything," Tim said.

"I sure will," the deputy replied.

When Lori wasn't teaching school, she remained busy helping Tim in the field or with the cattle.

"Lori, our operation is losing more money every day. The wheat is blowing out, the market is low, and the cows that sluffed their calves last spring haven't been able to gain any weight, although I'm feeding them expensive feed. I'm going to have to sell them as culls just to get rid of them. It would have been cheaper if they had just died at the beginning," Tim said.

Lori nodded her head to agree. She had heard the story before.

"Lori, we are so far behind with our bills that the only way out is to declare bankruptcy. I've never been a quitter, but it will be better to quit than to go to jail for the debts I can't pay," Tim tried to explain.

"What about the disaster loan that the FHA promised us a year ago when we lost our entire milo crop, and many of our cows in that terrible twenty-four hour storm?" Lori asked. "That's when we started charging most of our farm expenses. We were hoping to pay off the bills with that government aid," Lori said.

"The FHA office has a new man taking over this area. He has refused to sign our government loan," Tim explained.

"Tim, we owe so many people. Some of them are our friends. A bankruptcy would mean that we would never pay them back," Lori argued.

"I feel as bad about it as you do, but we have no other choice," Tim said.

"Tim, I'm scared," Lori whispered as she curled up in her husband's arms and went into a sleep of unhappy dreams.

Tim had just drifted off to sleep when the telephone started ringing. He opened his eyes and looked at the lighted, digital clock next to the bed. It was 11:30 p.m. <u>Someone must be sick</u>, Tim thought as he lifted the red telephone receiver.

"Are you going to be around your place tomorrow?" a gruff voice asked.

"I plan to be working in one of the fields twenty miles south of here," Tim replied. "Why?" he asked.

"As bad as I hated to, I promised you that I'd let you know if I needed to get in touch with you. You better be around your farm in the morning about ten," the deputy ordered.

"Do you need my help on the posse?" Tim asked.

"No, indeed not!" the deputy exclaimed.

"You sound serious. Is it that bad?" Tim asked.

"I'm not at liberty to say," the deputy said, and hung up the telephone.

Tim was wide awake by now. He dialed the other deputy who had been a friend for a long time. "I can't tell you anything," the deputy said.

Tim was shaking as he dialed the first deputy back. "Does this have anything to do with the Gonzales family?" he asked.

"Yes," the deputy said.

"Do I need a bondsman?" Tim asked.

"Yes. Now don't bother me anymore," the deputy said.

"Thanks for letting me know," Tim said and hung up.

"Lori! Lori!" Tim shouted, shaking his sleeping wife. "We have trouble!" he said.

Lori opened her eyes. Tim told her about his conversation with the deputy. "I can't believe it's <u>that</u> serious. Go back to sleep and we'll talk about it tomorrow," Lori said.

"It's serious. If I don't have bail money by tomorrow, <u>I'll go to jail</u>," Tim explained.

Lori sat up in bed. "Tim, we don't have any money. I don't know what we can do," she said.

"Do you know anyone who would lend us the money? They'll get the money back when everything is over," Tim asked Lori. He sounded desperate.

"My precious mother will loan us the money, but I hate to call her at this time of night," Lori answered.

"We have no other choice," Tim whispered. He felt himself breaking out in cold sweat.

Lori's hand felt like it weighed at least fifty pounds as she dialed the familiar number.

Arthur answered. "May I speak to mother, please?" Lori asked. She would have rather taken a beating than to have to explain to her mother their desperate situation and ask to borrow the money they needed.

Lori explained their situation to Elizabeth the best she could. She wasn't sure just what was happening.

"How much do you need, Lori?" Elizabeth asked. She sounded sleepy and concerned.

"We won't know until sometime tomorrow, I mean later this morning," Lori answered.

"Arthur and I will be by the telephone waiting for you to call, to see what we can do to help," Elizabeth said.

Lori felt ashamed and like crying when she hung up. She and Tim prayed that everything would turn out all right. Lori slept for a little while, but Tim was awake the rest of the night.

"Lori, will you please stay home with me?" Tim pleaded the next morning.

Lori called Mr. Wilson to report that she would not be in school that day. "I'm sorry to let you know so late. I hope you don't have any trouble finding a substitute for me," Lori said.

"Yes, I know. I already have someone to sub for you today," Mr. Wilson said.

"Thank you," Lori said and hung up. Then the shock hit her. "How, in the world, did Mr. Wilson know that I wasn't going to be in school today when I didn't even know it?" Lori asked.

"He's on the sheriff's posse, too," Tim reminded.

"I know, but I don't think he's the type to ever let anyone know what the posse is doing," Lori said.

Tim did a few chores outside while Lori read some scriptures. Lori fixed a light breakfast, but neither of them was able to eat.

Lori gave Kato and Lucky most of the breakfast, and straightened up the kitchen and house.

At 9:30, they both changed into better clothes. Tim and Lori were trying desperately to be calm, but when the sheriff's car turned into the driveway. Lori started to shake uncontrollably. She ran into the bedroom and shut the door. She felt like running for her life.

Tim answered the door and invited the two lawmen in for a cup of coffee.

"Sounds good to me," Deputy John said. He motioned for the other officer to follow.

Deputy Robert came out from the driver's side of the car. He had his hand on the butt of the gun hanging in the holster. "Get him out here!" he shouted.

"Let me tell Lori that I'm leaving," Tim said. He started back into the house.

"Don't go back into the house!" Deputy Robert ordered, taking another step toward Tim. He tightened his grip on his gun without taking it out of the holster.

Tim started to get into the back seat of the car.

Deputy Robert pointed to the front seat and said, "You know that prisoners have to ride in the front so they can be guarded from the back seat!"

Tim was searched for weapons and pushed into the front seat of the car. Deputy Robert read him his rights. ". . . and anything you say may, and will be used against you . . . You have the right to an attorney, or one will be appointed for you . . ." "Do you have anything to say?" he asked.

"The only thing I have to say is that innocent people don't need lawyers," Tim said. "What am I being accused of, anyway?" he asked.

Deputy Robert handed Tim a set of papers to read.

Lori was watching and listening from the kitchen window. She could not stay in the house any longer. She ran out of the house. "What's going on?" she asked, trying to sound calm.

Deputy Robert pushed the papers up into Lori's face. I'm glad this is just a bad dream, Lori thought as she read the papers. The papers read:

Tim Jones has been charged with child molesting twelve-year-old Rosita Gonzales, who is not his spouse, and who is more than three years younger . . . on the 21rst day of December, the defendant is accused of opening the bathroom door as the Plaintiff was getting out of the bath tub and tried to see her nude body . . .

On August 21, when the Plaintiff awoke in the morning, Tim Jones has been accused of standing over her with nothing on but his socks . . . Tim Jones had his hands on Rosita's private parts, and asked Rosita Gonzales to touch him in his private parts . . . .

At the end of the charges were the signatures of twelve people that had signed as witnesses. Lori personally knew ten of them. Besides Rosita and Carlos, the witnesses included Rita, Tim's ex-sister-in-law, the two deputies standing before her right now, another neighbor, Tim's ex-wife, Tim's daughter, Sally, the sheriff, and a school teacher in Plainsville, and Lori's' principal, Mr. Wilson.

"How can all of you be witnesses to something that never happened?" Lori shouted. "How about all the things Rosita has stolen from us!

Lori shouted again. "She even stole my wedding rings," Lori tried to explain.

The lawmen were not listening. The shiny, black car was already backing away from the house.

Lori felt angry, confused, sick, and terribly embarrassed by what she had just read. Her face felt awfully hot. What she had just shouted at the deputies was just plain dumb and had nothing to do with what was happening now. It seemed like everyone they knew had suddenly turned into monsters that were out to destroy her and Tim.

Lori felt weak as she saw Tim taken away in the police car just like a common criminal. "When your own law is out to get you, who can you turn to for safely?" Lori asked herself. She felt like she and Tim had just entered a war for survival, and that the odds were against them.

"I'm not guilty so I don't need a lawyer. I'll answer your questions the best I can," Tim said as the car traveled to the county seat and jail.

"You better take this serious, Mr. Jones. We're going to put you in jail and set your bail so high, it'll take a hellulva lot to ever get you out!" Deputy Robert shouted, making the first turn on the country road.

The two lawmen started firing all kinds of questions at Tim.

Lori ran into the house. She was angry, and called Rita. "What are you trying to do, destroy us!" she shouted over the telephone.

"What are you talking about?" Rita asked.

"You had Tim arrested and He's innocent!" Lori exclaimed.

"You know he's guilty, Lori. You even told me so, yourself," Rita replied.

"I _what_?" Lori shouted.

"Remember when you and Rosita came over to visit Pete after the last of school parties?" Rita asked.

"Of course I remember, but I didn't tell you that Tim was . . . Tim was," Lori stuttered, not even able to say the horrible words.

Rita continued her accusations. "Remember telling me you were going to take Rosita home the next week because school would be out? You said you hated to loose her because you loved her, and that Tim was fond of her?" Rita said.

"Surely, you couldn't have taken that statement the wrong way. People use that expression all the time. You make it sound like I knew it was going on, and that I thought it was okay!" Lori exclaimed.

"Ray told Mrs. Stone that Tim bought Rosita because he loves her," Rita said.

"Tim is innocent!" Lori shouted.

"How do you know?" Rita asked. "You weren't with him when it happened?" she said.

"Because I know why Ray said what he did, and I know Tim. Tim became a Christian before we were married, and I've never seen, or heard him say anything, that would make me believe that he isn't living for the Lord as well as he knows how. People just won't let his past reputation die," Lori tried to explain.

"He may be innocent this time, but he wasn't innocent with his daughter. He still needs to be punished for that," Rita said. "You'll be better off without him, Lori," she added.

"I don't believe that story either," Lori said.

"If he's a Christian, like you say he is, then prison is a good place for him to witness, just like Paul did in the Bible," Rita said.

"Paul was put in prison for preaching the Gospel, not for being accused of molesting a child," Lori protested.

"Lori, you need to get out of the county, and all the hurt you have gone through here. I remember all the things Hollis put you through, and then he married someone young enough to be your daughter. You see them every time you go to town.

The only thing that's going to get you through the hurt Tim is putting you through now is the Word of God.

You need to at least take a few days off from school, until you can get yourself pulled back together," Rita said.

Rita was still talking. "I know that you'd be happier somewhere else. I hear that you folks have gone broke anyway, and that you're going to have to sell the farm. We'd like to buy it when it comes up for sale," she said.

Lori could hardly believe what she was hearing. She and Rita had been friends for years.

"Lori, are you still there?" Rita asked, with a pause.

"Yes," Lori whispered. "We were talking about Tim's arrest, not our financial status," Lori said. "What do you, <u>really know</u>, about whether Tim is guilty or not?" she asked.

"I guess what I know is what I've heard, but I believe it anyway," Rita answered.

Lori felt depressed as she hung up the telephone, and called Mr. Wilson. "How did you know Tim was going to be arrested today, and what was your name doing on the paper as a witness?" Lori asked her boss.

"Because the sheriff's deputy was here at school and was establishing the fact that you were here in school on August 21, and that Rosita was not with you," Mr. Wilson explained. His words were kind, and he sounded concerned.

"I don't care if I was home or not that day, I know Tim is innocent. He's not perfect, but he would never do anything like they are accusing him of," Lori said.

"I don't know about that, but I do know this, whether you win or loose in court, you have already lost in this community," Mr. Wilson said. "People will always wonder when they see him, and people will want to keep their little girls away from him," he tried to explain. "Do you know what I mean?" Mr. Wilson asked.

"I'm afraid I do," Lori said. She started to cry.

"Lori, you need to take some days off from school until you can get yourself pulled back together again," Mr. Wilson said.

"I promise I won't come back to school and cry in front of my students, if that's what you are afraid of," Lori said and hung up the telephone. She should not have been so rude to Mr. Wilson when he was trying to be kind. Lori ran to the car and started her dreaded trip to the county jail.

<u>I wish there was someone I could talk to that would understand, before I have to go into the jail and see Tim</u>, Lori was thinking. She

thought of her close friend, Vera Lee, and stopped by her house in town.

Lori had gone to Vera Lee's house many times to talk when she went through her divorce with Hollis. Vera Lee had always made time in her busy schedule to help.

After Lori had sold her home and bought the mobile home, she moved it into Vera Lee's yard. The two women had taught school together, gone to church together, shopped out of town together, and rode many miles on their bicycles together. Vera Lee was now only teaching half days so she could spend more time with her two small children.

"This situation doesn't surprise me, because Rosita is capable of making up some pretty big stories," Vera Lee said. "Things will turn out okay.".

The two friends prayed over the situation, and that, "Lori would be strong in the Lord." Lori hurried on to her dreaded destination. She had done nothing wrong, yet Lori felt like a criminal when she walked into the sheriff's office. Her embarrassment was beyond description.

In one corner of the office was a large desk where a dark-haired dispatcher was working. One wall was covered with pictures of all the former sheriffs of the county, including Sheriff Wade. The rest of the room was filled with tan, leather-covered chairs and sofas. The dispatcher did not look up until Lori walked over to the desk.

Lori's voice was shaky when she asked, "May I see my husband, Tim Jones?"

""No Mam., Mr. Jones is being questioned by the sheriff and his deputies. No one can see him until they are finished and his bail is paid," the dispatcher replied.

"How much is his bail set for?" Lori asked.

"Five thousand dollars, cash," the lady said with a smile.

Lori clutched the corner of the desk to steady herself. She felt numb as she looked over the room for a telephone. She could barely see because of tears. There was a pay-phone in one corner of the room.

Lori's hand felt even heavier than before as she dialed her mother's number again.

Elizabeth answered the telephone immediately.

"The bail has been set at five thousand dollars," Lori heard herself saying.

"Don't worry Lori. We'll be there with the money as quickly as we can get there," Elizabeth said. "Just be strong in your faith,.".

It seemed more like six hours, rather than thirty minutes, before Elizabeth and Arthur came in. Elizabeth gently pulled Lori from the corner of a sofa that she had shrunk into, and led her over to the dispatcher's desk. "I'm ready to pay Tim Jones's bail," she said. Elizabeth took out her check book and started to fill in the blanks.

"Sorry, but it must be paid in cash, only," the lady said.

Elizabeth put her checkbook away. "Lori, why don't you come with us to the bank. You need to get out of here for awhile," Elizabeth said. She led Lori out of the jail building.

Arthur was holding Lori up as she made her way to their car. He drove up to one bank and let Elizabeth out before he drove to the bank where he did his business.

Lori waited in the car. She did not want to see anyone she knew.

When Arthur returned, he placed two hundred, and fifty dollars into Lori's hand. "Take this. You'll need it before this is all over," he said.

"I just can't take more than the bail money from you guys," Lori said, arguing.

"Don worry about it now," Arthur said. He stopped to pick up Elizabeth at the other bank. They were soon back in the sheriff's office.

Elizabeth handed the dispatcher the five one thousand dollar bills. "May I have a receipt for that?" she asked.

"Yes, of course, and you are supposed to watch me put it in the safe," the surprised dispatcher stammered.

The door at the end of the hall opened, and Sheriff Wade stomped out. He saw Lori and her folks. "What are you doing here!" he shouted.

"I'm waiting to see Tim, and mother has just paid his bail," Lori replied. "When can I see him?" she asked, trying to sound calm.

"Not until we get through with him," Sheriff Wade answered. "You shouldn't be here," Sheriff Wade told Lori's folks. "Let me know if anything develops," He shouted to the dispatcher as he stormed out the front door.

Tim was sitting on a small bed under a bright light. The rest of the room was dark. The deputies were sitting in chairs facing Tim. He had been interrogated with questions in the tiny back room for six straight hours.

"Can I please have something for my terrible headache?" Tim asked.

"Sign this confession, and we'll give you some aspirin," one deputy said.

"I can't admit to something I didn't do," Tim repeated for the hundredth time.

Sheriff Wade and the three deputies were taking turns with the questioning. Sheriff Wade returned to relieve one of the deputies. When the sheriff left the room thirty minutes later, Lori caught him as he rushed through the office. "How are things going?" she asked.

"He doesn't have a chance!" Sheriff Wade shouted. "His daughter came in yesterday. The dispatcher helped her write a confession," the sheriff explained. "We wouldn't have paid much attention to the Mexican girl's story, but with Sally's confession, we have it wrapped up pretty tight. Both are the same pattern," Sheriff Wade said. He walked back to the room and yelled, "Get a confession out of him, and quit babying him!"

Lori was angry over Sheriff Wade's comment about Rosita being just a Mexican girl. She remembered the comments that Samuel's parents had made about her sometimes daughter.

"I'm a married man, and I love my wife, but I'm not always true to her," one deputy said. "We all have our hang-ups, and you might as well admit yours," he said.

"I don't have a problem," Tim said again.

Sheriff Wade returned. "If you'll sign this confession, I'll take you to the state mental hospital for treatment this evening. If you don't sign, I'll see that you are put in prison for forty years, and I have the power to get it done!" the sheriff shouted. "No one who owes as much money as you do should be allowed to walk the streets of this county!" he exclaimed.

"We're not here to talk about my debts," Tim replied. "Please give me something for my headache. I can't stand it any longer," he pleaded.

One of the deputies handed Tim a piece of paper instead of an aspirin. Tim handed it back.

It was six o'clock when the dispatcher motioned for Lori to go to the back room. She entered the room, and a deputy handed her Tim's confession to read. It had been written by someone else, but it had Tim's signature. Tim was slumped down on the edge of the bed. He looked pale and haggard.

Lori read the confession. "I could have accidentally put my hands on Rosita when she was sleeping with us, thinking that it was my wife," it said. Lori stopped reading. "Tim, this can't be true. When Rosita slept with us, I slept in the middle, and you and Rosita were fully dressed. I had my arms around her all night to keep her from shaking," Lori said.

"That's right. I guess I forgot," Tim said weakly.

Lori read more of the confession. "I could have opened the bathroom door accidentally about the said time . . ." it said. Lori stopped again. "Tim, this can't be true, either. Rosita always locked the bathroom door. I haven't even seen her in the nude," Lori said.

"I guess I forgot that too," Tim replied.

"Tim, when the worst thing on your arrest papers was supposed to have happened, Rosita had that high-collar, long sleeved, blue, one-piece slack suit of mine on, so I could wash her dirty clothes. It would have been difficult for you to have been touching her in the wrong places with her wearing that," Lori explained. "Rosita was awake early that morning so she could call all the churches in town. She was calling those churches at the very time you have been accused of molesting her. Even if she had been asleep, you couldn't have gotten through her bedroom door without waking her up. She would have been shouting at you before you even reached her bed," Lori said, trying to remind Tim of the recent past.

"Rosita's confession said that if she told anyone what had happened, that you said that you would really get her. I've never heard you use that expression before," Lori added. "Tim, Rosita is trying to get even with us because she still thinks we had Dano arrested,"

"Don't blame the girl," a deputy said. "After your neighbor made such a scene, me and a deputy in Plainsville went to Rosita's school. We took Rosita and one of her woman teachers to a vacant room and questioned her. At first, Rosita said that nothing had happened. That's pretty common for a victim to say that. Then I started to suggest situations and she started to answer yes or no,"

Tim butted in. "You mean you put pictures in her mind like you tried to do to me today?" Tim asked.

"No, that's not what I meant!" exclaimed the deputy.

"What I think has happened, is that Rosita has told what happened the night you pulled her out of Samuel's bedroom. She has used you, Tim, instead of Samuel, in her story," Lori said.

Tim agreed and said,. "Samuel didn't have anything on but his socks just like Rosita has said in her confession about me."

"I don't believe a word of your story!" the deputy exclaimed. "I know you are guilty, Tim, and we're going to prove it," he said. "You can go home now, but you must appear at the first hearing in court. If you ever fail to appear when you are called, you will lose your bail money," the deputy said with a smile.

"Please call me the night before to remind me," Tim said, begging Deputy John. "I don't want to lose Lori's mother's money."

"I'll do it for her sake and not yours," Deputy John replied.

Tim and Lori were still talking to the deputies, when Arthur came in and said, "Lori, your mother has a headache. We're going to the cafe to eat supper. You guys join us as soon as you are through here."

Lori went back into the waiting room of the sheriff's office. She sat down and started to cry again. She managed to tell the clerk that she would meet Tim downtown at the cafe on Main Street. She just had to be alone and try to get control of her emotions. Way back in the corner of her mind was the thought, <u>what if Tim really is guiltily</u>.

Lori walked out of the police station. She felt the blowing sand stinging her face and legs as she walked beside a dirt street.

Through the howling wind, Lori thought she heard someone calling her name. She looked up and saw Sheriff Wade's wife motioning for her to get into her car.

"No thank you," Lori said and kept walking. "I guess I didn't have to be so rude when she was just trying to be nice," she told herself.

Lori felt confused, and her thoughts were on the recent past again. "After daddy died, and that man stole his tools, it was mother that had to get on the witness stand and identify the tools. The criminal didn't even have to get on the witness stand. He was protected and got off free to rob someone else within a matter of weeks. It was mother who was treated like a criminal, not him," Lori reminded herself.

"When Tim's mobile home was robbed, finger prints were taken, but not one item was found or returned. The insurance company didn't pay a dime, because Tim didn't have receipts to prove that he had bought the stuff that was stolen.

Some of our yearling calves were stolen. There were signs of portable pens and truck tracks. The sheriff's depart didn't seem to do much about that either," Lori whispered.

Lori was thinking, <u>The Foster Insurance Company wouldn't pay on cattle killed in a blizzard because the autopsies were performed a day too late. The storm had been so bad that the Vet couldn't get to the carcasses within twenty-four hours to determine the cause of death. By the time the Vet did get there, some of the carcasses had been in the sun for a couple of days. Some of the carcasses were still buried in snow-drifts. Decay was at different stages so the insurance company insisted that all the cattle didn't die at the same time. The insurance company tried to say that the cattle died of starvation and not the storm.</u>

We didn't want the oil company to drill on our land. It is a school section, and we would have never received an income from any oil or gas found on our land. The oil man told Tim that his company had enough money that they could drill anywhere they wanted to.

Tim asked the company to fence off the oil-slush pit so the cattle wouldn't wonder into it. The cattle broke through the electric fence during a storm and fell into the pit full of dirty water and harmful elements. Some died and the rest lost their calves. The company wouldn't even pay for the surface damages to the land., Lori was thinking.

"And, the nerve of Rita and her husband telling everyone that the cattle had starved to death. The cattle had been eating milo stalks, and it was the fat ones that died," Lori whispered.

I guess it's a dog eat dog world all right. It's a long way from what God has intended for it to be. It's frightening when you know your friends, and lawmen, are out to get you, and large companies push you around, Lori thought.

"I feel like I've been arrested right along with Tim. If people believe what Rita is saying, then they will think that I helped in the hideous act!" Lori shouted into the howling wind.

I have lived all my life in this county, and I have lived as pure as possible. Now I am hit by all these awful things just for trying to do what is right, Lori thought. "Why Lord?" she shouted.

Lori could feel that her face was covered with dirt from the blowing sand. "But, I don't care how dirty I am. I just don't care anymore," Lori said aloud. Everyone in the county knows by now that Tim has been arrested, and they know why, Lori was thinking. She felt too embarrassed to face anyone. She wished she could just disappear into the blowing sand and never come back.

Once again, Lori thought she heard her name being called through the howling of the wind. She looked up. Tim was waiting for her in the car. He had a big smile his face. How can he be smiling! Lori thought. "Well, if he can smile, so can I," Lori told herself and got into the car.

"Everything will be all right," Tim said.

Lori had heard that phrase millions of times.

Lori went straight to the rest-room as soon as they reached the cafe. She washed the dirty tear-streaks from her face, and put on some lipstick. She tried to smile as she joined the others at a table.

Tim ate a large supper. Lori had trouble swallowing the soup she had ordered. She kept her head turned toward the wall every time anyone entered the cafe, so she wouldn't be recognized.

"Tim, why don't you and Lori come out to the ranch with us for awhile tonight," Elizabeth was saying. "I'll fix us something cold to drink, and we can talk about what you kids should do next," she said.

CHAPTER XVIII

PANIC

Elizabeth fixed four glasses of lemon-aid. She put two of them on the kitchen table where Tim and Arthur were talking, and took the other two to the living room where Lori was laying on the sofa. Elizabeth set the lemon-aid on the coffee table in front of the sofa., and gently rubbed Lori's back. "You have always been such a good girl. I can't understand why you have to suffer so much," Elizabeth said.

"What are your plans to fight this situation?" Arthur asked Tim.

"I don't know. I didn't think I needed a lawyer because I'm not guilty. I didn't think innocent people needed lawyers," Tim answered.

"That not always true," Arthur said. "It looks to me like you're going to have to fight back with every thing you can, and with the best lawyer you can find," he advised.

"You're probably right, but Lori and I don't have any money to fight with right now, and Sheriff Wade knows it," Tim replied.

"You have to do what you can," Arthur said.

"Sheriff Wade told me that he was going to try to send me to prison for forty years. He told me he has the power to do it," Tim explained.

"It's hard to imagine Sheriff Wade talking like that, but I believe you, Tim," Arthur replied. "I could tell that he was pretty mad today."

Lori and Elizabeth joined the men in the kitchen. They all agreed that Tim was going to have to fight for his life. When it was time for Tim and Lori to go home, Arthur said, "Let's all join hands and pray."

They all joined hands while Arthur prayed, "Dear Lord, we are asking you to take care of this situation, and save Tim's life and show Tim and Lori what to do. Give them courage to go back and face the people who have hurt them, and those who believe the story is true. Help them to forgive and know Your will. In Jesus name we pray. Amen."

Each of the others prayed. While Tim and Lori were putting on their coats, Arthur said, "You kids go back and hold your heads high, because you don't have anything to be ashamed of."

"Keep us informed as to what is happening," Elizabeth said. She and Arthur waved good-bye as Tim and Lori drove out of the yard.

Lori and Tim were not able to sleep that night. The next morning, Lori was weak and had a bad case of diarrhea. She called Mr. Wilson to say she would not be in school that day.

"Tim, you must find a lawyer today," Lori said and handed Tim the telephone book.

"I guess, but I don't know of any criminal lawyers, so I sure don't know the <u>best</u> one," Tim replied.

Lori shivered at the word criminal.

Tim looked through the telephone book. He found "Attorney Information" and dialed the number. A lady answered. "Could you tell me who is the best criminal lawyer in the state?" Tim asked.

"Mr. Linden Freedman," the lady quickly replied.

"Can you tell me who is second best?" Tim asked.

"I can give you the names of about two thousand other good lawyers," the lady said.

"May I have Mr. Freedman's number?" Tim asked.

"You will have to call information for that number, sir. We are not allowed to give out any attorney's numbers," the lady answered.

Tim called information and wrote down the number, then dialed it.

"Mr. Freedman is too busy to talk to you," Mr. Freedman's secretary said. "He might have time to talk to you in a couple of weeks from now."

"Lady, I don't have two weeks!" Tim exclaimed.

"Most people we work with don't," the secretary said and hung up.

Tim called the number again. "I hear that Mr. Freedman is the best criminal lawyer in the state?" he asked.

"He is, because he very seldom looses a case," the lady replied before hanging up again.

Tim gave up and went out to see if the cattle had enough grain and water. He went on to the field and did a little farming, but came in early. He had lost all interest in anything.

Lori read from the Bible and prayed. She still felt terribly depressed. "I dread facing people at school. I think I'll stay home tomorrow, since its Friday, and try to make up for it next week. That will give me the weekend to start feeling better," she told Mr. Wilson over the phone later that evening.

"I think that's a good idea, Lori," Mr. Wilson said. "I sure hope things turn out okay for you and Tim," he said.

"Thanks," Lori said, and hung up the telephone. She had cried so much she couldn't cry any more. If Tim was taken away from her for forty years, what would be left for them? They would be in their late eighties when he got out of prison.

Lori fixed Tim a good supper. It was silent at the table. They went to bed early and tried to sleep in each others arms. They felt a little more rested the next morning. Tim waited until eight o'clock and started to dial Mr. Freedman's office again.

"Wait," Lori said. She took the telephone from Tim's hand and hung it up. "Let's pray before you make the call. I'm getting awfully tired of the devil pushing us around." she explained. "Heavenly Father, if this is the lawyer that Tim is supposed to have, let Tim be talking to him, not his secretary, this very minute, in Jesus name, Amen!" Lori prayed.

Tim made the call. Mr. Freedman answered. After he heard a little of Tim's case, he said, "I want you to be here in my office at ten o'clock in the morning."

"Tomorrow is Saturday. I didn't figure you would be open on Saturday," Tim said.

"We are closed on Saturdays," Mr. Freedman answered. "That's why I can spend a lot of time with you and hear your whole story tomorrow," the attorney explained.

"What do you charge?" Tim asked.

"Eight thousand dollars, if the case is not extra drawn out," Mr. Freedman answered.

"That's awfully high?" Tim exclaimed.

"How much is forty years of your life worth?" Mr. Freedman asked.

"I see what you mean," Tim said, nodding his head.

"You must bring me at least seven hundred, and fifty, dollars with you tomorrow as a down payment for me to get started on your case," Mr. Freedman ordered.

"Okay, we'll see you tomorrow," Tim answered.

Now, Lori knew why Arthur had given her the two hundred and fifty dollars. It would be enough money for the expense of the three hundred mile trip. "Tim, how are we going to get the $750 by tomorrow morning?" Lori asked.

"I was saving a small government deficiency check to pay some bills, and buy feed for the cattle. We'll just have to use it to pay Mr. Freedman. I don't know where we'll get the rest, later," Tim answered.

"Well, I don't have any doubts that Mr. Freedman is the lawyer we're supposed to have," Lori said.

"Me, neither," Tim replied. He went to the buffet cabinet in the dining room and took the check from its hiding place. "Somehow, things will work out, Lori," he said. Tim was trying to convince himself as much as encouraging Lori.

"It doesn't seem like things can get much worse," Lori said with a sigh.

It took six hours to drive to the state capital. Tim and Lori left two hours before sunup. Mr. Freedman's office was downtown, next to the state capital, and judicial buildings.

They were early when Tim started knocking on the door of the old two-story building. It took several times of knocking, and fifteen minutes, before a young man answered the door. He invited Tim and Lori in and introduced himself. "I'm Ted Smith, Mr. Freedman's assistant," the young man said.

The building looked old on the outside, but the inside had been completely remodeled. The old oak woodwork had been refinished and polished. The interior was decorated with thick Oriental carpets, partly covering the hard wood floors, and expensive Early American furniture. The drapes were made of a satin maroon-colored fabric. The furniture and drapes were the most beautiful Lori had ever seen. The interior of the building was a quiet, drastic change from the noisy, polluted streets outside. It was almost like stepping from one world into another.

The reception room was huge. It had a large reception island where an attractive secretary was sitting behind a large oak desk.

Mr. Smith spoke with the secretary, and the slender brunette led them up a winding stairway to the second floor of the building. Tim and Lori were ushered into a plush office. The large office had several large lounge chairs around a large executive desk.

"Mr. Freedman, this is Tim Jones, and his wife, Lori," the secretary said. She left the office and quickly descended the carpet covered stairs.

"Please sit down," Mr. Freedman said as he continued to study some papers on his desk.

Mr. Freedman was a small, Jewish-looking man. He looked like he could be in his late fifties, although he was in good physical condition. Mr. Freedman was about ready to speak when the telephone rang. He turned around in his large swivel chair and started talking to another client.

Tim and Lori felt like intruders. They could not help hearing Mr. Freedman's side of the conversation, even though he had his back turned toward them.

After several minutes of conversation, Mr. Freedman hung up the telephone. He turned around and looked at Tim and Lori. Mr. Freedman leaned over the desk to shake hands with his new clients. "Well, now, tell me Mr. Jones, are you guilty of the felony charges brought against you or not?" the attorney asked.

"No, I'm not guilty!" Tim exclaimed.

"That doesn't matter. The important thing is that you be perfectly honest with me on everything," Mr. Freedman said. "Don't hold back any information."

Lori was shocked. <u>What does he mean that it doesn't matter if Tim is guilty or not?</u> she wondered.

Tim and Lori talked to Mr. Freedman for two hours. Tim did most of the talking, with Lori adding a detail now and then. Mr. Freedman stopped Tim several times to ask specific questions.

"I'm worried over Tim's confession, that I know can't be true," Lori said.

"Why didn't you call me before you signed anything?" the attorney asked Tim.

"Because I thought only guilty people needed lawyers, and our cash flow is depleted right now," Tim answered.

"You did bring me $750 today, didn't you?" Mr. Freedman asked.

Tim showed the attorney the government check. "That's all I have right now," he explained. "We stopped by a drive-in bank when we got here, but they wouldn't cash it for us because today is Saturday," Tim said.

"You can cash it somewhere tomorrow and pay me before you leave town," the attorney ordered.

"What worries me is that our sheriff told me that he has the power to have me put in prison for forty years," Tim said.

"Don't worry about that. It's the DA and the judge that have the power from now on. Your sheriff's duty in this case is over," Mr. Freedman said, trying to assure Tim.

"He said that he has the power with the judge and DA to get about anything done that he wants to do," Tim argued.

"He can't have, so don't worry about it. Leave the worrying to me. That's what you're paying me for," Mr. Freedman said with a smile.

"I think we were 'set-up' the last time Rosita came to stay with us," Lori said. "If that's true, all someone would have to do now, is to wait until I'm in school, and send a young girl out to the farm. She could come back to town crying and saying that Tim tried to sexually molest her. It would just be his word against hers and who would believe Tim now? He would be arrested again," Lori tried to explain.

"Lori, it's your duty to see that no young girls are even around your place. Tim, if any come to your door, don't even answer the door. Don't take any chances until all this is over," Mr. Freedman ordered. "Stay away from that area as much as possible."

"That will be hard to do until we get rid of our farming and ranching responsibilities, and I get through teaching this year of school," Lori said.

"Be gone as much as you can," Mr. Freedman said again.

"I want you to go downstairs to my assistant's office and tell him your story. He will tape it for us to study," Mr. Freedman said.

"Can you do anything to keep my arrest from being put in the county paper?" Tim asked.

"I think so. I'll try anyway," Freedman answered. He pushed a small button on his desk and the young secretary returned.

"Follow me," the secretary said. She led them down the curving stairs, and into a smaller office where Mr. Smith was waiting for them at a large desk.

Tim and Lori spent the rest of the day with Mr. Smith. He taped their story and offered words of sympathy. "You guys have really been shafted to get into this much trouble just for trying to help that poor family?" he exclaimed. "It looks like a pretty good case to fight," he said. Tim and Lori felt like there might be some hope for them when they finally left the lawyer's office that Saturday evening.

For the first time since the trouble started, Lori was hungry. She and Tim celebrated over a patty-melt hamburger and went to bed early.

Tim could not cash the check until Monday. There was no way Lori could get home to teach school. She had to call Mr. Wilson again, and miss another day of school.

"I understand," Mr. Wilson said, again.

"I have so many sick days accumulated from years of teaching that I'll never use, I just hope the school will let me use some of them instead of docking my salary $98 a day for these three days that I've missed," Lori told Tim.

"I'm sure they will, since you have gone years without missing hardly any work," Tim replied, trying to sound cheerful.

Tim paid Mr. Freedman early Monday morning and received more words of encouragement. It was late when they drove into the dirt driveway of the farm.

"Lord, please help us through this terrible situation," Lori prayed as she snuggled up to Tim's warm back, and tried to go to sleep.

Lori tried to hold her head high and look happy when she went to school Tuesday morning. No one wanted to talk to her, or even speak to her. "It's just my imagination," Lori kept telling herself. The students were good, as usual, and Lori was happy as long as she was in her classroom. Lori avoided going into the teacher's room when anyone else was there. She avoided the other adults in the building as much as possible.

When Lori came in from school Thursday evening, Tim was sitting at the kitchen table. He had the county paper in his hand. Tim was extra pale. Without saying a word, Tim handed the paper to Lori.

"Where is it?" Lori asked.

"Right on the front page," Tim said.

Lori dropped down in a chair when she read the dreaded words, "Tim Jones was arrested last Wednesday on charges of child molesting. His bail has been set for $5,000."

As Lori read the article again, she noticed how easy it was to read it without seeing the words "on charges of". How many times have I read something like this about someone else and thought they were already guilty? Lori wondered. How many people have I judged to be guilty that were really innocent?"

Lori patted Tim's large arm. She could not think of anything to say.

"Everyone will think I'm guilty when they read this," Tim said looking down at the table. "Everyone in the county reads the county paper, too," he added.

"Our friends will know you are innocent," Lori said.

"Most of the people in this county don't really know me, and most of them believe everything they read," Tim said.

"Mr. Freedman will have to get the trial moved to another county, now. I won't have a chance in this one," Tim said with a sigh. He jumped up from the table and went into the bedroom to call his attorney.

The secretary answered. "Mr. Freedman is not here, but I can let you talk to Mr. Smith," she said. Tim felt his legs getting weak as he heard Mr. Smith say, "I'm sorry Tim, but the court has refused to let the trial be moved to another county."

"What chance do I have now?" Tim asked.

"I don't think you have anything to worry about, Tim. You still have the best attorney in the state," Mr. Smith said. "Did you see the headlines in the national newspapers today, where Mr. Freedman won another difficult case?" he asked.

"No, I didn't, but thanks for your vote of confidence, anyway," Tim said before he hung up.

Once again, Tim and Lori feared for Tim's life. They prayed and tried to make themselves believe that Tim would be found innocent, but the situation looked scary.

Lori went to school Friday morning. She heard a lot of teachers talking in the teacher's work room. Lori took a chance and walked in. Everyone stopped talking. The room was terribly quiet. Everyone looked at her in a strange way, as they left the room to go to their classes.

"It's just my imagination," Lori told herself again. Down deep inside, she was thinking, <u>What if they really do think that Tim is guilty, and that I had a part in it</u>. The very thought made her want to run and never stop, but she tried to act natural and went on to her first class.

During the second period, one of the teachers came to Lori's door. She motioned for Lori to step out into the hall. Lori told one of the students to read a page aloud from the textbook. "Listen carefully, because I will ask questions on it when I return," she said.

Lori joined her friend in the hall. <u>It will help to talk to someone</u>, she was thinking.

"Lori, you're still young you need to go somewhere else and get a fresh start. People will understand if you marry again, someday," Lori's Catholic friend said.

"Tim is innocent," Lori said. "He has just had some people that are out to destroy him. We're just praying God's blessing upon them, because that's what the Bible tells us to do," she explained.

"You can't do that!" the friend exclaimed. She looked at Lori with a puzzled look before walking away.

Lori felt alone the remainder of the day. She stopped by the mail box on her way into the house that evening. As she went through the usual amount of bills, she stopped. There was a letter from one of the teachers she had just seen that day.

Lori opened the envelope. It was a sympathy card. The card read as though Tim was <u>dead</u>. "All my friends think Tim is guilty, and they are expecting me to leave him," Lori whispered to herself. Lori plopped down in the large chair in the bedroom and rocked for awhile. She felt confused, hurt, and embarrassed for Tim, herself, and her family.

Tim and Lori stayed to themselves that weekend. They didn't even venture to church.

On Monday, Lori went straight to her room without even going past the teacher's room. She sat down at her desk to look over the day's plans. On top of her lesson-plan book was a book she had never seen before.

Lori picked up the small book and read the title, "What to do When the Situation Seems to be Impossible," by Kenneth Haggen". The inside cover had been signed by the superintendent's wife. With the signature was a note that read, "The Lord told me to give this to you this morning. Love and Prayers, Pat . . ."

Lori read part of the book at noon while she stayed in her classroom to be alone. In the middle of the afternoon, Lori looked up from her work to see another friend standing at her classroom door. Her friend motioned to her. The students were working on their reading workbooks, so Lori quietly slipped out of the room.

Lori had known Lupe for a long time. She was Spanish, and one of the cleanest people she had ever known. Lupe had cleaned Lori's house for many years before Lori and Holllis were divorced. Lupe and her family had lived next door to Tim and his first family.

Lori stepped into the hall and Lupe threw her arms around her and started to cry. "I know it isn't true, Lori. Tim wouldn't do anything like that," she sobbed. If I can do anything to help, please let me know," she said.

"Just pray for us. Pray that everyone will soon know the truth about Tim the way we do," Lori replied.

"I've already been praying, but let me know if there's anything else I can do," Lupe said, patting Lori's hand.

"Thanks. This is the time that friends like you mean so much," Lori said.

The next day Lori felt weak as she got ready for school. The ride on the bus made her stomach upset. When her planning period came, she didn't know if she felt well enough to finish the school day or not. After Lori dismissed her Social Studies class to go to PE, she went to see the school librarian. "Gina, I feel so tired and sick today. Would you please pray for me?" Lori asked.

Gina gently took Lori's hand and led her into the room at the back of the library. It was the room where the audiovisual equipment was stored. Gina closed the door and took both of Lori's hands and prayed, "Oh, Heavenly Father, give Lori the strength she needs, and help Tim in this time of tribulation, in Jesus name, Amen."

"Thanks Gina. I feel better already," Lori said.

Lori started to leave when Gina said, "Lori, you have lived through other terrible experiences in this community and learned to hold your head high. I know God will help you to do it again."

Lori nodded her head to agree. She felt much better and even went into the teacher's room for a cup of coffee.

There were three teachers in the workroom when Lori walked in. They stopped talking when they saw her. Two of the teachers said they had to get back to work and left the room. The other teacher started grading papers without even speaking to Lori.

"I'm just imagining things," Lori told herself again. Vera Lee came to school to teach her afternoon classes. She was just as friendly as ever, and she made Lori feel a little more at ease.

It's ridiculous to let what people think bother me so much, Lori was thinking as she went to her first afternoon class.

Tim called just before bus time. "Lori, I called Violet today to see if she had time to fix your hair at her shop this evening. She said for you to walk down there after school. I'll pick you up about five," Tim said. "I thought it might make you feel better to have your hair styled, and visit with Violet for awhile," he added.

"That sounds great. See you at five," Lori replied.

There was no one else in the shop. Violet started on Lori's hair right away. The head massage felt great, and the coconut aroma of the shampoo was refreshing. "How are you doing?" Violet asked. She sounded concerned.

"Fine, I guess," Lori answered.

"Lori, I've received a lot of phone calls this week. People are asking me whether I think Tim is guilty or not," Violet explained. "I'm concerned."

"Maybe some people still think he's innocent," Lori replied.

"The trouble is that so many people don't know Tim as well as we do, Lori, and most people think that he's guilty," Violet said. "I just thought you ought to know,."

I wonder if most of them think I knew about it and that I'm guilty too? Lori was thinking.

When Tim came to town that evening, it seemed like everyone avoided him. They only spoke to him when they had to in the stores. He felt very uncomfortable, and was anxious to get back to the farm. He and Lori went straight home after Lori's hair was finished.

When Lori came home a few days later, Tim was sitting at the kitchen table with his hands over his face. He heard her come in and handed her an envelope.

The letter was from Mr. Freedman's office. Lori pulled out the contents and read, "I'm sending you a copy of your daughter's confession. I thought it might help you to know what she said."

Lori looked at the handwritten letter. Sally's writing had not changed much since Sally had been in Lori's sixth grade.

The letter said, "Tim Jones, who is not my real dad, but my adopted dad, started getting into bed with me when I was about twelve years old. He tried to have sex with me. I would scream and scream. My mother never knew anything about it until I told her and my boyfriend when I was sixteen. At that time my boyfriend wanted to kill him and called him a S.O.B."

"Tim, how can anyone take this statement serious?" Lori asked. "You and your family lived in a cheap three bedroom mobile home with paper thin walls. Your ex-wife isn't deaf. How could Sally have screamed and screamed, and her mother never heard or knew?" Lori asked.

Tim was lying over the table with his hands still over his face. He didn't answer.

"I can't believe a confession like this could be used in court. It looks like Sally would have at least mentioned all the rodeo trips you two took together alone. It would have made a little better story," Lori said.

"The sheriff and his department believe the statement, and they are going to try to use it as evidence in court," Tim explained.

"One of your old neighbors told me that Sally wanted to be you all the time whether anyone else was around or not. She said that Sally didn't show any signs of being afraid of you, and after all, she did go with you to all those sheriff posse queen shows.

One of my friends was teaching at the high-school the very day Sally, and the rest of the kids, checked out. She said she asked Sally about all of you moving so suddenly. My friend said that Sally cried and told her that they were leaving you," Lori said, "It doesn't sound like she was afraid of you, or even hated you, the day they left."

"Yes, but Lori, I tried to come between Sally and Philip. She said she would never forgive me for that, and that she would get even with me," Tim explained. "I wish I had it all to do over again. I'd be a little more understanding."

"Sometimes I wish I could raise my boys all over again," Lori said. "I'd sure enjoy them more the second time around, and I'm sure I'd be a lot better mother now. But we never get a second chance," she said.

"Tim, do you remember when you got your divorce, and your ex-wife tried to accuse you of something like this? The story was so mixed up that the judge didn't even take it seriously. If I remember the story right, you were supposed to have tried to bother Sally, and a few months later, she was supposed to be afraid of you, or something like that," Lori said, trying to remember back a few years, "I do remember the one time your Ex came to your house. We were grilling some meat out doors. She came right up to me and told me it was a good thing that I had boys instead of girls because girls wouldn't be safe around you."

"Your Ex was angry and talking loudly. She said she had a hard time convincing your oldest son that you had tried to molest Sally. Then she turned right around and said that your oldest son had a hard time convincing her you had tried to molest Sally.

It sounded so mixed up that I never took it too seriously. I just thought she was angry because I was there, and I didn't feel like arguing with her," Lori explained.

"You shouldn't have been embarrassed, Lori," Tim said. "We didn't even know each other until quite awhile after they all left, and I needed someone to talk to."

"I also told your twins, the first time they came to visit you, that if they thought there was any chance of you and your ex getting back together, that I would walk out of your life right then," Lori said. "They told me there was no way you guys would ever get back together."

"Tim, I love you, and it would be devastating to do without you for forty years," Lori said.

Tim took Lori in his arms and said, "Everything will be okay. My Ex has used everything she could to turn my kids against me because she knows that's the only way she can hurt me." Tim held Lori in his arms for several minutes. "Would you like to go with me to check the cattle?" he asked.

"I think it would feel good to get outside for awhile," Lori answered. She put on her coat and followed Tim to the pickup.

The next day Lori picked up her check from her school mailbox located close to the superintendent's office. She took it to her room before she opened it. She wanted to look at it before the students came in from their noon recess. Lori moaned as she looked at the amount. Instead of using any of her accumulated sick leave days, the district had deducted $98 for each of the four days she had missed school. Two of the four days, Lori <u>had</u> been too sick to teach.

Each teacher was allowed eight sick days each year. Lori had taught in the district for almost fifteen years, and had never missed more than three days in one year. When a teacher accumulated more than forty days, the district bought the days back for $24 a day. At a time like, it seemed so unfair.

<u>I guess they are just following rules, and I'm not going to lie about being sick when I'm not, no matter what happens</u>, Lori thought.

"With my check almost $400 short, how are we going to pay the utilities, and buy groceries?" Lori asked herself. She could feel more fear swelling up inside her.

After school that evening, Tim sent Lori to one pasture to check the cattle, while he checked a pasture in the opposite direction.

On her way back, Lori stopped to visit Lena, a Christian friend. Lena and her husband had just remodeled an old farm house. It was now a lovely home. The yard was beautiful with flowers planted around the large trees.

Lori visited with Lena while Lena folded clothes in her lovely laundry room. Lena had not heard about Tim's arrest. Lori told her friend about all that had happened to them. "I can't understand why Tim's family is still trying to destroy him," Lori said.

"Lori, if Tim has to go to prison and you <u>would</u> happen to leave this area, what would happen to your farm?" Lena asked.

"I don't know. It would probably go to our creditors," Lori answered.

"Maybe, just maybe, Tim's family thinks that if you guys were out of the way, they would get the farm," Lena said.

"I never thought of that?" Lori exclaimed. "I just keep thinking that there is a point in time when people stop hating and hurting each other. It took me a long time to heal from my divorce."

The women prayed together, and Lori hurried home to fix Tim's supper.

Late one night the telephone rang. It was Deputy John. "Tim, as bad as I hate to help you, I <u>did</u> promise you I'd call you and let you know when you're supposed to show up in court again. You're scheduled to appear before the judge at ten in the morning," Deputy John said.

"There must be some mistake!" Tim exclaimed. "My attorney called me and told me that he had made arrangements for the hearing to be postponed until next week because he's too busy to come tomorrow," Tim tried to explain. "I'm sure my attorney hasn't made arrangement to be there tomorrow."

"That's your problem," Deputy John said, and hung up.

Tim immediately called the county clerk's house. The deputy was right. "I have to appear before the judge in the morning to plead guilty or not guilty," Tim told Lori. "If Deputy John hadn't called me, your mother would have lost her $5000."

Tim called Mr. Freedman at his residence. "I know it's terribly late, but I have to appear in court tomorrow morning," Tim explained. "Are you planning on being here?" he asked.

"There is no way I can be there," Mr. Freedman said. I asked that DA to postpone the hearing until Tuesday of next week because I'm wrapping up another case this week. You would not have caught me at home after tonight!" the attorney exclaimed. "The DA promised me that he would take care of it, and that's why I haven't thought any more about it. I should have known better than to trust a DA that is also an acting attorney in the same area. That's not legal either!" Mr. Freedman shouted. "I'm used to attorneys keeping their word." "I'm sorry Tim.

It's not your fault, but there's no way I can be there, or even send my assistant by tomorrow morning. You're just too far away."

"You'll have to appear before the judge alone tomorrow, Tim. All you have to do is just plead not guilty," Mr. Freedman said. "This is turning out to be much more of a case than I thought it would be. When I first heard your story, I didn't think it was serious enough to even make it to a jury trial. With this many foul-ups, it won't be as easy as I thought," the attorney said. He sounded concerned.

"You mean we <u>could</u> lose?" Tim asked.

"There's still a good chance to settle out of court, so don't worry," Freedman said,

Lori wanted to go with Tim, but she could not afford to loose another $98 by missing another day of school. Tim went alone. He visited with some neighbors, who seemed friendly, while they were waiting to be called before the judge. The neighbors were having trouble collecting rent and regaining possession of a house they owned in town.

Tim tried to act calm when his name was called, but all he could think of was what it would be like to be locked up for forty years.

A man read the number of the case and handed the judge a stack of papers. The judge was a small, older man that had an air of confidence.

It took the judge several minutes to look over the papers, before he looked up at Tim over glasses that had slid down his nose. After looking straight at Tim a few minutes, the judge looked at the papers again.

Tim had the feeling that the judge was reading Rosita's statement over again.

Looking back at Tim, the judge said, "Three charges of felony? There's no evidence of any kind of force put on the girl." "Why are the charges so high?" he asked.

"That's the way the sheriff wanted it, Your Honor," Tim answered.

"How do you plead?" the judge asked, looking Tim straight in the one eye looking in his direction.

"Not guilty Your Honor," Tim answered. "I'm not guilty of anything except flipping her on the seat a few times, Your Honor," he said.

"You can go to prison for doing that, if the minor brings charges against you," the judge commented.

"I didn't know that, Your Honor," Tim replied.

"Since there is no sign of force, I'm going to reduce the charges two degrees to match the said crime," the judge announced.

"What does that mean, Your Honor?" Tim asked.

"To put it in layman's terms, it means that you can't be sentenced to more than four years in prison instead of forty years," the judge explained.

"Thank you, Your Honor," Tim said.

"I'll see you here one month from today," the judge said. "Next case, please," he ordered.

"Pardon me, Your Honor, but how much of a chance does this case have of reaching a full jury trial?" Tim asked.

"All the DA has to prove is that there was a possibility that it could have happened. In your case, you have no witnesses. It's just your word against the girl's, so it'll go to court, at least to a preliminary hearing," the judge explained.

"Does this mean, Your Honor, that anytime a man is alone with a girl under age, possibility can be proven, and he can be charged with anything, if the girl wants to bring charges?" Tim asked.

"That's right," the judge said. "Next case," he called again.

Tim felt both relieved, and perplexed. Was there no protection for a man's word against a bitter child's? Has the law, in trying to protect children, given too much authority to the kids? Tim wondered.

Tim was on the front page of the county paper again. It read, "Tim Jones appeared before the judge this week on charges of child molesting." Most of the people reading the paper would be convinced that he was guilty now. "What chance do I have before a jury in this county?" Tim asked himself again.

Tim started to use the telephone on Friday. The country telephones were still party lines. Someone was on the line, so Tim started to hang up the phone when he heard one of the neighbors say, ". . . and isn't it just awful that Tim Jones has hurt some little kid."

Lori found Tim staring at the newspaper when she came in from school. He was depressed, and frightened. "Let's go visit Violet and Charles tonight, and try to get our minds on something else for awhile," Lori suggested.

The four adults were sitting around the kitchen table discussing Tim's situation. "If only Rita hadn't insisted that Tim be arrested," Lori was saying.

"That's too bad, considering what you did for her husband," Violet said.

"What do you mean?" Lori asked.

"I guess you've forgotten, Lori, but remember about two and half years ago. The old sheriff called you at school one day. He asked you how well you knew Rita and Ted, and . . . ." Violet said.

"That right. I told him I thought I knew them pretty well because Rita and I had gone to college together. He asked if I would go out and check on her because she had just called the police department and wanted Ted arrested for beating her up. Sheriff Bob said that if anyone from his department went out there, Ted would have a criminal record, and he didn't think it was really that serious.

I went out there right after school, because Tim had asked me to go to Huntington to pick up a grain check at one of the elevators there. Rita's farm was right on the way. I talked Rita into going to Huntington with me.

Rita's legs were badly bruised. Before we got back to her place, I told her that the sheriff had called me. Rita said that she had decided not to have Ted arrested, or to leave him, because Pete needed his grandfather.

I told her I admired her for staying with him, and thinking about her grandson before she thought of herself. I suggested to her that the next time Ted started to hit her, for her to say, 'in the name of Jesus, you can't hit me'.

I don't know whether she ever tried that or not, but they seem to be getting along these last two years," Lori said, finishing her story. "I had forgotten all about it."

"You kept her husband from having a criminal record, and just because you were trying to help those poor kids, she has caused Tim to have a criminal record," Violet said.

"It's funny that you reminded me about that. Outside of Tim, I think you are the only one I ever told that story to. I didn't want it to be something that people could gossip about," Lori said.

"You just called me to pray for you while you went out there," Violet said.

"Speaking of a criminal record, when they arrested me, they took a mug shot of me, and then they asked me if I wanted one for a souvenir," Tim said.

""You've got to be kidding," Lori, Violet, and Charles said all at once.

CHAPTER XIX

TIM'S ARREST

Tim and Lori were getting ready for bed late Thursday night when the telephone rang. Tim was apprehensive as he picked up the receiver. It seemed like every call turned out to be bad news.

"I just want you to know, son, they brought your father back to the Nursing Home from the hospital yesterday. The nurses think he's doing fine, but he will probably die tonight," Sarah said. "He told me good-bye when I left the Home this evening. We both knew it was our last good-bye," she explained. "He could last a couple of days, but I don't think I will ever see him alive again,"

"How can you be so sure when the doctor and nurses think he is getting better?" Tim asked.

"I just know," Sarah replied.

"Do you need for us to come over to be with you tonight?" Tim asked.

"No, I'll be okay, but be prepared for the call," Sarah said, with a tired sigh.

Sarah went right to bed. She was tired and was soon asleep. At 4 a.m., she was awakened by someone pounding on the front door of her mobile home. She reached for the lamp and found the knob.

Sarah waited for her eyes to adjust to the bright light before she found her glasses. Her body was too tired to look for her robe. She answered the door with only her night gown on. Sarah recognized the white uniform, and the face, of one of the lady workers from the Nursing Home.

"Get your clothes on, dear. You're needed at the Home," the lady said, gently.

Without asking any questions, Sarah dressed and followed her friend out to the lady's car. They drove the short distance over to the familiar large building. The lady took Sarah's arm and led her to Daddy Andy's room.

Sarah looked at her husband of sixty-eight years. He looked peaceful, and small, lying on the white bed sheets. She could remember when he weighed over 300 pounds. Now he weighed less than a hundred.

Sarah did not cry. She squeezed the hand that now felt like cold stone. "Nurse, I want him left here like this until my son and his wife get here," Sarah said.

"Do they live close to the Home?" the nurse asked.

"No, they will have to come sixty-five miles to get here," Sarah answered. "What time did he die?" she asked.

"We aren't sure. The nurse on duty checked on him about 1:30 this morning. He seemed to be sleeping. When she came back later, he was already gone," the nurse explained. "If you think you will be all right, give me your son's telephone number, and I'll call him for you," the nurse said.

Sarah handed the nurse and small piece of paper she had tucked in the billfold of her purse. The nurse walked to the Nurses station to call Tim and Lori.

Sarah moved a chair close to the bed and sit up close to Daddy Andy's body. She begain to softly pat the cold, stiff hands.

A few minutes later, a tall, slender man came in. "Excuse me, mam, I'm here from the funeral home. I've come to pick up this body," the man said.

"I want him left here until my son and his wife gets here," Sarah requested again.

"The sooner we take care of him, the better he will look," He explained. "We only have a certain amount of time to move him out of the Nursing Home, but I'll leave him here as long as I can," he said. The man left the room to talk to a doctor in the hall.

The nurse returned. She stood at the back of the room and watched Sarah pat Daddy Andy's hands. "I've called your son. They will be here as soon as possible," the nurse said.

The tall man returned thirty minutes later. "I'm sorry, mam, but the time is up. I must take him now," he said.

"If that's what you have to do, then do it," Sarah said. She watched Daddy Andy's face as it was covered with a white sheet, and his body put onto a stretcher.

Sarah was suddenly aware that three of her friends were standing beside her. They were leading her from the room, when the nurse said, "Be sure she drinks plenty of water to keep her from becoming dehydrated because of stress."

Tim shook Lori. As soon as Lori opened her eyes, Tim whispered, "Daddy Andy is dead."

Lori got up and helped Tim call his brother, sister, and some other relatives. She had to call Mr. Wilson to tell him she would be missing more school. "Hopefully, I'll be back in school on Monday," Lori said.

Two hours after they had received the death call, Tim and Lori entered the Nursing Home.

The arrangements for the body took a lot of legal papers and expense. The body was transported to another state for the funeral, then to Texas for burial. Tim and Lori picked out a nice casket and some flowers. They tried to keep the expenses down.

Twenty-five relatives arrived two days before the funeral. Lori would have had a difficult time feeding everyone, but relatives, friends, and neighbors brought in a lot of food. She was doing all the cooking and dish washing to give the rest of the family a chance to visit during their rare time together.

"Who is writing the obituary?" Lori asked Tim's sister the day before the funeral.

"We thought that you would do a good job on it," Ann answered.

"I haven't been in the family very long. I probably know less to write about Daddy Andy than anyone else," Lori replied.

"We still want you to write it. If you need any information, you can ask any of us for it," Ann explained.

Between cooking, serving, and dishes, Lori started writing the history of a man she had dearly loved. Aunt Martha and Elizabeth had written obituaries before. They came to the farm to help Lori write the obituary and to help with some of the other work. With their help, they put together Daddy Andy's history in a way that was satisfactory to Lori and the family.

Lori had a feeling deep inside her to write a poem in honor of the father-in-law she had only known for three years. She titled it, "The Big, Big Man in the Overalls".

The poem told how this big man had loved people, especially children. Lori told of how he had finally made Jesus the Lord of his life when he was eighty-three years old. The poem said that Daddy Andy no longer had a body that was paralyzed on one side, and no longer had some fingers missing from a gasoline fire many years ago, but "He had a new body given to him by God. Now he could talk, walk, and sing again."

Everyone loved the poem and wanted a copy of it.

Elizabeth and Aunt Martha were bringing in more food. Elizabeth called Lori into the bathroom just before they left. "How are things going for you, financially?" she asked.

"Okay," Lori whispered.

"Here's fifty dollars anyway, to help on groceries or in any other place you might need it," Elizabeth said. She placed the cash in Lori's hand.

"Thanks, mother. I don't know what Tim and I would do without you and Arthur," Lori said, trying not to cry. She felt so ashamed to always be needing money.

On the day of the funeral, Tim and Lori went to the church early to check on the arrangements. Lena and her husband were scheduled to sing for the funeral. They both had terrible colds. "I don't think we can sing more than one song, and I'm not sure we can do a good job with that. We don't know what to do," Lena told Lori.

"Daddy Andy loved your music," the Lord seemed to say to Lori. "Daddy Andy would be happy if you would sing two of his favorites," Lori felt down deep in her heart.

Lori felt embarrassed to offer her help, but everyone else thought it was a great idea.

It was hard for Lori to sing instead of cry. She sat down at the church piano and played and sung two of Daddy Andy's favorite songs. There was a mirror on top of the piano placed in a position where Lori could see the crowd without turning around and facing them. She almost forgot the words of the second song when she looked out over the crowd and saw Timmy and Tommy, and the rest of Tim's first family.

Timmy and Tommy had changed from being boys to young men. Lori hardly recognized them.

Lori finished her song and played softly for the crowd to file out of the beautiful new church. She found Tim standing beside the hearse all alone. "Where's the rest of the family?" Lori asked.

"Over there," Tim answered. He pointed across the street. "I told my family to go over there and talk to my kids while they have a chance," Tim explained.

"And, here you are, standing all alone beside the casket. It's too bad they couldn't visit Daddy Andy while he was alive," Lori said. She felt angry over the situation.

"It's not my kid's fault," Tim replied.

Lori and Tim climbed into the rose-colored Cadillac, and started down the street to pick up Sarah and Daddy Andy's sister. The hearse was ready to start the two-hundred mile journey to Texas for the burial. It was waiting for the cars of the family to line up behind it.

Sarah was standing at the side of the road talking to Sally. Sally looked up and saw Tim. She screamed and ran across the street and stood close to her husband,.

Lori could see the hurt on Tim's face, but he didn't say anything. Sarah waved good-bye to Tim's first family and crawled into the car with

Aunt Mary. The large procession started their slow journey to the Texas cemetery. Tim looked back to see his kids for the last time.

The funeral and burial were soon over. All the relatives had gone home. Sarah went back east to live with Ann. Tim and Lori were expecting some of the relatives to help with the tremendous expenses. Everyone else had more money than they did. Elizabeth's fifty dollars was the only help Tim and Lori received.

Daddy Andy had not had any life insurance. At the time Tim and Lori were wondering how they were going to buy groceries, pay utility bills, feed cattle and farm, and pay court costs, they were left with a $3,500 funeral bill.

Tim and Lori were still staying away from people as much as possible. They even stayed home Thanksgiving Day. Tim had to appear in court every month, and the hearing was set on a day in March. Mr. Freedman, or his assistant, was always present to go before the judge with Tim, after the first appearing.

In an effort to get away, Lori and Tim decided to be gone for Christmas. Tim had been talking to eye specialists at Oral Robert's University in Tulsa, Oklahoma. The doctors thought they could operate on Tim's eyes and bring them together. This would help his appearance, and maybe his sight. Lori's school insurance would cover most of the cost of the surgeries.

"If I can get my eyes straightened, and some implanted lenses where I don't have to wear these thick glasses, I know it'll help me get a better job. I will have more than just tunnel vision too. My appearance has not been so important working with cattle and on a tractor, but when we leave the farm, my appearance will bother some people. I need to have this done before I look for another line of work," Tim said.

The day school was out for Christmas vacation, and Lori received her teaching check, she and Tim left for the City of Faith in Tulsa. They were excited about something, for a change.

The weather was warm and rainy when they entered southern Oklahoma. It felt good to be able to relax away from the terrible problems at home. Lori and Tim walked, arm in arm, across the lawns toward the beautiful City of Faith's hospital.

The damp air smelled refreshing. It had been a long time since Lori had felt so relaxed. She squeezed Tim's arm. <u>At last Tim is going to have his eyes fixed so that he will look like other people</u>, Lori thought. <u>I wonder what he'll look like without his thick glasses</u>, she was thinking.

Tim was thinking the same thing. He was excited, anxious, and afraid. He remembered how his eyes-balls had hurt with stitches when they were operated on the first time.

The hospital was still under construction. The finished part of it was beautiful. Tim and Lori had to ask directions three times before they found the right office on the fifth floor. They sit down in an opened-ended, unfinished reception room to wait to see a doctor.

Soon, a young surgeon, dressed in white, was examining Tim's eyes. He put drops in Tim's eyes to dilate them, and examined them again.

Tim and Lori waited for the surgeon to put his information together.

"When I talked to you on the telephone a few days ago, I thought we could probably do something with your eyes through surgery," the surgeon said. "Your eyes are turned out worse than any I've ever seen. They have been that way for so long, that if we straighten them out, even perfectly according to our instruments, your brain could not adjust to such a tremendous change. You would see double. I don't think we should do surgery on your eyes," the doctor explained.

"What about the implanted lenses?" Tim asked. He was still hanging onto the last ray of hope.

"Your eyes have been so damaged by your former surgeries, that they are not round enough to take implants," the young doctor tried to explain. "It would cause infection that would cause you to loose what sight you have left. You <u>do know</u> that the surgeries have caused deterioration in your eyes and that you are gradually going to be blind, anyway," the surgeon explained. He sounded sympathetic.

Tim nodded his head that he knew he was eventually going to be blind. He was so disappointed that he could hardly talk. "Doctor, what can I do?" he asked.

"There is nothing humanly possible we can do. I guess the way you are now is better than being blind at this time," the doctor answered. "Are you folks Christians?" he asked.

"Yes, and I've seen a lot of people healed, but when Oral prayed for my eyes a couple of years ago, they weren't healed. Since that time I just haven't been able to believe for the healing of my eyes," Tim explained.

"Believing for your sight is the hardest thing to believe for," the doctor replied. "You can act like you're healed until you are healed from a lot of sicknesses. When it comes to your eyes, you can't pretend you can see when you can't see," he explained.

"What I would like to do is pray with you that you'll be able to believe for a <u>creative miracle of brand new eyes</u>. That's the only thing that will take care of your problem. The eyes you now have are beyond repair," the young doctor explained. "If God created everything, like we know he did, try to believe that He can create another tiny set of eyes for you,".

The doctor laid his surgical hands on Tim's head and prayed for the creative miracle. He also prayed for any other problems that the Joneses might have.

<u>If he only knew how many things that he is praying for right now, but God knows and that's what is important</u>, Lori was thinking.

Tim felt defeated again as he walked to the car with Lori. His eyes were so dilated, he could not see. Lori had to help him out of the building, and to the car. He felt like he was already blind as they climbed into the car. The fresh rain did not smell as refreshing now.

"I thought I would be in the hospital most of the week, and we wouldn't have to go home. I'm not ready to go home," Tim said. "Lori, what would you like to do," he asked.

"Whatever you want to do," Lori answered.

Tim thought for awhile. "I have Lonny taking care of the cattle until we get back," Tim said. "What do you think about going to Illinois to see mom, and Ann and her family.?" he asked.

"Do we have enough money to go that far?" Lori asked.

"Well, we were planning on expenses for you staying in a motel this week while I was supposed to be in the hospital. There won't be any expenses while we are at Ann's" Tim replied. "It shouldn't cost any more than what he had figured on to stay here in Tulsa. If we're careful, I think we could manage to get to Illinois and home before our money runs out," he explained.

"Let's find a motel room and call Ann," Lori replied.

"We can't possibly be there before Christmas Eve, but that's better than going home," Tim said.

They found a cheap room and called Ann. "We'll wait to open our gifts until you get here. See you tomorrow," Ann said.

Tim and Lori were ready to leave for Illinois early the next morning.

"Tim, I hate to go there for Christmas because we don't have any money to buy your family any Christmas gifts," Lori said.

"The only other choice we have is to go back home," Tim replied.

"Let's head east and not north!" Lori exclaimed.

It felt nice to be heading away from problems. The Missouri countryside was beautiful. It had been a long time since Tim and Lori had seen such green country. Lori was driving because Tim could not see well enough. He had to keep his eyes closed most of the time to keep from having a headache from his dilated eyes. He was relaxed and almost asleep.

"Tim, the car is knocking and jerking!" Lori shouted.

"I still can't see well enough to drive, or to look under the hood," Tim said. "We'll just have to stop in the next town and have a mechanic check the car to see what's wrong with it!"

The trouble grew worse, and the rose-colored Cadillac would not go over forty miles an hour. The engine sounded like it was going to explode.

"Tim, years ago Hollis and I had an old car that sounded like this. It turned out to be a busted rod in the engine," Lori said. She moaned thinking about extra expenses that they could not afford.

"That's what it sounds like to me too," Tim said. "I sure hope it isn't or we'll have to buy a new engine if that what's wrong," Tim explained.

Lori parked the car in front of a garage in the next town. Tim got out of the car to look for a mechanic.

Lori was afraid to turn off the car. It was knocking and jerking so drastically now, that people on the street stopped to stare at her. I wish I could hide, Lori was thinking.

"Whatever it is, it's bad, but we can't help you," the young mechanic said. He turned around and walked back into his shop without saying another word.

The car sputtered and jerked to the next town. The next mechanic seemed to be a little more experienced. "It is a rod and the car shouldn't be driven anymore," he said. The second mechanic also returned to his shop without offering to help any further.

"Here we are stranded in the middle of Missouri, so what do we do now," Lori asked.

"I'll just have to call my brother-in-law, Carl, and tell him our situation. Maybe he can help," Tim answered. They found a public telephone. Lori had to dial the number for Tim.

"Stay right there," Carl said. "I'll send one of my workers and a vehicle after you. They can pull you the rest of the way here. You can get the car fixed in St. Louis after Christmas. My worker will be there by eight in the morning," he said.

"Thanks," Tim said and hung up.

Tim and Lori found a cheap motel within walking distance of the car. Carl's man showed up at 7:30 the next morning, but Tim and Lori were already up and ready to go. Lori stayed at the car while Tim and the man looked all over the small town to find a tow bar. They came back an hour later.

"We have looked everywhere, and we can't find a tow bar," Tim explained to Lori.

"Lori, you will have to guide the car while I pull you all to the next town. We can get a tow bar there," Carl's worker said.

They stopped in every town, but no one had a tow bar to rent.

Lori guided the car while they were pulled through the beautiful Ozark country. She could not enjoy the scenery because she had to watch the pickup pulling them every minute. She had to see every turn and coming stop, so she could make the same moves as the pickup. It took all Lori's strength to drive the Cadillac without the power steering and power brakes. Her arm muscles begin to ache.

By evening, they were crossing the Mississippi River into Illinois. Tim was beginning to see a little better, and enjoyed the scenery.

Lori took her eyes off of the pickup long enough to glance at the river. "It's much smaller than I remember it," she said. "Maybe this is its low time of the year. The last time I saw it was at the Memphis crossing, and maybe it's larger there,"

Lori felt exhausted when they were finally pulled into Ann's yard. It was dark, and the family was just beginning to open their packages. Lori's eyes hurt and her body ached all over.

"I wish we had some gifts to take in to them," Lori said.

"They will understand," Tim replied.

"I guess I did the right thing before we left home, anyway, even though we don't have any Christmas money." Lori said.

"What was that?" Tim asked.

"I guess I forgot to tell you, when I gave Pete that $120 cash for a new bicycle to replace the one Ray tore up," Lori answered.

"How did you give it to him?" Tim asked.

"I found a card and wrote a letter of apology, and put it in the envelope with the money. I thought I'd give it to him at school. Then I decided it would be safer to give it to him on the way home on the bus. I ended up taking it over and giving it to Rita to be sure she knew we had tried to make things right," Lori explained.

"Rita was still angry, and said that no amount of money would ever replace Pete's bike or heal him from the terrible experience," Lori said, as she lead Tim through the dark to the brightly lighted and decorated house of Tim's relatives.

There were short greetings and the rest of the packages were handed out. Ann's two grandsons had dozens of packages to open. They squealed in delight over each one.

Tim received a nice shirt and some after-shave. Lori received a purse from Sarah, a pocket camera from Ann, and some warm, heavy sock from the grandsons.

"We really appreciate this but you shouldn't have . . . We weren't able to . . ." Lori stammered.

"Don't worry about it. We understand," Ann said. "It's time to eat," she called to everyone.

Lori had never seen so much food. Ham, beef, turkey, all kinds of seafood, salads, pies, cakes, cookies, and candy filled the dining room, kitchen, back porch, and one bedroom.

Lori and Tim were nervous about their situation and they had nothing to do for three days but sit and eat. The pounds Lori had worked so hard to get off, quickly returned. She couldn't button any of the clothes she had brought with her and she avoided looking into the mirror as much as possible.

When Carl went into East St. Louis to work again, he rode with his son and let Tim and Lori borrow his pickup. They used the pickup to look for transportation to get home. They had trouble finding a rebuilt engine at a reasonable price, and even considered trading in the Cadillac for an older vehicle. No one would trade cars with them because Tim and Lori's car was not running and they could not even see it. Nothing seemed to work out the first day.

The second day, Tim and Lori found a rebuilt engine for five hundred dollars.

"How are we going to pay for it?" Lori asked Tim.

"Maybe I can borrow a little cash from Carl and Ann until we get home. Then we'll have to sell your grain that's in the elevator from your dad's estate to pay them back. We'll just have to hope there is enough grain to pay for the engine and expenses," Tim said. He sounded very depressed.

"I guess that's all we can do. We have to get back home somehow," Lori replied.

Carl used the pickup to pull the car into East St. Louis and into the gas station where it was to be repaired. "I have so manna workas gone fo Christmas, we's can't getcha fixed uptil afta New Yers," the man told Tim.

"If they don't get it fixed until then, I'll have to ride a cross country bus home, so I won't miss anymore days of school," Lori said. She felt fear rising up within her again.

"They will have it finished in time for us to start back home the day before school starts. We can drive straight through if we have to," Tim explained.

Carl and Ann, along with their son and his family, lived sixty miles from the city where Carl's factory was located. The men either had to commute five days a week, or the whole family stayed in a mobile home and large motor home located inside the factory compound.

Lori rode to East St. Louis the next day with Carl, his son, Trent, and Tim. The city was quite different from the St. Louis across the Mississippi River. East St. Luis was ninety-five percent black. The poverty was immediately visible. They passed many huge factories that were now closed and boarded up. Most of the houses were small, close together, and in need of paint. The only pretty spot Lori saw was a small park. Very few houses had grass, or even a yard, around them.

Carl noticed Lori's interest, and started telling her and Tim about their city.

"Most of the people in this area are out of work, and there is a lot of crime. When we first opened our factory, we didn't think we needed guards or guard dogs. We were robbed so many times that we decided that the guards and guard dogs were cheaper than replacing equipment. The high fence around our complex wasn't enough to protect our property," Carl said.

Carl continued his story, "Last week, two ten-year-old boys broke into a neighboring factory complex. One of them got away, but the guard dogs killed the other one. It's a sad way to have to live. The Negroes seem to accept us pretty well, and we have been able to create jobs for a lot of them. We still have the mobile home and motor-home we live in parked behind the fence, guards, and guard dogs."

Carl talked about their new business and plant. "Our place was once a glass factory where millions of pop bottles were made. When pop factories started using aluminum cans instead of bottles, the factory went broke and closed.

We bought the whole, huge complex for only fifty thousand dollars down. We have turned it into a recycling plant. We buy leftover paints from the automobile factories in Detroit, and other wastes, and reprocess the material into useable fuel. Sometimes companies pay us just to pick up their wastes and we are paid well for the fuel we make because other types of fuel are so expensive.

We are expanding, as quickly as the government will let us, to meet the demands of the market. Our complex is so large that we'll never have to worry about expanding outside of our own area. We even have one new warehouse that is four hundred feet wide and six hundred feet long, that has never been used. I'd like to show you the whole complex as soon as I get my men to work," Carl said.

The main street of the city ran parallel to the railroad tracks. Lori saw a high fence ahead, with many buildings behind it. The buildings were so large they seemed to be unreal in the gray dawn of the cold, winter morning.

Carl drove up to the large gate and was met by a black guard. The guard was wearing a black halter around his slender waist, housing a pistol. Another, wearing a uniform and armor, came out of a pill-box to greet them. The guards had broad smiles on their thick, black lips. Four large German Shepherds dogs stopped barking when they recognized Carl.

"This is Jack and Miko. They are two of my best men," Carl said.

"Glad to meets Car's kinfolk from ways out west," one guard said. Both guards held out their large dark hands for Tim and Lori to shake. The black guys showed a lot of respect for Carl.

"Sure hopes ya-all has a nice visit in dis hah, our city," The tall guard, wearing a Swedish hat, said.

Carl gave out orders for the day, then drove the car to a large red brick building about a hundred yards from the gate. It was a two story building with a basement high enough off the ground to have windows as large as the rest of the building. All the windows had heavy frames, screens, and cross bars.

Lori bent over to pet the dogs.

"Those are young ones still in training. We have other dogs delivered here at night that guard the place. I want to raise my own dogs because the other dogs are so dangerous. Last week the dog trainer went to one of the factories to pick up his dogs. He forgot to wear his protective clothes, and padded leather gloves. One of his own dogs mangled both arms, and he's still in the hospital," Car explained. He held the front door of the office building open for the others to walk through.

"Since I have my little grandsons around here, I decided it would be safer to train dogs with the kids around," Carl said.

There were several offices in the first building. The rooms were furnished with thick, red carpets. Carl's office was extra nice, with a pretty, young, black secretary sitting at a desk in an area in front of the office.

Besides expensive furniture, Carl's office was decorated with his hunting trophies displayed on one wall. There was a mounted wild boar's head with his mouth open and tusks protruding. There were also the heads of mountain goats and sheep, and the head of a wild longhorn ram, displayed.

Lori's attention was on the mounted head of a Tennessee angora sheep. Its fur looked like white silk. "Wasn't it hard to shoot something this beautiful?" Lori asked.

"Yes, but I knew how pretty he'd look mounted, and I shot him with a rifle I bought that Clark Gable once owned," Carl said, proudly.

The temperature was below zero as Carl showed them the rest of the buildings. Most of them were unheated. Lori was thankful for her new, heavy socks inside her wool-lined, winter boots.

"This is the largest stove I ever saw," Lori said with a laugh, as the entered one of the four kilns. The kiln was two stories tall, and about thirty feet square.

"Yes, it heated hundreds of pop bottles at once, when the old bottle factory was running," Carl replied.

After Tim and Lori completed their tour, they stayed in Carl's office long enough to warm their freezing feet, before they drove across the Mississippi to the other St. Louis. They were still hoping to find a place that would trade cars with them without seeing their Cadillac. If they were successful, they could go home earlier.

Many salesmen even laughed when they heard Tim explain their situation. No place was interested in trading for a car they could not see. Discouraged, Tim and Lori drove back across the river into East St. Louis.

"Let's stop by a sandwich place," Tim said.

"It seems like I'm always hungry," Lori replied.

The waiter in the old drive-in took their orders from behind a bullet-proof glass. The money and food were exchanged through a slanted tray in the wall between the two rooms. There were no chairs so Tim and Lori ate their sandwich in the pickup.

"Tim, I feel so sorry for the children that have to grow up in an environment like this. It would be terrible to live in a community where you have to be afraid all of the time," Lori said.

Lori told Carl about the place where they had eaten.

"I told you there was a lot of crime in this neighborhood," Carl said. "The people are so poor they are burning anything they can find to keep their houses warm. At least one house a day burns down in this city," he explained.

"See those large tanks out there?" Carl asked, pointing to the west part of his property. "They hold the fuel we make. One tank was faulty and exploded a few weeks ago. Three houses on that street were heavily damaged.

Our insurance paid for the damages, but it was unreal how well the Negroes took it. One old man said he was sitting in his rocking chair when he heard the terrible noise, and the doors of his house flew off, and the windows exploded. He said that there was no reason to get all excited. He just thought the world had ended, and it was now the Great Judgment Day," Carl said.

They left one of the vehicles at the factory compound, and rode back together that night with Carl and Trent. Carl told Tim and Lori about the way the Negroes fix pig-snouts. "There's a place about four blocks from our factory where you can try some if you want to," Carl explained.

Tim and Lori gave up looking for a different car at about two o'clock the next afternoon. They went back across the river. "Let's stop here and try some of those pig-snouts," Tim said. "They sounded pretty good when Carl was telling us about them,"

Tim parked the pickup, and Lori followed him to the door of the tiny cafe that was located next to the busy main street. The door was still locked. Tim knocked several times before Lori noticed a sign that read, "Open at 4 p.m.". They were walking back to the pickup when they noticed a very large black man crossing the street.

The man was walking toward them. "Hey!" he shouted.

"Hi," Tim shouted back, while walking to the pickup. Tim did not realize how different he must have looked with his large cowboy hat, and western-style clothes.

Lori said, "Hello" and waited for Tim to unlock her door.

Tim had just unlocked Lori's door, and was walking to his side of the pickup when the poorly dressed man walked up to him. The man was wearing a light-weight sweat shirt with the hood pulled down tightly around his face. He had both hands pushed down in his pockets.

He must be very cold, Lori was thinking.

"My name's Rob," the man said.

Tim smiled and said, "Hi. My name is Tim."

The man pointed something at Tim through his sweatshirt pocket. "Does ya knows what dis is?" he asked.

"It could be your finger," Tim calmly answered.

The man cursed and pulled his hand out of his pocket. He was holding a large revolver. Lori stood in shock. She saw the expensive carving on the barrel of the gun as the man pushed the weapon into Tim's chest.

There had been so many times in the last few months that Lori felt like she was having a nightmare, but like all the other times had been, this was reality. Shall I try to run for help, or should I try to sneak into the pickup and try to help Tim from there, Lori wondered. He will want my purse when he's finished with Tim. I must get the important things out of my purse and toss them into the pickup before he comes over here Lori was thinking.

Lori tried to find the things she wanted to keep and take them out of her purse before it was too late. If I can just toss my driver's license, pictures, credit cards, and money into the floor of the pickup before he come over, maybe I can save them, Lori thought. Her hands were shaking as she tried not to move enough to get the man's attention.

Lori saw cars going by just a few feet away. She knew people could see what was happening. Why doesn't someone stop and help us she wondered.

"Gives me ya-alls wallet!" the man shouted.

"I don't carry a wallet. You can check me and see," Tim said. He moved his hands down his body to prove that he did not have a wallet. Should I try to knock the gun out of his hand, Tim was wondering. If I try, and it doesn't work, he might start shooting, and Lori might get hit, Tim was thinking.

The man shoved the gun further into Tim's body. "Gives me your rings!" the man ordered, looking at the diamond ring Tim's mother had given him, and his wedding ring.

"I can't get them off because they're too tight," Tim replied. "Would you like to try to get them off?" Tim asked, holding out his hand.

The man thought Tim was swinging at his gun. He jumped back and clicked a shell into the chamber. "Then boogie man!" the man shouted.

"Burger Man, where?" Tim asked, feeling rather stunned. Tim was serious because he could not understand his assailant's strange dialect. The man thought Tim was making fun of him. He was cursing and his hands were shaking.

The man grabbed Tim with his free hand and threw him across the top of the pickup. "Puts ya hands as faw overs da truck as ua cans, man, and keeps dem dere!" he shouted, as he pushed Tim against the top of the pickup.

The man pointed his gun at Lori and walked around to her side of the pickup. He jerked her from the pickup and held the gun between her eyes, about an inch from her forehead. Lori could see the carved ivory handle of the gun. It was a design she would never forget. The barrel of the gun was black and dirty.

"Yo pouse!" the man shouted.

"My purse has our credit cards in it, and we don't have any other way to get home," Lori said.

"Gives me yo pouse!" the man shouted louder. He grabbed Lori's purse. Before he could step back, Lori grabbed her purse back. "Let me get my credit cards and pictures out, and you can have the rest," Lori said.

The man was shaking and cursing. He pushed the cold gun barrel against Lori's forehead, and tried to pull the trigger.

A scripture flashed through Lori's mind, "Lo, I am with you always, even unto the utter most part of the earth." <u>The Lord is not going to let this guy kill us</u>, Lori knew in her heart. <u>There's a New Testament in my purse, and maybe he'll read it and get saved</u>, she was thinking. The gun was hurting Lori's forehead as the man's hands were trembling, and he was trying to squeeze the trigger.

The man grabbed the purse for the second time without moving the gun from Lori's head.

Lori grabbed it back and said, "My mother-in-law just gave me this purse for Christmas. I want to keep it."

The man now had both hands on the gun in an effort to squeeze the trigger. He looked so angry and confused. After a few seconds, the man grabbed Lori's purse for the third time. He stepped back while still pointing the gun at her.

The new camera fell out of the purse and landed on the sidewalk. Lori picked up the camera and asked, "Can I at least keep this?" She started to take the man's picture, but another scripture verse came to her mind, "Thou shall not tempt the Lord thy God." "The Lord expects me to use some common sense," Lori told herself.

The man kept the gun pointed at Lori's head as he ran backwards. He reached the corner of a building and disappeared behind it.

Tim and Lori jumped into the pickup and drove down the alley where they saw their assailant disappear. The alley was completely deserted. There were at least fifty doors on each side of the alley's road. Beside each door was a trash can so full that the trash was running out into the alley.

Tim and Lori hurried to Carl's factory. Tim told the two guards what had happened. Miko ran into the pill-box and called the police. As soon as he returned, he said, "Ya-all must be rights with da Man Upstairs cause nobodies gets robbed in East St. Louis and lives to tells abouts it. Theys neva leaves witnesses."

"We are," Lori answered with a smile. Then she thought about what had just happened and started to shake and sob. "Thank you for Your protection, Lord," she said.

Two black policemen came to get a full report of the hold-up, and a description of the robber and stolen goods. The report was written down, and a carbon copy was given to Tim.

After the police left, Amos, one of the guards, asked, "Wouldcha all likes to goes back to dat street, and drives around to sees if ya-all cans sees the dude that robs ya?" He soon had his shiny, old Cadillac pulled up to the gate for Tim and Lori to get in. They drove over the area several times, but did not recognize any of the people they saw on the crowded streets. They did not find the purse in any of the alleys, and returned to the factory gate.

"The mayor of the city just called to offer his condolences over your robbery," Carl told Tim and Lori. "He said that he felt bad that you were robbed in his city. He also said that his police department is doing everything they can to catch the thief," he explained.

Lori felt too tired to ride back to the country that night. She and Tim stayed with Trent and his family in their motor-home parked safely behind the guards and fence.

Trent's boys were two and four years old and his wife was eight months pregnant. Lori was trying to forget the day's events and go to sleep when she heard, "Mom, I need a dry diaper."

"You mean you need a <u>baby</u> diaper?" the mother asked.

"No! Give me another kind! I'm not a baby!" the child yelled.

Tim and Lori were laughing when they heard the other little boy ask, "Mom, will the baby get cold if you sleep with your stomach out from under the covers?"

Lori and Tim laughed again. It felt good to relax from the day's events with laughter.

The workers were just reporting for work the next morning. One old black gentleman was talking to Carl's secretary when Tim and Lori came into the office.

"Last nights on ma ways home from woak, I wus a walken down dis hea alley when dis hea dude walkes up to me and saz his name's Rob" the old gentlemen said. "I tells him my name's Hamburger, but nots da kind ya eats. He din sticks dis hea gun in mys side and I thoughts I was a having a oplipsi fit, cause da fust thing I noze, my feets was a moven so fast dat my body couldn'ts catches up. I ranz to my houze and locked ma doorz and stoods theres a shaken in my shoez!"

<u>Who would want to rob a poor old man like Hamburger?</u> Lori wondered. His clothes were old and much too large for him. He was extra skinny, and his shoes did not fit at all. He was so very poor. <u>This is a different world than I have lived in all my life</u>, Lori thought.

That night, the news on TV showed a bank robbery. The security cameras had taken pictures of the thief. Lori and Tim thought the man looked familiar.

Tim talked the mechanics into fixing the car early. The day before New Years, They packed their clothes and waited for the mechanic to call before they rode to the city with Carl. Carl was almost late when the mechanic finally called.

"I dun't know whatza matta with the motoa, but it wontz run," the mechanic said.

"It ran all right when I bought it," Tim said.

"Well, its not a runnen now, sa," the mechanic repeated.

"Take it back out, and I'll see if I can find another engine for you to put in tomorrow," Tim said.

Tim found a second motor in a wrecking yard. He did not have to pay for the first engine, but he had to pay for the hours the mechanics spent changing the three engines. It came to an extra two hundred dollars.

Lori did not have time to make bus connection now, so she had to call Mr. Wilson again. It would be a loss of almost two hundred dollars from her next paycheck. Tim and Lori had both lost their driver's licenses in the robbery. They hoped they would not get stopped by any patrolman on their way home.

It was snowing and blowing, and fifty degrees below zero, when Tim and Lori finally left St. Louis. Lori had to drive again, because Tim could not see well enough in the white blowing snow.

They had crossed Missouri and were ten miles from Topeka.

"Let's stop at the next eating place and get something to eat," Tim said.

"I feel like I need some coffee, too," Lori replied. She parked the car in front of a nice looking restaurant. Immediately, a white Cadillac, with a Wyoming license, pulled in behind them. Lori was stretching her legs and not paying any attention to the other car until she heard someone yelling at Tim.

"Hey, Pardna, come here!" a black man yelled.

Tim turned around and saw two men sitting in the white car. They were wearing cowboy hats. The driver had his window down and his arm was lying partly out of the window. He yelled at Tim again.

Tim and Lori both saw a gun in the man's right hand. The barrel was resting on his left arm. The gun was pointed directly at them.

<u>Here we go again</u>, Tim and Lori were both thinking.

"Keep walking into the restaurant. Don't stop or look back," Tim said. He followed Lori through the front door.

The man yelled several times for them to stop.

When Tim and Lori were safely inside, they ran to a window and looked out. The men were still in their car, but they had parked their car beside the Jones's car instead of behind it.

Tim ran to the restaurant counter where a waitress was working. "May I borrow your telephone?" he asked.

The woman pointed to a telephone booth close to the front door. Tim ran to it and tried to dial the police. The phone was not working. He asked another waitress if she knew the telephones were dead. The waitress just shrugged her shoulders and kept walking toward a table with her arms full of food.

Tim asked the first waitress if he could see the manager. She nodded her head in a certain direction. Tim ran into a small office where a man was sitting behind a desk. He explained about the men, gun, and dead telephones.

"I know our phones are down. I suggest that you go across the street and use the one at the gas station over there," the young man said. He showed no concern.

"Your restaurant might be in danger," Tim said.

"I don't believe your story so don't bother me!" the man shouted. "Can't you see that I'm busy!" he yelled.

Lori watched the two men come into the restaurant. They went to the counter and ordered two cups of coffee. As soon as Tim came out of the office, Lori pointed to the two men. They ran to the car. Lori backed away from their parking place while Tim wrote down the license plate number of the white car.

Five miles from Topeka, Tim flagged down a patrolman. He told the state trooper about the two men in the white Cadillac, and gave him the license number. Tim made the mistake of telling the patrolman about their robbery in East St. Louis.

"Sounds like you are just paranoiac from your robbery and are starting to imagine things. But, I'll check it out when I get time," the patrolman said. He crawled back into his car with the "cherry" on top, and headed in the opposite direction of the restaurant.

Just before Lori and Tim reached Topeka, they met three State Patrol cars. The cars had their light and sirens on. They were speeding in the direction of the restaurant.

Maybe it is a wreck on the Interstate Highway, and maybe it is a robbery, Tim and Lori were both thinking.

The trip Tim and Lori had planned to be economical, and restful, had turned out to be very expensive and stressful. It was a trip they would never forget. Now they had to face the problems at home.

CHAPTER XX

A NEED FOR A LAWYER

Lori's grain check barely covered the expenses of the new engine for the car. No matter how bad things were, the Lord took care of them. When there wasn't enough money to buy butane, they had enough electricity to stay warm with two portable electric heaters. When the electricity was shut off because Tim and Lori could no longer pay their bill, Tim "borrowed" fuel from a neighbor's tractor that was sitting in a field close to the house.

"Tim, I don't want you to take that fuel. It seems too much like stealing," Lori had said.

"The fuel is in a tank that my neighbor borrowed from me a few years ago. He never returned the tank, and I know the tank is more valuable than the fuel I'm taking," Tim tried to explain.

It seemed that there was always just enough money for needed groceries. When there was no grocery money, there seemed to be some surplus in the large pantry that Lori could put together for meals. They never went hungry.

Lori had gained too much weight to wear her school clothes. She found some of Sarah's old clothes, that she could get into, to wear to work. The clothes were in good condition, but were out of style.

Some of the teachers were in the workroom talking about hard times. Lori looked at their pretty clothes and wondered if they knew what hard times really were. She and Tim were trying to cover up the hard times they were going through. They didn't want to worry Lori's family, or let the community know how defeated they were.

Lori tried to always look neat and wear a smile.

All the while that Sarah lived in Lori's mobile home, Tim and Lori paid the space rent and utilities. Sarah always claimed she was too broke to support herself. When Lori cleaned out the mobile home after Sarah moved to Illinois with Ann, she found a new sewing machine, microwave oven, and twenty-five brand new dresses that had never been worn.

Tim and Lori found out later that Sarah had a reasonable Social Security check, and an oil lease check coming in every month. She was spending her money buying anything she wanted.

Sarah was gone now, but the mobile home was too full of her furniture to move to the farm. They could not afford to have the home and furniture moved, and eventually, they could not afford the space rent any longer.

Tim had not seen, or heard, from his brother since Daddy Andy's funeral. Tim called Bud and asked him if he could move their mother's things and have them stored in the Texas town where he lived. If the furniture was moved, Tim and Lori could move the mobile home to the farm and stop the lot rent expenses.

The night before Tim had to be in court again, Bud called. He had just finished moving Sarah's things. He was tried and angry. He cursed Tim for not taking better care of their parents.

Tim was hurt. "I paid off a hundred thousand dollar debt so dad could die in peace. We also paid off hospital bills, therapist bills, and mom's full support for almost two years," Tim explained. "How can you be so upset?" he asked.

Bud was still cursing.

"Bud, after paying most of the debts, Lori and I spent over $2,000 a month for two years to keep dad in the Nursing Home and provide a home for mom," Tim explained again. "If we were doing such a terrible job, why didn't you do something?" Tim asked.

"I don't believe in putting good money after bad," Bud shouted loud enough for Lori to hear clear across the room.

Lori grabbed the telephone. "Let me tell you a thing or two. Tim and I have lost everything we have, trying to take care of your folks. At the very time we are going bankrupt, you and your family left us with all the expenses of Daddy Andy's funeral, and anything else there happened to be. As far as I'm concerned, you have no right to criticize anyone until you have done your part!" Lori shouted.

Lori started to cry. Tim took the phone again. He had every reason to be angry, but he felt no anger toward his brother. Tim felt sorry for Bud, and quietly explained that he and Lori had done their best.

Bud started to cool off. The two brothers said a friendly "good-bye".

"Why did he have to call tonight, of all nights?" Tim asked. "Tomorrow is the day I go to court and fight for my life. This is the time I need some encouragement from my family, and not calls like this," he said.

Lori patted Tim's large arm. "My family is behind you, anyway," she said. "Are you sure you don't want me to go to court with you and Mr. Freedman tomorrow?" Lori asked.

"Yes, I want you to go, but I think its best that you don't," Tim said as he put his arm around his wife and drew her close. "We can't stand any more of your ninety-eight dollar a day deductions, and remember what Carl told us just before we left Illinois," Tim said.

"He said that there are a lot of people that would like to prove that I was a part of your 'said crime', in allowing Rosita to be abused. He said I needed to stay out of it as much as possible," Lori replied.

Tim and Lori prayed before she left for school the next morning.

"Everything will be all right," Lori said, just before she boarded the school bus. She prayed quietly every chance she had that morning. I know I should trust the Lord and not worry, but this whole situation is so scary and embarrassing, she was thinking.

Lori dismissed her class for PE at ten o'clock and went to the teacher's room to work on the next week's lesson plans. She poured herself a cup of coffee and sit down at one of the long work tables. She was engrossed in her planning when she heard someone call her name. She looked up and saw the school secretary.

"Lori, you're wanted on the telephone," the secretary said.

I know it's from Tim. Will the news be good or bad? Lori was thinking.

"Lori, you have to get over here to the county courthouse right now. Mr. Freedman says it's very important for you to be here for the hearing," Tim said. He sounded desperate.

"I'm at school without any transportation, Tim. Remember." Lori replied. "I don't have anyone to take my classes for the rest of the day. Even if I could find someone, I don't have any way to get there," she said. "Could you come over and get me?" Lori asked.

"I can't come after you. Mr. Freedman just got here, and he has to brief me on too many things," Tim explained.

"I'll see what I can do," Lori whispered, and hung up. Lori suddenly realized why she was whispering. She had developed a case of laryngitis, and could not talk above a whisper. Lori also had a headache, and she didn't feel well.

Lori ran to Mr. Wilson's Math class. She motioned for him to come out into the hall. Lori explained that she was needed at the courthouse as soon as possible.

"I'll be glad to take your classes this afternoon, but you'll have to find your own transportation to the courthouse," Mr. Wilson said with a kindly smile.

"Thanks," Lori said. She returned to the school office. "What can I do next?" Lori asked herself. Mike, Mitch, and Stacy are all at work. Even if they weren't, I'd be too embarrassed to ask them to take me, Lori was thinking.

Lori remembered some friends that lived close to the school. They were ministers of another church. They had been kind to Lori and Tim when it seemed like the whole town had turned against them.

Lori called the number and talked to Jeri. "I'm in a terrible predicament," Lori whispered as loudly as she could. She explained the situation.

"I'll let you talk to Les," Jeri said.

Lori repeated her story in a desperate whisper. "I know its twenty-two miles away, but I don't know who else I can turn to," she whispered.

"Don't worry. I'll pick you up at school in fifteen minutes, and we'll do anything else we can to help," Pastor Wes said.

"Thanks, but I can't leave until I finish my morning classes. I'll just walk over to your house as soon as I can," Lori whispered.

"I've been studying about health and prosperity," Les was saying. "I believe in healing, and I know God wants some people to be healed and prosperous. I know many Christians aren't in perfect health or prosperous. When people believe that God wants them healthy and prosperous, and they aren't, then they tend to doubt their salvation, too," Wes said as he drove Lori to the county seat and courthouse.

"I can understand what you're saying, but I know these things that are happening to Tim and me are because we haven't spent enough time studying the Bible. We don't speak the Scriptures over our situations enough. We haven't praised the Lord enough to defeat the devil, and what he is doing to us," Lori tried to explain in a whisper.

"Although I sound sick today, Tim is in court, and our finances have run out, I still know God wants us healthy and prosperous according to His Word. God corrects us with His Word, not by allowing us to be hurt by things like this," Lori whispered.

"Don't feel condemned if you don't see all good things from now on," Les said kindly. He parked the car in front of the courthouse. "Are you sure you don't want me to go with you and be with you and Tim this afternoon?" Pastor Les asked again.

"I'm sure, but I appreciate your offer," Lori whispered. "Just pray for us," she said.

Lori found Tim and Mr. Freedman sitting on the brick railing on the south side of the courthouse. They were talking and laughing. They looked like they were there just to enjoy the early spring sunshine and a sandwich.

Mr. Freedman explained to Lori, "It'll be better if you don't say anything. I'll try to keep you from getting on the witness stand, but I think Rosita will do a better job of telling the truth when she sees you. She probably feels closer to you than she does Tim."

Lori heard a car door open behind her. She turned around and watched Carlos and Rosita get out of the blue Chivvy. "She looks so much older," Lori said.

Tim had been told that Carlos was carrying a gun, and that he had sworn he would kill Tim on sight.

Carlos and Rosita came up the courthouse steps and told Tim and Lori hello. There was no sign of bitterness, or anger.

Lori wanted to put her arms around the girl that had cost them so much pain and money. Whoever said that blood is thicker than water, or that you can't love someone as much as if they were of your own blood? Lori thought. I guess I'll always love her, no matter what she does or says, Lori was thinking as she walked over to Rosita.

"Don't talk to them!" Mr. Freedman shouted.

Tim and Lori turned around and followed their attorney into the courthouse. They walked up the two sets of wide stairs that led to the large courtroom. The old marble floors were well preserved and clean.

Mr. Freedman motioned for them to set down close to the courtroom door to wait for the hearing. It seemed like they sit there a long time, waiting for the hearing to begin. Lori and Tim tried not to look in the direction where Carlos, Rosita, and some other people were sitting. "I don't know what is taking so long," Mr. Freedman said.

The District Attorney's assistant came out of one of the side doors in the large waiting room. "The DA wants to talk to you, Mr. Freedman," he said.

Mr. Freedman returned twenty minutes later. He sat down beside Tim. "The DA wanted you to sign a confession, and in return, they would lesson the penalty," he explained.

"What did you tell them?" Tim asked.

"I told them that you wouldn't confess to a crime that you weren't guilty of in the first place," Mr. Freedman said.

"That exactly what I would have told them," Tim said.

A man in a police uniform opened the courtroom door. He motioned for the crowd to come inside. Lori shuddered when she thought of facing the people that had signed as witnesses on Tim's arrest papers, especially Rita and Sally. At least she knew Mr. Wilson would not be there.

After everyone was seated, Lori looked around the large room to see how many of the twelve "witnesses" had showed up to testify. There was no one in the courtroom besides those directly involved in the case. The only witnesses, besides the deputies, were poor little Rosita, and Carlos. The neighbor that had caused so much trouble wasn't even there, nor was any of Tim's former family.

Lori was sitting at a small table next to Tim. Tim was sitting next to Mr. Freedman. Across the front of the room, not very far away, sit Rosita between the DA and his assistant. Carlos was the only person sitting in the audience area.

How different everything looks from here, Lori was thinking. She remembered the many times she had brought her school classes to see a court in session, as a part of their study of the United States government. "Praise the Lord, there aren't any school kids visiting today. Maybe it's because Rosita is still a minor," Lori said to herself.

"All rise," the bailiff said loudly.

Everyone stood up as the judge entered the room and sit down behind his large desk located above the front of the room. He tapped his gavial twice, and the bailiff said, "All may be seated. Court of the Honorable Judge Stone is now is session."

"This is the pre-trial hearing of case #3577893, in which Rosita Gonzales, the Plaintiff, brings charges of child sexual molestation against Mr. Tim T. Jones, the Defendant. Mr. Jones is represented by his attorney, Mr. Linden Freedman. Rosita Gonzales is represented by the honorable District Attorney of this county, Mr. Frank. Fuller.

Mr. District Attorney, will you please present your case," the judge said.

Mr. Fuller stood up and read the charges that were brought against Tim. "I would like to call my first witness, Sheriff's Deputy Jay Robert, to the witness stand, your Honor.

Deputy Robert stepped forward and placed his hand on a Bible held by the bailiff. "Do you swear to tell the truth, and nothing but the truth, so help you God?" the bailiff asked.

"I do!" the deputy said loud and clear. He walked over to the witness stand, and sit down, proudly, in the chair.

"Now Mr. Deputy, tell us everything you know about this case," the DA instructed.

"One of Tim Jones neighbors told us several months ago that she suspected that Rosita Gonzales was being sexually abused by Mr. Jones," Deputy Robert said with a western drawl. He sounded like he was in the center of a great western movie. "At that time our department couldn't find any evidence of the said crime," Deputy Robert explained. "Then the Plaintiff's brother, who was staying with the Joneses at that time, stole their neighbor's bicycle. When the neighbor reported the theft, she said she had proof that Rosita Gonzales was being sexually abused by Mr. Jones," he said.

"We apprehended the Plaintiff's brother and returned the stolen goods. We picked up the evidence that we needed on this case, so we went to the Joneses to pick up the Plaintiff. Rosita wasn't there, but Mr. Jones acted scared. He told us several times, that if the girl said anything, to not believe her," Deputy Robert explained, looking straight at Tim.

Lori and Tim shook their heads in disbelief. How could Deputy Robert lie like that under oath, they were both wondering. The only thing Tim had said was to let them know as soon as they found Rosita and if she was all right, Lori remembered distinctly.

Tim and Lori had not known why the deputy was so angry and hostile that day. They did not know about Rita's complaints, or that Ray had talked to the neighbor about Rosita.

Deputy Robert was still speaking. "A few days later, I went to Plainsville. Me and a deputy from Plainsville went to the Plaintiff's school. We asked a lady teacher to join us while we questioned the girl and help her write a confession," he explained.

"When I first begin to question the Plaintiff, she denied everything. But after awhile, I got her to say yes on some very definite questions," the deputy said.

"Thank you, Mr. Deputy. Now Mr. Freedman, you may cross examine the witness, if you wish," the judge said.

Mr. Freedman shook his head "no". "Not at this time, Your Honor. I would like to reserve the right to call the witness later, if it pleases Your Honor," he said.

"Permission granted. Next witness," the judge said.

It suddenly seemed terribly hot in the courtroom as Rosita took the stand. Everyone in the courtroom had a glass of water sitting in front of them. Lori was drinking a lot of water to make her throat feel better.

Rosita was pale and shaking.

Lori wanted to go to the front of the courtroom and throw her arms around the frightened girl. I wish there was some way I could take her out of this terrifying experience, Lori was thinking.

The DA begin asking Rosita questions. He was very stern in his questioning, and Rosita became even more frightened. "Rosita!" he said loudly. "Do you see the man that harmed you, Mr. Tim T. Jones, in this courtroom?" the DA asked.

"Yes," Rosita whispered, while looking down at her lap.

"Will you please point to him!" the DA ordered.

Rosita pointed a shaking, slender finger at Tim.

"Are you pointing to the man in the dark brown suit with the thick glasses?" the DA asked.

"Yes," Rosita whispered.

"Your Honor, I want to specify that the Plaintiff has pointed out the Defendant, Mr. Tim T. Jones," the DA said.

"Acknowledged," replied the judge.

"Rosita, did Tim Jones ever open the bathroom door, and try to look at your nude body?" the DA asked.

"No, he did not!" Rosita shouted.

Lori had never felt so embarrassed, as the DA loudly read Rosita's statement and handed it to the judge as evidence.

"May I remind you of <u>your</u> own written statement," the DA told Rosita in a gruff voice. He questioned Rosita again. "Did the Defendant, Mr. Tim T. Jones, ever open the bathroom door and try to look at you nude body?" he asked.

"I don't know," Rosita said.

The third time the DA asked the question, Rosita shouted, "No!"

Deputy Robert yelled, "Rosita, don't you remember what you're supposed to say?" He shook the written statement at her.

"No," Rosita whispered. She looked like a frightened child, twisting her cotton T-shirt between her shaking hands.

"Sir, you are not to speak, unless you are on the witness stand," the judge said, warning Deputy Robert.

"Your Honor, I would like to call for a recess," the DA said.

"Granted. A fifteen minute recess," the judge announced. Everyone stood up for the judge to exit.

"I've never heard anything like this Kangaroo court!" Mr. Freedman exclaimed, shaking his head with disgust. He led Tim and Lori out of the courtroom and into the hall that led to the public rest-rooms.

During the recess, Tim and Lori watched the DA working with Rosita in a corner at the end of along hall. He was telling her what to say when the court was back in session.

Rosita was nodding her head up and down like a robot.

Everyone stood up for the judge to enter. Rosita was put back on the witness stand. The DA continued his horrible questioning. He was receiving the same confusing answers. "Rosita, tell the judge what Tim Jones did to you!" he shouted.

"I don't remember nuthin!" Rosita shouted at the DA in anger. She looked over at Lori with pleading eyes. "Please help me, Lori," Lori read from the child's frightened face.

"I wish I could, Babe, but I can't," Lori tried to tell Rosita without words.

It was the frustrated DA that shouted this time, "Rosita, don't you remember what you're supposed to say?"

"No," Rosita whispered without taking her eyes from Lori's.

The DA asked for another recess, and it was granted. He talked to Rosita in the hall again. Lori, Tim, and Mr. Freedman saw Rosita nodding her head up and down, again.

Mr. Freedman was disgusted, and said he was going to the restroom. Lori and Tim waited by the courtroom door.

Mr. Freedman had not returned when everyone entered the courtroom, and stood up for the judge to enter. Tim and Lori were apprehensive about their attorney's absence.

The judge was looking over some papers when the sheriff burst into the courtroom. Sheriff Wade stomped up to the front of the room, and grabbed some papers off the table in front of the DA He almost knocked the DA off of his chair in the process.

"It looks like I'm going to have to handle this myself!" Sheriff Wade shouted. He shook the papers at the judge and threw them down on the judge's bench. "Look at these!" he ordered.

The judge looked over Sally's confession. "I don't think this is relative to this case, the judge said meekly. He reached for a book on the shelf behind his bench's desk.

The judge was looking through the book when Mr. Freedman walked into the room. "I believe this is the statue that Your Honor is looking for: LAW 4926490, 1981," he said, and held up two copies of information.

"Yes, thank you," the judge said and motioned for Mr. Freedman to approach the bench.

Sheriff Wade looked surprised, and stomped out of the courtroom.

The judge completely ignored Sheriff Wade's rude approach into the courtroom, and stomping up to the Judges bench without permission. He was looking down at the paper Mr. Freedman had handed him.

The frustrated DA called Rosita back to the stand and started questioning her again.

Rosita tried to answer the questions as well as she could. She knew she was not doing what the DA wanted her to do. <u>What am I doing here hurting the people that have been so good to me?</u> she wondered <u>I didn't know I would cause Tim and Lori so much trouble. They always seemed to be able to work out our problems before</u>, Rosita thought.

The courtroom temperature was getting uncomfortably warm. The DA's voice was hoarse and dry as he asked again, "Rosita, don't you remember what you are supposed to say?"

"No!" Rosita shouted. She begain to sob and cough.

Lori heard a commotion beside her.

Before Mr. Freedman knew what was happening, Tim was standing before the judge. "Your Honor," Tim was saying.

The judge looked shocked.

Mr. Freedman jumped up, ran across the room, and grabbed Tim's arm. He pulled Tim back to his chair and pushed Tim into the chair "Tim, no one can approach the bench without being recognized. The only way you can stand up there is on the witness stand, and you have to be called to do even that!" Mr. Freedman exclaimed.

"Mr. Freedman . . ." the judge said.

"I'm sorry, Your Honor, I'll keep my client in his chair from now on," Mr. Freedman said.

"See that you do! One more time, and he will be charged for contempt of court!" the judge shouted.

"That means you will go to jail," Mr. Freedman told Tim.

"All I wanted to do is to request that Rosita be served a glass of water like the rest of us have," Tim said.

"You're unbelievable!" Freedman exclaimed. He requested permission to approach the bench. The judge gave the permission.

"Your Honor, my client would like to request that the Plaintiff be given a glass of water," Mr. Freedman said, sheepishly.

The judge's frown turned into a smile, then into a chuckle. "I think that can be arranged," he said. Several snickers could be heard across the room. A man soon appeared with a glass of water for Rosita.

After more questioning, the DA gave up and went back to his chair, exhausted.

"Mr. Freedman, do you wish to cross examine the witness?" the judge asked.

"Yes, Your Honor," Freedman replied. He walked slowly over to Rosita. "Rosita, I know you are very embarrassed, and frightened. I'll try to ask my questions in the nicest way I can," the attorney said softly.

Rosita begin to relax and turned loose of her shirt tail.

"Rosita, please take your time to answer my questions, because they are very important. Try to remember back when you were living with the Joneses," Mr. Freedman said. "Rosita, did Tim Jones ever try to look at you when you didn't have any clothes on?" Mr. Freedman asked.

"I don't think so, that I can remember," Rosita said, looking at Lori.

"Rosita, this is very important, so answer slowly," Mr. Freedman begin again. "Did Tim Jones ever touch you on the breasts, or between your legs?" the attorney asked.

"No!" Rosita exclaimed in anger. She never took her eyes from Lori's. Lori nodded for her to tell the truth.

"Rosita, did Tim Jones <u>ever</u> touch you in any of the wrong places?" Mr. Freedman asked.

Rosita continued to look at Lori instead of the person that was asking her questions. A smile crossed her face. "He could have without meaning to, when we were all wrestling, sometime," Rosita answered.

Freedman waited a minute before he continued. "Rosita, has Tim Jones ever done anything, or said anything, that embarrassed you?" he asked, softly.

"No," Rosita said. She was smiling now.

"Rosita, were you happy living with the Joneses?" Mr. Freedman asked.

"Yes," Rosita answered, leaning toward Lori.

"Rosita, if Tim Jones has only done good things for you, then why is he about to go to prison, now?" Mr. Freedman asked.

"Because . . . . Because . . . ." Rosita started to answer. She looked at Tim then back at Lori. Her countenance changed. She looked angry and wild.

<u>Oh, no. This is the other Rosita</u>, Tim and Lori were both thinking.

"Because he <u>did</u> do something to me! I just can't remember what it was!" Rosita shouted.

"That is all, Your Honor," Mr. Freedman said. He went back and sat down beside Tim.

"Mr. DA, do you want to question the witness again?" the judge asked.

"No, Your Honor," the DA replied. He sounded like he knew he had already lost the case.

"Then we will adjourn for a short recess. I will have my decision when we come back," the judge said.

After the judge had left the room, the young DA walked over to Mr. Freedman. "It doesn't look like we have much of a case," he said.

"You did a good job in presenting what little you <u>did</u> have," Mr. Freedman said, as he shook the DA's hand.

Mr. Freedman returned to the table where Tim and Lori were waiting, "They have nothing to continue the case with, Tim," he said with a victory smile. "Anyone can see that the girl would like to be back living with you guys right now,"

"All rise," the bailiff announced.

After everyone was seated, Tim was told to stand and face the judge.

The judge looked at Tim. "I've given this much consideration. I'm dropping the charges that were supposed to have taken place on December tenth of last year, the charges of trying to see the Plaintiff's nude body," he explained.

"However, "I'm keeping the serious charge of August of this year, where you are charged with touching the Plaintiff's body, and wanting the Plaintiff to touch you," the judge continued. "I'm turning this case over to the next highest court. This case will come to a jury trial on June 10," the judge said.

Everyone stood up for the judge to leave the room.

The DA was as surprised as Mr. Freedman. At one time during the hearing, the judge had even said that there wasn't much evidence that anything ever happened between Tim and Rosita. The Judges attitude had changed from the very time the sheriff had entered the courtroom.

Mr. Freedman was still shaking his head in disbelief at what the judge had just announced. The young DA came over to shake his hand again. "We just got lucky to have a trial set over such a flimsy case as this," he said.

"You're right," Mr. Freedman replied. "You have a lot of work to do before the trial."

"How can this happen when the girl said that nothing happened, and she wished she was still living with you guys?" Mr. Freedman asked. "That _is_ what she said, isn't it?" he exclaimed. "I'm sure it is, and we can get a tape of her testimony," Freeman said, answering his own question.

"Don't worry Tim. We'll give them more than they can handle in court during the trial. We'll make it last two weeks. They don't have a chance and they know it. The trial will make the National Press like my last case did. You just watch and see," Freedman said, not giving anyone a chance to interrupt his thoughts.

On the way out of the courthouse, Rosita saw Tim and Lori coming down the hall. She and Carlos started toward them. Carlos looked like he had lost his last friend.

"Keep going!" Mr. Freedman shouted. "How can you still think so much of that girl?" he asked as they were crawling into the car.

"It's not her fault that this is happening," Tim said.

Tim and Lori started their fifty mile trip to take Mr. Freedman back to the nearest large airport. He was scheduled to fly back to the state capital that evening. The attorney loved a good fight. He was talking and laughing all the way.

"After all the publicity Tim has gotten in the county paper, do you think there are enough people left in the area to make up a jury, one that hasn't already made up their minds that Tim is guilty?" Lori asked.

Freedman did not answer.

"Do you think he can ever have a fair trial here?" Lori asked. "The only people that still think he is innocent are our friends and relatives. According to the law, that makes them ineligible to be chosen to be on the jury."

"I still think Tim has a ninety-eight percent chance of winning", Freedman said with confidence.

"What about the other two percent?" Tim asked.

"There's always a chance that a person won't win. The attorney that tells you differently is only fooling himself," Freedman explained.

"How much will a long trial like this cost?" Lori asked.

"Only about $8,000 more, and that's awfully cheap for what you will be getting," Mr. Freedman said, smiling.

"I hate to put Rosita through two more weeks of what she has been through today," Tim said.

"I still can't believe how much you guys think of her!" Mr. Freedman exclaimed. "Is she more important than your freedom, Tim?" he asked.

"As we told you before, we don't blame her for what has happened," Lori said. "She just got into a trap planned by older people. She didn't mean to hurt us," she explained.

"I think we have time to eat before your plane is due," Tim said. "What kind of food do you like, Mr. Freedman," he asked.

"Any kind," the attorney said. "I'm not a very big eater," he explained.

Tim parked the car in front of a restaurant and they went inside. The attorney told Tim and Lori a little about himself over a large meal of Mexican food.

"I'm dating one of my secretaries. I thought I had a good marriage until my wife, of many years, told me she was tired of being an attorney's wife. She said she wanted a divorce," Mr. Freedman said. "I didn' feel like taking the time to fight her, so I had divorce papers served on her that very afternoon," Mr. Freedman said with a laugh. "I guess I <u>had</u> been pretty busy with my work, and I <u>had</u> been away from home a lot working on several different cases,"

Mr. Freedman boarded the small passenger plane. "Everything is going to be okay, so don't worry," he yelled just before the door was closed.

The new hopes were soon gone and the old fears were back when Lori went to school the next morning. The fears grew as the hearing made the front page again. To most people reading the county paper, it sounded like Tim had already been found guilty and sentenced.

"I have some good news," Tim said when Lori came home from school that evening. "You remember the storm that cost us about $450,000 in twenty-four hours?" he asked.

"How could I forget that one. It destroyed the prettiest milo crop I ever saw at just the very time we were getting ready to harvest it," Lori replied.

"It looks like we are going to get that five percent disaster loan to continue our farming and ranch operation after all," Tim explained. It was the first time he had felt like smiling for a long time.

"When are we going to get the loan?" Lori asked.

"I don't know, but maybe it won't be too much longer," Tim replied.

"It better be soon, because we need the money now to start farming, feed the cattle, and to pay Mr. Freedman, and just to live on," Lori said.

"All I know is that the president <u>did</u> declare this area a disaster after the storm, and the FHA office said that we will get the loan. We'll just have to charge our fuel, cattle feed, and try to survive on your salary. We'll just pray that the loan comes through in time to pay Mr. Freedman, and everyone else," Tim said. "We have no other choice."

Tim went to the FHA office the next week to check on the loan's progress, and give additional information on their farming and ranching operations. The office personnel promised that the loan would soon be available.

Tim and Lori did not hear from the FHA. Tim talked Lori into going in to check on the loan and update the information the second week. There was still no loan.

Tim went in the third week, and Lori the fourth week. The loan was always promised.

Lori stopped by the office one day and picked up some more papers that Tim needed to fill out. The new administrator was standing by his office window and saw Lori leave. "Who is that lady?" he asked his secretary.

"That is Tim Jones's wife," the secretary said.

"Would you please catch her before she gets into her car? I want to talk to her," the FHA agent said.

Lori was backing the car away from the curb when the secretary caught her. "Mr. Woodman wants to talk to you, Lori," she yelled from the sidewalk.

Lori was surprised. She and Tim, along with a lot of other ranchers and farmers, had asked to talk to Mr. Woodman many times. They were always told he was too busy to talk to them. Now the agent had asked to talk to her? Lori hurried back into Mr. Woodman's office.

"Please sit down, Mrs. Jones," the agent said, pointing to a chair next to his desk. After Lori sit down, the agent said, "I'd like to ask you what you think about the enormous loan you folks have applied for."

"We must have the loan to pay off our farming and ranching bills, and to keep operating," Lori said with determination.

"What will you do if the loan doesn't go through?" Mr. Woodman asked.

"I can teach school, so we won't starve, but I don't know how we can pay off the people we owe, if you don't endorse that loan," Lori answered.

"How could anyone ever get in debt as far as you people have/" Mr. Woodman asked.

"Blizzards, grasshoppers, no rain, oil slush pits, wind damage, supporting parents, and a poor economy," Lori answered,

"That is a lot of reasons!" Mr. Woodman exclaimed.

"Mr. Woodman, I'd like to ask you something," Lori said.

"I guess it's your turn," Woodman said with a smile.

"If we don't get this loan, we'll lose our land. There are a lot of other farmers and ranchers in the same predicament. I know of some instances where the government is even taking away land from people that have farmed it for many years, and letting people farm it that have never farmed before. By the way the economy is going, the government could end up owning almost all the farmland in this country," Lori explained, "What will they do with it, and how close will this situation be to a communist economy?" Lori asked.

"I can answer that question," Mr. Woodman's assistant said as he walked into the room. "The government knows they'll end up with the land. They will rent it back to the farmers because no one else will work that hard on the land," the man said. "And, it will be too darn close to a communist economy."

"My next question is, do we get the loan?" Lori asked.

"I'm thinking about helping you guys stay in business one more year if you, not Mr. Jones, will make all the decisions concerning money matters from now on," Mr. Woodman said.

"Tim wouldn't agree to that, and I don't know that much about farming and ranching," Lori replied.

"Let me know if you change your mind," Mr. Woodman said. He stood up as a sign for Lori to leave.

Lori told Tim what Mr. Woodman had said. Tim was angry, and hurt. A week later, they were notified that their loan had been turned down.

Tim heard about the new Federal Crop Insurance that some farmers were buying. As a last resort, he called the agent to find out more about it.

"You don't have to pay for the insurance until the crop is harvested. Then you'll have the money to pay for it. If you don't raise a crop, you'll receive money from the insurance to keep your operation going," the insurance agent explained.

"I'll take it", Tim said. "When can you be here for me to sign the papers?" he asked.

"I'll see you about eight o'clock tonight," the agent said before he hung up.

It was almost eleven o'clock that night when the agent drove into the yard with the papers to sign. There had been a lightning storm, and the electricity was out. The signing had to be done by kerosene lamps.

"I'm sorry I'm so late," the agent said, apologizing. "They had my bankruptcy sale today, and I had to get my family relocated. We lost our house along with the land. It seems like everything has gone wrong today," he explained.

Jim Wilson was an attractive man that Tim and Lori had known for a long time. He had always been optimistic, and laughed a lot, but tonight, he looked tired, old, and defeated.

The papers were soon signed. Mr. Wilson shook hands with Tim and Lori and left.

Two weeks later, Tim received a letter explaining that the insurance policy had to be rewritten, because he was farming land in two different states. Tim signed the papers at the back of the letter and mailed them back to the insurance agent.

It had been extremely dry that spring,. The wheat crop blew out before it could root well. Tim called the insurance adjuster out to the south fields to show him that there was no crop coming up, and that is was too dry and windy to plant it over.

"You didn't work your ground well enough!" the man exclaimed.

Tim asked the older man to walk out into the field with him. "Now pick up some handfuls of soil and see how well the ground has been worked," Tim said. "We had to work it several times because the vine weed was so bad," Tim explained.

"The ground is soft. I'll take your report back to the head office and let you know," the adjuster said.

A few days later, a younger adjuster came by the farm to talk to Tim. "I want to inform you that your wheat didn't germinate, and that's why you didn't raise a crop. You should have tested it before you planted it," the man explained. "You won't be receiving any insurance money from us."

"I used seed wheat that had done well the year before. I even had a neighbor, who was used to farming in that area, to come over and see if he agreed with the way I was planting. He also looked at the seed," Tim explained.

"You should have tested your seed before you planted it!" the adjuster shouted.

"The policy didn't say I had to test the seed. It's supposed to pay for all circumstantial loss of crops!" Tim shouted back.

"Plant the crop over!" the adjuster ordered.

"It's too late and there's not enough moisture to pant it over!" Tim exclaimed.

"You still aren't eligible for a payment," the young man said. He jumped into his new car and spun out of the yard.

A few days later the sheriff issued papers to Tim and Lori. The bank was foreclosing on everything they owned. The papers ordered them to sell all the cattle and turn the money over to the bank.

The papers that showed business transactions of their operation were two years out of date. They showed that Tim and Lori still owned the cattle that had died in the storms, and the cattle that Tim had to sell as culls after they lost their calves. Each of the cows, living and dead, were listed as a cow and a yearling calf, and that the cows were ready to calve again.

"We have reported everything to the bank. Why haven't they kept a record of it?" Lori asked.

Tim shrugged his shoulders and said, "They don't even show the equipment trade I made to get the new drills last fall, and I had the bank okay it first."

Tim read every page carefully. The first page said that they had thirty days to answer the summons. Page five said a hearing was set for the following Friday in a town eighty miles from where they had any farmland.

Lori and Tim had to find a lawyer immediately. They found a new lady attorney that had time to work with them. Lori had to miss school again for the court hearing. The judge dismissed the hearing because it had been set up in the wrong county. Lori had missed another day school for nothing.

Tim and Lori left the courthouse feeling exhausted. The wind was blowing and the dust was starting to cover things. "Lori, I need for you to drive. You know how hard it is for me to see in a dust storm," Tim said.

Lori was driving home when they were caught in a terrible dust storm. She strained her eyes to see the white line in the middle of the highway. The sand sounded like buckshot pounding against the outside of the car.

It was even hard to breathe inside the car because of the dust.

Lori was driving slowly, but she was afraid to stop because a car could easily hit her from behind. Although it was in the middle of the afternoon, it was almost dark. Lori turned on all the lights, including the flashing emergency light and turning signals.

There were many cars feeling their way along the dangerous US. highway. It was almost impossible to see any of them. Even the large eighteen-wheeler trucks were barely visible in the fog of light colored dust.

Tim was trying to protect his weak eyes from the dust. Lori felt dust on her face, and grit between her teeth. There was soil from wheat fields, and tumble weeds blowing across the road for miles. Their only relief from the storm was where there was pasture land of buffalo grass on both sides of the road to keep the soil from blowing.

"Lori, look out!" Tim shouted above the roar of the wind. "There's a car passing another car! It's coming right toward us! You'll have to go into the ditch to miss it!" he yelled.

Lori pulled into the sloping ditch. If it had happened at any other place, the ditch would have been too steep to pull into without turning over.

"Some people have to hurry whether they can see or not!" Lori shouted. She slowly pulled the car back upon the highway.

The dirt was blowing so hard that it looked like the sun had set. There seemed to be no letup in the howling wind and blowing sand.

"Are the eighties going to be a repeat of the 'Dirty Thirties'?" Lori shouted.

"I hope not!" Tim yelled back.

I read something that I couldn't forget the other day," Lori shouted.

Tim leaned over against Lori so he could hear above the howling wind.

"This guy said that he was about thirteen years old in the 'Thirties', and when the bank foreclosed on his dad's farm. He said his dad had been a strong, proud, hard working man, until the day of the foreclosure," Lori said.

"He said that his dad really died the day they lost their farm although his body lasted a few more years. His dad was so broken hearted over the loss of the farm that he begain to drink. His mother divorced him and moved to town. She tried to support her children by doing other people's washing. His mother ended up getting married again, but his dad ended up dyeing as a drunk in a ditch close to the farm," Lori explained.

"I imagine there were a lot of stories like that in the 'Dust Bowl' period," Tim said above the raging wind.

"Tim we should get some money from our landlord that owns the south fields. Dean said that he would pay us for our expenses, and labor, for cleaning up the land, and getting it in shape to farm or sell. We have spent a lot of days digging up old posts and fences, and leveling the land. I remember the day it took me four hours to get an old tire-chain out of the planting shank so I could go ahead and plant the rest of the milo. The fields are larger, and easier to farm, and the land should be a lot easier to sell now," Lori said.

"Lori, I hate to tell you this, but that land sold three months ago, and our former landlord won't talk to me when I try to call him," Tim explained. "He never was very friendly after that situation between Samuel and Rosita, anyway."

"I guess a person needs to always get a written contract on things like that," Lori replied. She felt so disappointed. "I guess I knew that he hasn't wanted to talk to you since the night you took Rosita out of his son's bed."

Lori and Tim were both thinking the same thing, <u>There was no way they could get the money to pay Mr. Freedman for the trial Tim was facing</u>.

As time for the trial grew nearer, Tim felt more and more uneasy. <u>The few people in the county that aren't sure if I'm guilty or not, might vote against me just because I owe them money</u>, Tim was thinking.

Lori was thinking about the time her father had been on a jury. The thief had been caught in the very act of stealing grain out of a local grain elevator, and selling it in another part of the state. Everyone knew he was guilty, and it was proven in court. Every person on the jury voted that the guy was guilty except for one man.

The trial took place in winter. The jury had to stay in the part of the jail that was cold. They were not allowed to see their families, or to talk to anyone until the verdict was given. One by one, the jury members changed their votes so they could go home and see their families, and return to their work. The group decided that the man was not guilty so they could be dismissed.

Lori's father had been bothered for a long time about the unfairness of the whole thing. "You never know for sure how things are going to turn out in a court of law," her father had said several times.

"Lori, watch that car!" Tim shouted.

Lori was brought back into the miserable present. She pulled the car closer to the ditch. The storm was letting up a little, and they could see their next destination. It had taken them four hours to drive the forty-eight miles to the next town.

Lori glanced at the man that had been her husband for four years. He wasn't rich, or famous, or handsome, with his plump figure and thick glasses, but Tim had given her a love like she had never known before. She could never doubt is love. He was always near to give her a shoulder to cry on when life got too rough. Tim had married her at a time he knew she still had a love for Hollis, and maybe she always would. Tim had never gone anywhere without her.

Lori could not stand the thought of Tim going to prison, even for four years. Their lives would be ruined. "Oh God, please help us to find our way out of this terrible nightmare," she prayed.

They were stopped by a man on the road. "The US highway going south is closed because of poor visibility," the man said.

"We're turning east at the intersection," Lori explained.

The man waved for them to go on.

Lori's eyes felt sun burned by the time they reached the farm. They had seen a few accidents, but they had gotten home without even a scratch on the car.

Lori walked into the house and moaned. She had left the house clean and shiny that morning. Now she could write her name in the dirt on the dark brown sofa. "You can't even tell what color the bright gold-colored carpet in the living room is supposed to be," Lori sobbed.

The wind let up enough by morning that school was not canceled. It started blowing again that afternoon, and school was dismissed early.

When Lori came in from work, she found Tim in the bathroom. He was trying to replace a window that the wind had blown out. Tim's eyes were filled with dirt. The dust was so thick in the small bathroom that it was impossible to see from one wall to the other.

Lori had cleaned house again the night before. Everything was covered with dirt again. She felt like it was the end of the world, and she did not have any more energy left to fight. Lori jumped into bed with her school clothes still on. She covered up her head and tried to get away from the never ending dirt. Lori tried to daydream that they were living safely in a beautiful, green somewhere.

The strong wind made it impossible for Tim to replace the window. He nailed up the opening on the outside with a large piece of plywood, and taped cardboard on the inside.

Tim cleaned off a small spot on the table and fixed himself some soup. There was sand in the soup before he finished eating it. The roar of the wind was giving him a terrible headache. Tim left the sandy soup on the table, and jumped in bed with Lori.

The wind let up during the night. While Lori was in school the next day, Tim used their grocery money to buy enough gas to chisel the worst blowing pieces of ground around the house.

CHAPTER XXI

MORE FEARS AND RESPONSIBILITIES

The school bus had just pulled off the main road, and onto the side road going to the farm. Lori saw them from the bus window. Several large cattle trucks were parked in the farmyard. They had come to pick up the rest of the cattle and take them to market.

Lori stepped off the bus and waved good-bye to the bus driver. She slowly walked past the first cattle truck. Then she stopped. Tears rolled down her face once more. She could see the nine beautiful seminal bulls through the slats of the truck trailer.

Lori remembered the many times she had chased the bulls back into the pastures. She remembered how Tim put treats in his shirt pockets, and there would be nine, 2,000 pound bulls trying to get the treats out of his pockets. Only one of the bulls had been too wild to be petted.

"You have grown so much since we bought you last year," Lori said through her tears. She pushed her fingers through the slats and patted each of their soft noses. "Good-bye Ugly Head, Whitey, Longhorn, and Baby. Baby, do you still cry when the others fight?" Lori sobbed. "Good-bye Curly, Pretty, and Little Longhorn. How many times have I chased you over a four wire fence, Little Longhorn, and as soon as I left, you just jumped back out again?" Lori said, patting the large head and horns.

"Good-bye Ears. Why did you always act like a scared Brahma instead of acting like the others?" Lori asked.

"I'll miss all of you," Lori said. She ran into the house to cry.

Tim tried to be cheerful when he came in for supper. "Do you know what Ears did when the cowboys started to load him on the truck?" he asked, laughing.

"Knowing Ears, I'm afraid to guess," Lori answered, trying to smile.

"He put three good cowboys off their horses and running for the fence. They scrambled to safety several times before they got Ears into the truck," Tim explained.

"I felt like he would have liked to have charged me a few times when I was chasing the cattle on foot, but he never did, or I wouldn't be here today," Lori said. "Thank you Lord," she said. "What will happen to the bulls now?" Lori asked.

"There is a chance they may be sold for hamburger. There isn't a demand for breeding bulls on the market right now. It's hard to imagine since they are registered and at the prime of their breeding life," Tim said with a sigh.

<u>The farm seems so deathly still tonight without the sounds of the cattle in the pens</u>, Lori was thinking as she was trying to go to sleep beside Tim's warm body.

The telephone was ringing when Tim came in from work the next evening. "Can you come up here right away?" Mr. Freedman asked.

"I guess I can if it's that important. But, I'd rather wait until Friday evening so Lori can come with me, if that's okay," Tim answered. "What's so important?" he asked.

"I don't need to tell you until you get here. It might be good news, but I need to talk to you first. I'll see you early Saturday morning," Mr. Freedman said.

Tim and Lori counted what little money they had left from Lori's short check, and the money Elizabeth and Arthur had given them. It would take all they had to make the familiar trip to the state capital and back. They felt nervous as they entered the large office building and were able to usher themselves into Mr. Freedman's office this time.

"The DA still wants to negotiate," Mr. Freedman explained. "They still want you to sign a confession, and they will go lighter on the punishment," he said.

"I'm tired of fighting, and I don't have any more money to fight with, anyway," Tim said.

"That's why I called you up here. I think they want a confession bad enough that I might be able to work out something with them this time," the attorney said.

"I'm not sure I can go through confessing to something I didn't do, but I don't want a two week trial either. I can't afford to pay you. I don't want to put Rosita through a trial. I know, without a doubt, that I can never get a fair trial in the county. You can't get the trial moved to an area that hasn't been covered by the news about me. Just work out what you think is best," Tim said. He covered his face with his hands and laid his head on Mr. Freedman's desk

Mr. Freedman was involved in several telephone calls from other clients before he was able to get the DA. While they were waiting, Lori and Tim walked around the office to try to settle their nervousness.

When Tim and Lori walked back into Freedman's office, the attorney shouted, "What do you have in that little county of yours, <u>a tail that wags a dog</u>!"

"What are you talking about?" Tim asked.

"Every time I talk to the DA and make an offer, he makes me wait until he talks to that sheriff of yours and asks him what he should do. I've never heard of such a thing!" Mr. Freedman shouted. He threw his hands up into the air. "Things like that just aren't done!" he exclaimed.

"I tried to tell you that when you first took the case," Tim said. "You just laughed at me and said I was just paranoid."

"This is the first time I've believed you when you told me that the sheriff stomped into the courtroom and up to the judge, and got by with it," Mr. Freedman said. "I just couldn't believe it had happened even though I got back from the rest-room in time to see him stomp out of the courtroom, No sheriff should be able to tell a DA what to do!" Mr.

Freedman tried to calm down as he looked over the papers again. "Tim, my advice to you, is to go a NON-CONTENDRA," he said.

"What is that?" Tim asked.

"It means that you don't legally deny that you did the said crime. In other words, on paper, you are admitting you did it," the lawyer explained.

Tim thought quietly for a few minutes. "If I do this, then what?" he asked, gripping the arms of his chair.

"Then they will reduce the charges to a misdemeanor. You'll have one year's unsupervised probation, and the whole thing will be over," Freedman explained. "They really want your confession."

"What will be on my record?" Tim asked.

"This is one reason I'm advising you to do this. It will be on your record for a short time, but your record will eventually be clean. The only way you can break parole is to be charged with the same crime again," Mr. Freedman said.

"I didn't do it the first time, and I sure won't do anything like it. I won't even flip a girl on the seat," Tim replied.

"Mr. Freedman, I hate to keep repeating myself, but we feel that Tim was framed the first time," Lori explained. "What would happen if anyone accused him of the same thing within that year's probation?" Lori asked.

"The chances wouldn't be good for Tim. Your best chance is to get away from that area for good, or at least until the year's probation is over," Mr. Freedman replied.

"There goes my job, and our lives as we have known them," Lori said with a sob. "I guess we have no other choice."

Tim leaned over and squeezed Lori's hand. "It looks like we have lost our farming and ranch operation anyway. But, everything will be all right," Tim said. He signed some papers for Mr. Freedman, and he and Lori were soon on their way home again.

Lori was still working with people that wondered why she didn't leave the "child molester". She tried to hold her head high and finish the school year the best she could.

It was time for next year's contracts to be issued. Lori received her contract when she picked up her mail from her school mail box. She did not open it up until she got home that evening.

Lori cleaned up the kitchen from the supper mess before she sat down to look at her new contract. There was a letter in with it which was unusual. Lori pulled the letter out of the envelope and unfolded it.

Parts of the letter read:

"We realize that you have had things come up this year that has kept you from giving your job all it needed. We hired a teacher, not a film projector. We feel that you show too many movies and film strips in your classes because you are not prepared for regular lessons.

We have talked to some parents, former students, Junior High teachers, and they all agree that you show too many AV materials, and you aren't teaching your students enough. We have even had complaints from parents and students, You have poor communication with your students and they can't understand your assignments.

We have not seen you at any of the school's activities this year. We feel it is important for our teachers to be seen outside of the classroom. You have been told many times not to be so religious in the classroom, but you haven't completely done this. We are renewing your contract for the next year, but if these problems continue, we will have to do something about it next year."

Lori was crying too hard to read the rest of the letter. <u>Have I worked in this school and done my best all of these years and I haven't been any better teacher than this</u>? Lori wondered.

Tim heard Lori crying and came into the kitchen. "What's the matter, Honey?" he asked as Lori fell exhausted over his large shoulder. "You are a good teacher, so what are you crying about?"

Lori handed Tim the letter.

"Lori, didn't you tell me, sometime this year, that your principal told you that the achievement tests showed that your students had an average increase of knowledge of three years the two years you work with them?" Tim asked.

"Yes. Maybe I do show a lot of films, and film-strips, but how many lecture words would it take to tell them what it would be like to live in Israel, for example. I can show a thirty minute film and they can see it for themselves. Besides, I have tests over the films and film-strips I show. They are not just entertainment," Lori explained.

"Maybe that is why the students complained," Tim said, trying to be funny.

"My sixth graders always finish the large book that is required by the school. They also finish a small book about the Roman Empire that isn't required. I cover that book so my students will understand more about our government. The sixth graders also have to know sixty country's locations and capitals to pass my final test.

My fifth graders even go through an extra book. They have to know the states and capital besides other countries in the Western Hemisphere. They have to fill out blank maps. I feel that it's important for kids to know the world they live in so they can at least listen to the news intelligently," Lori explained.

"You don't have to convince me, Lori," Tim said with a smile. "I know you are a good teacher. You taught all four of my kids, remember? If you weren't a good teacher, you would have gotten acquainted with me whether you wanted to or not," he explained. "I always gave teachers a bad time when I didn't think my kids were learning all they should in school."

"One of the seventh grade teachers told me just last week that my former students were fun to teach because they have so much basic knowledge that she can teach in more detail." Lori said. She felt angry now. Sometimes one of former students will come back and thank me for being a good teacher, and because they learned a lot in my classes, it made future classes easier," Lori said.

"I go over my assignments and ask if the kids have any questions. Sometimes, I even write the assignments on the chalk board," Lori explained.

"I surely do something right!" Lori screamed. "I'm tired and I think I'm going to go to bed."

Although Lori went to bed early, she did not sleep at all that night. <u>When will this terrible dream be over and things will start working out right, again</u>, she wondered.

"Don't let that letter bother you," Tim said the next morning. "We'll be leaving as soon as school is out, anyway," he said.

"Tim, my teaching is not just a job, but a big part of my life. It hurts to know that I'm not wanted at my school, anymore," Lori said with a sigh.

"You've had disagreements with your principal before, but I imagine the main reason you received that letter is . . . because of my reputation," Tim said.

"I just don't know anymore," Lori replied. It was even harder than before to go to school and face everyone again.

Lori taught her best each day. She was able to finish the school year covering all she had planned to cover at the beginning of the year. No matter how well the day went with her students, she never forgot that she was not wanted in the school system anymore.

Some parents heard about Lori's letter. They called to say that they appreciated the work she had done with their kids, and that they didn't agree with the school board's letter.

"I'm going to the board and tell them what a good teacher we think you are," Judy said over the telephone.

"Thanks. I appreciate any help you want to give me," Lori replied.

Lori went to talk to her superintendent before school was dismissed for the summer. Mr. Boner was a professional individual. Lori felt that he might try to help her.

"I was wondering if you could help me obtain a Year's Leave of Absence." Lori asked.

"I'll present it to the board for you," Lori," Mr. Boner said.

"Thanks. It's so hard to just walk away from my job after all these years," Lori said. "Maybe after a year, I'll know what I want to do," she added.

Lori's request was granted. It was still difficult to sign the papers saying she would not be back the following year. She had not realized, until now, how important her profession was to her. There had been times of discouragement when she thought she might like to quit and find some other line of work, especially after her divorce from Hollis. "I don't think anything, outside of Tim, could make me leave my job of fifteen years," Lori told herself.

The fifth grade class was busy finishing their reading workbooks. "Mrs. Jones, will you let us write long stories next year like your sixth graders did this year?" a student asked.

"I won't be your teacher next year," Lori answered.

The room became quiet.

"Gee Whiz! Why not?" one boy asked.

"Who will be our teacher next year?" another student asked.

"I don't know, but I know they will be a good teacher," Lori told her class.

"But, we want you!" another students exclaimed.

Lori did not want her students to know how much she wished she could be there teacher for the coming year. She assigned a little more work to keep her students busy. Lori did not want them asking any more questions, or notice the tears in her eyes.

Hollis's step daughter came up to Lori's desk. Carla was a beautiful, blonde young lady. She was also timid and had poor self-esteem. Carla was highly intelligent and always had her work neatly finished before the other students, but she didn't have enough self confidence to do well on tests.

"Mrs. Jones, May I spend the rest of the period writing a story?" Carla asked.

"I think that is a great idea since you have all your work finished," Lori replied.

Lori dismissed the students to go to PE one more time. Carla put her story on Lori's desk and stood close for Lori to read what she had written.

The story read: I once had a teacher that was really nice. I always had fun in her class. I feel sad because she will not be my teacher for the sixth grade. Her name is Mrs. Jones.

"It's people like you that make it so hard to leave," Lori said with a forced smile. She patted the pretty blonde head. They walked out of the room together hand in hand. Neither teacher, nor student, was smiling.

I hope she will have a teacher next year that will encourage her and help her see how talented she is, Lori was thinking as she watched Carla walk down the hall to PE

Tim would not go to town unless he went with Lori, and then he sat in the car and waited for her to do what they both needed to do. He felt like everyone was staring at him as they walked down the sidewalk past the car, or drove down Main Street.

Although Lori felt uncomfortable around adults at school, she enjoyed her last weeks with her precious students. In April, she took the sixth grade to see an old extinct volcano 150 miles away.

The students were all well behaved. The day was relaxing as well as educational. It was her last trip to the old mountain after ten years of trips with former students.

The other sixth grade teacher, Mr. Sanchez, had gone with her for eight of those ten years. He was an outstanding teacher. Mr. Sanchez had been kind and supportive to Lori through all these long, terrifying months. He was always willing to do more than his share of work and responsibilities. Mr. Sanchez had always had something encouraging to say at the right time. He had always been a lot of fun to teach with.

Lori smiled as she remembered the time some boys threw Mr. Sanchez into a creek pond. Lori had been laughing when Mr. Sanchez talked the girls into throwing her into the water, too. Some of the girls were larger than Lori, and they did not have any trouble getting her soaking wet. They had a wonderful time. Lori's bra was still wet when she got home that night.

These trips, and the teachers, and other people she worked with, would always have a loving spot in Lori's heart.

"Why don't you teach just one more year and then you can retire the same year I do," Mr. Miliano, the bus driver, said.

"You've been to this old mountain about as many times as I have, haven't you?" Lori said with a laugh. Mr. Miliano was an attractive man with dark skin and curly hair. He loved kids and always had a refreshing chuckle.

"Yeah, you even brought my boys here when they were young, and in school," Mr. Miliano said with his Spanish accent.

Lori enjoyed the ride home in the dusty bus. She enjoyed visiting with her two dear friends that she probably would not see many times again.

The sixth grade went skating for their Last Day of School Party. Lori hand not planned to skate because she had gained so much weight. It had been a long time since she had been on skates, and she did not want to embarrass herself in front of her students.

"Mrs. Jones, if you'll skate with us, I'll pay your way," a voice said from behind.

Lori turned around. It was Ralph, one of the poorest kids in school. He was Spanish. When Ralph had discovered that Rosita was not coming back he had asked Lori if he could live on the farm with her and Tim. He loved the country, but had to live in town. He was also having trouble getting along with his new step father.

"I'll pay for it myself, Ralph, but thanks anyway," Lori said. Little did she know that Ralph would be killed in a car accident the next summer.

Lori skated the rest of the two hours. She skated with different students. Her presence on the floor gave the students that did not know how to skate, the courage to try harder. Everyone had a wonderful time. There was not one argument among the students that day.

Lori was so thankful that she had the opportunity to come back after a year. Among other things, it kept the other teachers from giving her a "farewell luncheon" like they had given all the other teachers that had left the school. Lori knew she would have cried, and she had cried enough the past year to last a lifetime.

There was no money to farm. Tim cash leased the farm land until the bank took over. He started to work for a new company, selling vitamins and holding meetings in all the surrounding towns.

The first night Lori spent on the farm alone was one to remember. She had started reading a good book sitting in the large chair next to their bed when she fell asleep. "I think I will get ready for bed and read some more. That way if I am sleepy again, I can just fall into bed," Lori told herself. She went into the kitchen and put some water on the stove. The water pipes had frozen and she needed warm water to wash her face and brush her teeth.

Lori was walking across the kitchen when she realized that the two dogs were barking like they did when someone came to the house. She realized she was way out in the country alone and could be in danger. Lori rushed around and turned all the lights off hoping, that if someone was outside, they would think no one was at home. After turning off the last light, Lori ran to the window by the eating space in the kitchen where she could see the back step. She saw a man's figure in the dark with the help of the yard light. The person was carrying a large flashlight. Lori heard something like a knock and knuckles sliding down the door. It sounded like someone said, "Ma." She ran toward the door thinking it might be Mike or Mitch. She stopped and decided she should get a better look at the intruder. When the person turned around the flashlight shined on its face. It looked like Lori's dad.

"Mother must be sick," Lori said as she went to the door. Then she realized that her father had been dead for several years. She ran back to the window again and looked out. The figure wasn't there but she watched the back lights of a Buick leave the yard. Her Dad had always driven a Buick.

Lori thought that she might be dreaming so she called her friend, Vera Lee, in town. "Am I dreaming or am I really talking to you?" She asked.

"Lori, you are not dreaming. I want you to come to town and stay with me until Tim gets home. I don't like that place and the last time I was there I had a vision of my youngest son being killed on that place.

That is why I haven't been back. And, besides, there are a lot of people in the area that would like to get even with Tim because they think he really did hurt Rosita," Vera Lee said.

"I probably need to stay safe in the house and besides I'm not really scared. It was someone that needed to use the phone or something and I was too much of a coward to help," Lori explained. She checked with several people that week to try and find out who had been at her door. She couldn't find anyone that had been there.

Lori traveled with Tim as soon as school ended. She had wondered about the person she had not helped that night when the Lord let her see what really happened. She saw the whole incident over again. The dogs were biting through whatever was there. It had come to harm her. When it touched the door of the Christian home, the power of God was there and it lost all of its power. Lori thought back to the church service she and Tim had gone to. One of the guests stood up to be healed. The minister said that only Jesus could heal and he had to believe differently to be healed. The man shouted that they had tapes and pictures of the dead people they talk to. The minister had to ask the man to leave.

Lori and Tim had felt sorry for the man and followed him out to his car with some scriptures to show that his believe was wrong. He told them that they could pray for him and he would be healed. "I wouldn't miss $40,000 if you two would pray for me," the man had said. When Tim and Lori said they couldn't pray for him under the circumstances, he said, "Well, you are good kids. You are happy with what you believe and I am happy with what I believe."

"I don't think you are," Lori had replied.

"What do you mean?" the man asked.

"If you are satisfied in the way you believe, then what are you doing here at this meeting today," Lori asked.

The man slammed his Bible into the back seat and drove off angry.

Lori also remembered other things strange about the place they had just lost. One friend had to spend the night at the farm because it had rained and she couldn't get home over the muddy roads. She told Lori that she woke up in the middle of the night and it felt like there were hands all over her. She was frightened and prayed the rest of the night on the knees.

Another young couple had come to look at a Pickup that Tim had for sale. Tim and Lori were not home at the time. The wife called later and said they were no longer interested in the Pickup. "When I watched my husband and kids walking to the pickup I could see the pickup covered with blood. I screamed and we left your place as quickly as we could." She said.

Lori remembered the time she and Tim were almost asleep when it sounded like alarm clocks started ringing all over the house. Tim had panicked. Lori had shouted, "In the name of Jesus, you leave here and don't you ever come back!" It was immediately quiet and stayed that way.

"How about the time that we had some friends working for us and living on our other place?" Lori asked herself. Johnny's wife, Jane, had helped Lori clean the old large farmhouse and they were burning some dirty magazines and an Ouija board. The board started crying so loudly that Tim and Johnny came running across the yard to see what was making the noise. Lori and Jane had been so frightened that they started singing, "Greater is He that is in me than he That Is in the World."

Lori had found a starved, stray dog on one of the places they rented. She took the dog home with her. The dog acted more like a cat by rubbing up against their legs and walking on the wooden cattle pens and switching his tail. The dog jumped on one of the young pigs and tried to kill it.

Tim had told Johnny to take the dog with him and shoot it somewhere on the five mile trip home. Johnny called the next morning. He said he had shot the dog between the eyes about three miles from where they lived. The next morning when they got up the dog was looking through the screen door at them. The dog looked terrible and they were afraid to go outside. Tim told Johnny to shoot the dog again through the screen door and he would pay for the repairs.

"Most of the things that had happened to her and Tim on the farm were bad enough to seem strange," Lori said to herself, "I wonder if there is any connection?"

It would be six months before the bank could take over after the bankruptcy was final and take possession of the land and turn it over to the new owner. There were no cattle to take care of, so Tim and Lori were able to travel several days at a time.

The foreclosure day finally came. Tim and Lori lost everything they had except their furniture. The bank took the farmhouse, and Lori's mobile home that had been completely paid for before she met Tim. They thought they had hired the best bankruptcy lawyer in the country. Tim and Lori were supposed to be left a residence but it did not work out that way.

Lori had given Elizabeth back her part of her father's estate when she and Tim begin to have financial problems.

A few weeks before the bankruptcy was final, Lori wrecked the rose-colored Cadillac one night coming home from town. The road had been freshly graded and very dusty. A black cow was standing in the middle of the road. When the car lights reflected in the cow's eyes as she swung her head low and looked around, Lori thought it was a skunk. She slammed on the brakes. When she saw the outline of the large cow, she hit it on the highest part of the front of the car so the cow would not come through the windshield.

One of Lori's former students crawled into the car with her and waited for the police to arrive. She was concerned about the bump on Lori's forehead caused from the impact on the windshield. Lori was all right, but the car was totaled.

Tim and Lori had to pay $1500 to the bank to be able to keep their older car. The bank had to do this, but took all the other forms of transportation away from them.

CHAPTER XXII

COURT AND BANKRUPTCY

The day before Tim's hearing in the District Court, Mr. Freedman called. "Tim, I'm tied up in court here in the city tomorrow. I'm sending my new assistant to fill in for me. There's nothing left besides the formalities, anyway," Mr. Freedman said. "Everything will be just the same as if I was there," he said.

This time Lori did not have to worry about missing school to go to court with Tim. They drove the eighty-five miles, and to the small air port to pick up the new attorney.

"Hello, I'm your attorney for today. My name is Fred Wilson," the young man said with an extended hand. He was wearing an expensive three-piece suit, and an important smile.

The three shook hands and started for the courthouse.

"Now explain what is going to happen today," Tim said.

The young attorney went over the case about the same way that Mr. Freedman had explained it. "It looks like a pretty safe way to go," the attorney said.

Tim parked the car in front of the marble, historical looking building. He gripped the steering wheel and said, "I just can't admit, even on paper, to a crime I didn't commit."

"It's too late to do anything else, now," the startled attorney replied.

Tim ran into the courthouse building and up to a large counter. He told a clerk that he wanted to change his confession.

"The papers have already been signed. They have already been sent to the judge," the lady said. "It's too late to change anything now," she explained.

There were only five other people in the courtroom when Tim and Lori sit down beside their attorney. At exactly 2 p.m., everyone stood up for Judge Stark to enter.

"It isn't right for a case like this to be settled without a trial. Mr. Jones, if you are guilty, you should be <u>found</u> guilty. You should have a chance to prove yourself innocent and clear your name if you are innocent!" the judge exclaimed.

Judge Stark looked through the papers on his desk. He looked up at Tim above his reading glasses. "Mr. Jones, I want you to know that during this year of probation, if you have any misdemeanor, outside of a traffic ticket, that you will go directly to prison, without a trial, for not less that one year," Judge Stark said.

Tim stood up in shock. "That's not the way it was explained to me, Your Honor," he said, and fell back into his chair. Tim felt sweat on his cold hands. He looked at his attorney for help.

"That's not the way it was explained to Mr. Freedman, Your Honor," the young attorney stammered.

"That's the way the decree reads and nothing can be done about it now," Judge Stark said. "Tim Jones, stand up and face the court," the judge ordered.

Tim stood up and faced the old judge.

"How do you plead, Mr. Tim T. Jones?" Judge Stark asked.

"Non, Non, Non CONTENDRA, Your Honor," Tim finally managed to say through clenched teeth.

"Therefore, Mr. Tim T. Jones, you are hereby found guilty of child molesting and you are sentenced to two years to be served in the State Penitentiary," Judge Stark announced.

Tim and Lori were both hanging onto the back of the bench in front of them. Lori thought she was going to faint, or vomit, or both. Large beads of seat were dropping from Tim's forehead.

The judge was still talking. "However, since this is your first offense, I'm lifting the sentence to one year probation. The probation is to be unsupervised, but if probation is broken, you will go directly to the State prison without any further right to defend yourself," Judge Star said. "Case ended!" he shouted.

Everyone stood up for the judge to exit.

Tim turned to his new attorney. "Mr. Wilson, do you realize that if someone picks a fight with me, or brings any charges against me, that I'll be sent directly to prison?" Tim asked desperately. "It could be something as simple as my dog killing a neighbor's chicken, or someone accusing me of any number of things," He said.

"That's not the way we understood it at the office, Tim," Fred Wilson repeated.

The attorney was soon flying back to the city. It was after dark when Tim and Lori drove back to the farm.

Tim made the front page of the county paper again the next week. It now stated that Tim Jones was found guilty of child molesting. Even the few people that thought Tim was innocent now believed he was guilty. People just knew that "Innocent people can't be found guilty in a court of law".

The only time Tim and Lori returned to the farm was when no one knew they were going to be there. They entered the house late at night, after putting the old car in the garage and out of sight. Tim and Lori sorted through several days of mail, fed the chickens, Kato and Lucky, and the pups, and would leave under darkness of the next night.

"Lori, according to this mail, we need to sit down and make some decisions before we leave this time," Tim said.

Lori wiped the dust off a kitchen chair and sit down.

Tim continued. "The bank and government have taken over the farm. None of our insurance companies are answering any of our claims. The government refuses to help us even to have a residence. We need to make definite plans to move somewhere else as soon as possible," Tim explained.

"I know you can never feel comfortable in this area again, and you aren't safe here, anyway," Lori said. "The fact is, that we're being run out of the area that has been our home almost all of our lives," she added.

"I've never been one to run, but I don't see any future here for us," Tim admitted.

"Do you remember what Violet told us a few weeks ago?" Lori asked. Tim shook his head no. "She said its one thing to run away, but it's another thing to try to stay and let the devil camp on our doorstep," Lori said.

"You're right. I'll never feel safe here," Tim replied. "I think we should look for a place in Thomasville. It's only 250 miles away, and maybe we can make a new start there," he said.

"I don't know if Thomasville is the right place or not. I read in the paper that a lot of teachers are out of work there," Lori replied.

"I think we should go in that direction and do some looking next week, anyway," Tim said. "There is a lot of population there and our new business should do well," he explained.

The next week Tim and Lori rented a place in Georgetown, forty miles further away than Thomasville.

It was hard to go back and start packing. They had so many dreams of how they would successfully run the farm. They had dreamed of a beautiful yard with a duck pond nearby. Tim had dreamed of irrigating the land someday.

Tim and Lori had dreamed that the old house would be filled with the laughter of <u>all</u> their children and grandchildren. Now their dreams were all blown away like the harsh wind blowing dirt against the outside of the house.

Lori and Tim did not feel comfortable enough to ask anyone to help them move. Tim backed the U-Haul trailer up to the front door. Together, he and Lori loaded their only belongings.

"Lori, something has to be done about the dogs before we leave. We can't take more than two of them with us," Tim said.

"I know. Do what you have to do," Lori replied.

Tim gently put Lucky and two of the almost grown pups in the car and drove out into the field. When he let the dogs out, they started to follow the car. Tim shot each of them between the eyes as they looked up at him.

Lori went to the hen house. Something had killed all the laying hens but one. The animal was lying on her side, gasping for air. Lori took the hen to the house and forced some water down her throat. She stood up and started to eat some grain.

Tim returned to the house and found Lori with the old hen. He gently took the animal outside. Lori heard the gun discharge.

Tim walked back into the house. He and Lori fell into each others arms and cried together. When they felt better, they loaded Kato and Bingo, and started for the city. The farm was soon out of sight.

The farm was now deserted. The yard where the sound of farm machinery was once heard, and hens chattered happily, is now still. The place where dogs ran and played, and the sound of cattle were heard, is now still except for the howling wind.

The old house that once had the sound of music and a young girl's laughter with her "sometimes family" is now silent except for the tiny mice running across the dusty floor.

What about the three that made the music and laughter? What has happened to the little girl with the brown skin and coal black hair, that Tim and Lori loved so dearly? Will she live a normal life or run away like some of her sisters?

What about Tim who will never be able to return to his homeland without suspicion from the people in the community.

What about Lori, who was forced to choose between a fifteen year old job and her family, and the man she loved?

How many others, who are innocent, have been found guilty in a court of law? How many other people have been hurt by the media? Lori wondered.

"The only justice you and I have found, Tim, was God's promise when he said, 'There is no temptation come to you but what is common to man, but God has made <u>a way of escape that you may be able to</u> <u>bear it</u>," Lori said.

Lori looked over at her husband. She tried to release the past and relax. She smiled as she squeezed Tim's large arm. She knew as long as she and Tim had each other, that things would work out okay. "I know that Tim is innocent and there's nothing that can ever make me believe that he is guilty," Lori told herself.

Lori, if you only knew . . . but, women <u>do</u> have the right to change their minds, don't they?

THE END